Modern World History

for Edexcel

SYLLABUS A

Malcolm Chandler
John Wright

EDEXCEL
FOUNDATION
ED
EXCEL

Heinemann

Heinemann Educational Publishers

Halley Court, Jordan Hill, Oxford, OX2 8EJ
a division of Reed Educational & Professional
Publishing Ltd

Heinemann is a registered trademark of Reed
Educational & Professional Publishing Ltd

OXFORD MELBOURNE AUCKLAND
JOHANNESBURG BLANTYRE GABARONE
IBADAN PORTSMOUTH NH (USA) CHICAGO

© Malcolm Chandler and John Wright 1999

First published 1999

ISBN 0 435 31138 7

02 01 00 99

10 9 8 7 6 5 4 3 2

Designed by Kasa Design

Illustrated by Greig Sutton

Cover design by Carla Turchini

Printed and bound in Spain by Edelvive

Photographic acknowledgements

The authors and publisher would like to thank
the following for permission to reproduce
photographs:

Cover photograph: *Atom bomb,* courtesy of
Telegraph Colour Library

AKG: 69E, 70C, 75F, 76C.

Archive Photos: 108C.

Associated Press: 125F, 181E.

Birmingham (Alabama) Public Library: 179B.

Camera Press: 110A, 123E.

Corbis: 56C, 92C, 114B, 132C, 149B, 170E, 172G,
175B, 178A, 184J, 190C, 194C, 195A, 223C, 225A,
227C, 257F.

David King: 33F, 35F, 43F, 201C, 202A, 207A,
208B, 209A, 210C, 213F.

Ewan MacNaughton: 133F.

Hulton Getty: 37F, 72B, 72C, 136A, 145C, 155C,
156A, 157B, 162A, 167A, 169C, 217A, 232B,
243A, 245B.

Illustrated London News: 86D.

Imperial War Museum: 150A.

Kobal Collection: 219B.

Low/Centre for the Study of Cartoon and
Caricature: 153C, 234D.

Mary Evans: 140A.

Novosti: 226B.

Peter Newark: 176D, 185K, 186A, 187D.

Popperfoto: 38C, 54C, 154A, 158A, 241E,
251B, 253D.

Punch: 238E.

Solo Syndication/Centre for the Study of Cartoon
and Caricature: 250A.

Telegraph Colour Library: 189A, 191D.

Topham: 104C, 106B, 111F, 161C, 165B, 171F,
193A, 197C, 198E, 215A, 223A, 242B, 252C.

United Nations: 127F.

Written sources acknowledgements

The authors and publishers gratefully acknowledge the following publications from which written sources in the book are drawn. In some sources the wording or sentence has been simplified.

Blackpool Herald, 1915: 14H.

Marshall Cavendish, *Great Battles of World War II,* 1995: 94A, 94B.

Winston Churchill, *The World Crisis,* 1923: 19F.

G. Craig, *Germany, 1866~45,* Oxford University Press, 1975: 72A, 73E;

The *Daily Express,* 1938: 87E.

Daily Mail, 3 July 1943: 165C.

Daniel David, *The 1914 Campaign,* Combined Books, 1987: 14D.

Dardenelles Driveller, 1915: 19D.

O. Downes and E. Sigmeister, *A Treasury of American Song,* Consolidated Music, in Keith Feiling, *The Life of Neville Chamberlain,* London, 1946: 86B.

Fighting Forces, magazine, 1918: 20D.

Charles Freeman, *The Rise of the Nazis,* Wayland, 1997: 72F.

M. Gibson, *Spotlight on the First World War,* Evans, 1997: 20B.

R.G. Grant, *Hiroshima and Nagasaki,* Wayland, 1997: 97F.

Anne Grimshaw, *D-Day,* Dryad, 1988: 94C, 95F.

H.R. Haldeman, *The Ends of Power,* 1978: 115D.

Sarah Harris, *The Second World War,* Dryad, 1989: 92B.

Michael Hickey, *Gallipoli,* 1995: 18A, 18B, 19E.

L.F. Hobley, *The First World War,* Blackie, 1971: 22A, 22C, 23E.

Gwyneth Hughes and Simon Welfare, *Red Empire,* YTV/Weidenfeld and Nicholson, 1990: 90B.

Johannesburg Business Day, 1986: 129F.

N. Kelly, *The First World War,* Heinemann, 1989: 21F.

Kitchberger, *The First World War,* 1992: 14B, 15F., 22B, 24E.

Los Angeles Times, Sunday 5 May, 1974: 196B.

Peter Mantin, *Questions of Evidence,* Hutchinson, 1987: 97E.

Nixon Library: 196B.

Punch, August 1918: 24A.

Richard Rhodes, *The Making of the Atomoic Bomb,* Penguin 1988: 96B.

Martin Roberts, *Britain and Europe, 1848~80,* Longman, 1986: 86A, 86C.

Stewart Ross, *The First World War,* 1997: 23F.

Jane Shuter, *Christabel Bielenberg and Nazi Germany,* Heinemann, 1994: 71E.

David Stewart and James Fitzgerald, *The Great War,* Nelson, 1987: 16A, 16B, 16C, 17E.

John Terraine, *Mons,* Pan Books, 1960: 14A, 14C.

The Times, December 1917: 145E.

John Toland, *No Man's Land,* Macdonald, 1980: 24B, 24C, 24D.

Publishers Inc., 1943: 61F.

Guy Wint and Peter Calvorocessi, *Total War,* 1972: 87F.

With thanks to John and Andrew Frost at John Frost Historical Newspaper Service for the loan of the newspapers used in 169A and 198E.

The publishers have made every effort to trace copyright holders of material in this book. Any omissions will be rectified in subsequent printings if notice is given to the publisher.

The publishers would like to thank Dr James Ellison for his comments on the original manuscript.

DEPTH STUDIES CONTENTS

Depth Studies

Chapter 1:
The war to end wars, 1914~19

Chapter 2:
The Russian Revolution c. 1910~24

Chapter 3:
Depression and the New Deal:
the USA, 1929~41

Chapter 4:
Nazi Germany, c. 1930~9

Chapter 5:
The world at war, 1938~45

Chapter 6:
Conflict in Vietnam, c. 1963~75

Chapter 7:
The end of apartheid in South Africa, 1982~94

Outline studies

Depth Studies

All seven Depth Studies listed in the syllabus are included in this book. In each case the chapter begins with a section headed 'Essential Information'. This is divided into six sections, which match the bullet points set out in the syllabus. Each of these sections could be the basis of an examination question.

Essential Information

The purpose of the 'Essential Information' is to provide the basic knowledge required to cover the unit and to tackle questions in examination papers. In particular, it provides the knowledge and understanding necessary to answer questions that require you to 'use your own knowledge'. In the examination each of the questions testing the Depth Studies has two sub-parts requiring candidates to use their own knowledge. If you use the 'Essential Information' correctly, you will always be able to answer these effectively.

Exam Questions

At the end of each chapter there is a series of examination questions, one for each of the six bullet points in the syllabus. These questions are set in exactly the style as the questions that you will face in the GCSE examinations. They allow you to practise answering the sort of questions that will be set in Paper Two. All possible types of questions are included.

You may also find that your coursework assignments are based on the Depth Studies, and this will make these chapters even more useful.

Depth Studies

Depth Studies: A Summary

The war to end wars, 1914~19
This covers the campaigns at the beginning of the war, the nature of the fighting on the different fronts during the Great War and the controversies that have arisen since.

The Russian Revolution, c. 1910~24
This covers the problems faced by Tsar Nicholas II and his efforts to solve them, the reasons for his overthrow and the effects that Bolshevik rule had on Russia.

Depression and New Deal: the USA, 1929~41
This covers the impact of the Wall Street Crash and the Depression upon the economy and the people of the USA and the attempts made by President Roosevelt to tackle the Depression.

Nazi Germany, 1930~39
This covers the reasons for the Nazi rise to power and the impact of Nazi rule upon the people of Germany.

The world at war, 1938~45
This covers the events that led to the outbreak of the Second World War in 1939, the nature of the conflict in the years to 1945 and the reasons for the victory of the Allies.

Conflict in Vietnam, c. 1963~75
This covers the reasons for US involvement in Vietnam, the nature of the fighting and the consequences of the war for the peoples of the USA and Vietnam.

The end of apartheid in South Africa, 1982~94
This covers the background to the development of apartheid in South Africa, its impact upon the lives of the peoples of South Africa and the reasons for its collapse in the 1990s.

CHAPTER 1

The war to end wars: 1914~19

Essential Information

From 28 July to 12 August 1914, the countries of Europe declared war on each other with great enthusiasm. In every country there was a strong belief that war was justified, and that it could and would be won quickly and easily. Governments, peoples and newspapers all greeted news of war with joy. One ex-soldier summed up the mood in Britain with the comment, 'The great emotion was excitement.'

In Germany and France one reason for such enthusiasm was the plans that had been prepared for an outbreak of war. In France, Plan 17, a direct attack across the German border into Alsace-Lorraine, went into immediate effect. In Germany, the Schlieffen Plan, drawn up by the German Chief of Staff, Count Alfred von Schlieffen, in 1905, was set in motion. It was intended to win the war in the west in six weeks.

The failure of the Schlieffen Plan

In August 1914, Germany faced war on two fronts: in the east an attack by Russia and in the west an attack by France. The Schlieffen Plan had been drawn up to deal with this situation. In Germany it was assumed that the more dangerous opponent would be Russia, so the Plan aimed to defeat France before the Russian army was ready to advance. Schlieffen believed that the Russians would need six weeks to mobilise. This period could be used to deal with France. An army of 1,500,000 men would advance through Belgium, outflanking the French army drawn up along the German border. It would encircle Paris, then attack the French army from the rear. France would collapse. Then the Russians could be dealt with.

What went wrong?

While the Plan looked good on paper, Schlieffen had not taken account of the distances the

Who fought against whom?

The war was between the major powers of Europe. On one side there were the Allied Powers (led by Britain, France and Russia). On the other side there were the Central Powers (Germany, Austria-Hungary, and later Turkey and Bulgaria).

German armies had to cover in the strict timetable he laid down.

First, the German troops on the extreme right were exhausted after several weeks of marching and fighting, and were unable to keep up the pace.

Second, even before 1914, the Plan was changed. Von Moltke, the new Chief of Staff, withdrew forces from the right wing of the German army to strengthen the left. Even so, the main aim of the Plan stayed the same.

On 4 August, Germany declared war on Belgium and German forces crossed the border. However, unexpected problems occurred immediately. The Belgian government appealed to Great Britain for help. As far back as 1839, at the Treaty of Westminster, Britain, along with the other nations of Europe, had guaranteed to defend Belgium against any foreign attack. This promise was kept and within three weeks the British Expeditionary Force of 80,000 men was taking up position in Belgium. The German army also met much stronger opposition in Belgium than had been expected. The Belgian forts at Liège held out for twelve days and Brussels was not occupied until 20 August. The British met the Germans at Mons on 23 August and again at Le Cateau on 26 August. The British were professional soldiers equipped with the new Lee Enfield Mark III guns. They were heavily outnumbered but their rapid, accurate rifle fire slowed down the advance of the German

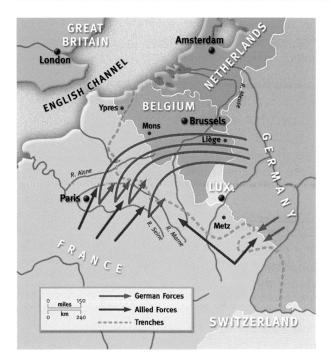

▲ The Schlieffen plan in action.

Aisne led to the 'Race for the Sea'. From 10 October 1914 onwards the two armies attempted to outflank each other by advancing to the North Sea. This was important because the Germans took Ghent, Bruges and Ostend, but failed to take any of the Channel ports. By the end of the year a front line had been established that was to remain largely in place until early 1918. As each side had built trenches sideways in order to try to outflank each other, the complex system of trenches, with connecting, reserve and communication trenches, soon extended for miles across Belgium and France. Despite a series of the biggest battles in history, neither side was able to advance more than ten miles in either direction.

Stalemate

Why was there a stalemate on the Western Front for three years? The basic problem was that army commanders in every country had not done their homework. It was assumed that the war would over quickly, like the Franco-Prussian War in 1870, but the machine guns and barbed wire made quick advances increasingly difficult. They also made the use of cavalry, which most armies believed would be the decisive weapon, almost impossible. The two British Commanders in Chief, Sir John French and Douglas Haig, were both cavalry officers and kept large cavalry forces in reserve behind the front line waiting for the big breakthrough which never came.

The main tactic used by both sides from 1914 to 1918 was frontal assault. First an artillery barrage was used to flatten the enemy's defences. This was almost always disastrous. The barrage usually failed to destroy enemy positions and the attackers found themselves advancing into a hail of machine gun fire. The British army made soldiers advance in order at a steady pace,

conscripts. One German officer wrote in a letter, 'It seemed as though there was a machine gun behind every bush.'

In the meantime, the Russian army had taken the Germans by surprise and had mobilised in two weeks. To meet this threat, on 25 August reinforcements were taken from the armies in Belgium and France and sent to the east. This overstretched the right flank of the German advance. The Commander of the German First Army on the extreme right gave up the attempt to encircle Paris and turned south.

As the Germans turned south they were attacked from Paris itself and then met French forces on 5 September along the River Marne. In a battle lasting eight days, the Germans were forced to fall back to the River Aisne. The Schlieffen Plan had failed. But there were still over one million German soldiers in France who now 'dug in' for protection. The Allied forces also did the same.

Stalemate, trench warfare and Haig

The failure of the Schlieffen Plan and of Allied attempts to drive the Germans back from the

Explain the German and French plans of attack in 1914.

Why did the Schlieffen Plan fail?

What was the 'Race to the Sea'?

creating an even better target for the enemy. Around Ypres (Wipers as the British called it), in an area called Flanders, heavy bombardments smashed the drainage systems, and thousands of wounded soldiers disappeared into the mud.

Trench warfare

Life in the 'trenches' could be extremely uncomfortable, as this soldier's lament explained:

> Far, far from WIpers I long to be,
> Where German snipers can't get at me.
> Cold is my dugout; damp are my feet,
> Waiting for a whizzbang to put me to sleep.

Whizzbangs (high-speed shells fired from guns which made a whizzing noise before you heard them explode) and snipers were only two of the risks. At Hooge, just along the Menin Road, where the front lines were only fifteen metres apart, 500 British soldiers were killed when the Germans exploded a massive mine under the British lines. Elsewhere, particularly if the front lines were wide apart, life in the trenches could be quite different, even boring, with just the rats, fleas, mud, dirty water, cold food and the stench of dead bodies to worry about.

But if a soldier found himself in the front line at the start of one of the major battles, he knew what to expect. Some 30 per cent of the troops who went 'over the top' at the first whistle would be killed and another 40 per cent would be wounded.

The role of Haig

Douglas Haig became Commander in Chief of the British forces on the Western Front in December 1915. He believed in the Big Push, that the enemy could be overwhelmed by sheer weight of numbers. On 1 July 1916 his first great battle began along the banks of the Somme. It was an attempt to take pressure off the French, who were involved in heavy fighting with the Germans at Verdun, but it was a disaster. The week-long bombardment failed to destroy the enemy defences and the British lost 70,000 casualties on the first day. When Haig eventually called off the attack in November, less than five miles had been gained and casualties were high

on all sides with approximately 650,000 German, 200,000 French and 420,000 British soldiers killed, missing or wounded.

In Haig's defence. It is true that he had only about half the forces that he believed he needed, but on the other hand, he allowed the army to go on attacking long after it was clear that no real progress was being made. At the same time, the French on the British right made much more impressive advances.

In 1917, Haig ordered a second major attack at Passchendaele, just north of Ypres. This time four miles were gained in three months, across a battlefield that was a sea of mud. When Haig visited the battlefield in late November, he said, 'My God, did I send men to fight in that?'

Haig appears to have been inflexible and lacking new ideas, but so were most commanders in the Great War. He remained convinced until the end of the war that cavalry was the key to victory.

Haig's tactics of the Big Push failed. In 1918, victory was won by surprise attacks without massive bombardments.

The war at sea

From 1900 to 1914, Britain and Germany engaged in a 'Naval Arms Race', each trying to build more Dreadnought battleships than the other. By 1914 Britain had 26 and Germany had 16. But both sides were afraid that their navies might be destroyed so there were few naval battles.

In 1914, there were a number of German raiders at sea. These were cruisers that preyed on merchant ships. The most famous was the *Emden*, which was sunk by *HMAS Sydney* in November. Much more of a danger was the squadron under Admiral von Spee, which defeated a British squadron at Coronel in November 1914, but was then itself destroyed at the Falkland Islands a month later.

The British Grand Fleet and the German High Seas fleet met only once in open battle. This was at Jutland. The Germans had 110 ships and the British had 145. The battle itself was fought mostly at long range and the result was indecisive. More British ships were sunk or damaged than German ships, but it was the Germans who broke off the battle and returned to their base. The German fleet never emerged from port again. It was possible, therefore, for both sides to claim victory.

The failure to defeat the Grand Fleet led the Germans to declare unrestricted submarine warfare in 1916. Merchantmen crossing the Atlantic were attacked by U-boats. David Lloyd George, the prime minister, forced the Admiralty to provide escorts for convoys and the number of losses fell dramatically.

The British Navy's other main role was to blockade Germany and strangle its trade. This was so effective that by early 1918 there were severe food shortages throughout the country and it was a major factor in Germany's collapse. Its people complained bitterly that they did not have enough to eat.

The Gallipoli campaign

In April 1915 British, French and Commonwealth troops landed on the Gallipoli peninsula in Turkey. Their aim was to attack Turkey and knock the country out of the war, then attack Austria and send supplies to Russia. The landings were the idea of the **Easterners**, led by Winston Churchill; it was their answer to the deadlock on the Western Front.

The landings were disastrous. In February the Navy had destroyed four Turkish forts at the entrance to the Dardanelles, the narrow opening to the Black Sea that was controlled by the Turks, but the Navy waited another month before destroying others. This delay meant that the Turks had time to strengthen their positions and, although the initial landings were unopposed, the troops were unable to make any progress inland. They were faced by high cliffs and Turkish defenders, who were well dug in.

In August 1915, a second landing was made at Suvla Bay, but with little effect. Eventually it was decided to withdraw the entire force. The evacuation, the most successful part of the whole operation, was carried out without any loss of life in December 1915, but 150,000 soldiers had been killed already through sickness and fighting.

The impact of new technology

Submarines
The significance of the submarine in warfare was shown almost immediately at the outbreak of the war when a German U-boat sank three British cruisers. At the beginning of 1917 the Germans had 120 submarines at sea and in April 1917 they sank more than 875,000 tonnes of Allied shipping. From May 1917, the Admiralty had to supply escorts for convoys sailing across the Atlantic. In addition, armed ships (called Q-ships) were disguised as merchant ships to catch out the submarines. Mines were also laid across the English Channel. By October 1917, the Germans had lost more than 50 submarines and the danger was over.

Tanks
The first tanks appeared in action during the Battle of the Somme on 15 September 1916. The army had resisted their use up till then. One reason for this was that they would scare the cavalry horses. The immediate impact of the first tanks was to terrify the German infantry. But the tanks were too few in number, only eighteen altogether, and they broke down all too easily on the muddy battlefield. Much more successful was the use of tanks at Cambrai on 20 November 1917. Some 380 tanks broke completely through the German lines, but the troops were unable to follow this up.

Tanks played a vital role in the great Allied offensive in August 1918. At Amiens, 450 tanks drove the Germans back eight miles and this began the wholesale retreat of the German forces. However, only 25 of the tanks were still

What problems did soldiers have to face in the trenches?

What percentage of soldiers were killed or wounded when they went 'over the top'?

List the ways in which the Royal Navy helped to win the war.

What were the advantages and disadvantages of tanks in the First World War?

in action four days later, a sign that the tank had not yet completely come of age.

Aircraft

At the beginning of the war aircraft were used mainly for reconnaissance (flying over enemy lines and reporting back on what was seen). At this time aeroplanes were not very strong. They made from wood and canvas and were held together by piano wire. From September British planes raided German airfields and in December 1914 German planes carried out an air raid on Dover. Heavy bombing of London began with the use of Zeppelins in 1915 and it was not until April 1916 that the first of these was shot down. From late 1916 Gotha bombers began to raid Britain. Altogether during the war there were 103 air raids, killing about 1,400 people. The numbers killed were relatively high as there were few ways of protecting people from bombing.

Dogfights began in France in the summer of 1915. These were aerial battles between fighter planes from Britain, France and Germany. From October the Germans had a distinct advantage with the invention of a device that allowed the pilot to shoot through the propeller. In July 1916, however, the British took command of the air and held it to the end of the war. By then many of the features of future aerial battles had developed, including formation flying, but air power had little effect on the war as a whole.

Gas

On 22 April 1915, at Langemarck just north of Ypres, the Germans used poison gas for the first time. Around 9,000 soldiers were killed. The gas proved to be a fearsome but unreliable weapon. At first it was spectacularly successful, but as better respirators were developed, and all armies developed large stocks, its use became more and more restricted. Attackers needed to wear respirators, which were clumsy and awkward, and made visibility very difficult. Gas was also unpredictable; on more than one occasion it was blown backwards into the faces of the attackers. By the end of the war it was still used in surprise attacks, but it no longer had the effects that it had had in 1915.

US intervention: the collapse of Russia

In November 1917, there was a revolution in Russia and Tsar Nicholas was overthrown. The Bolsheviks had seized power and immediately announced their intention to leave the war. Their leader, Lenin, expected civil war to break out in Russia at any minute and was determined to end the war against Germany, so that he could deal with his enemies. In March 1918, Russia signed the Treaty of Brest-Litovsk with Germany, handing over vast areas of land. Then the Germans moved a million men from the Eastern Front to France.

The USA had declared war on Germany in April 1917. Many Americans, including President Woodrow Wilson, had wanted to keep out of the war in Europe, but in March 1917 four US ships were sunk by German U-boats and the Zimmermann Telegram was discovered. This was an attempt by Germany to form an alliance with Mexico and begin an invasion of the USA.

The US declaration of war convinced the German High Command of the need to win the war quickly. 'Operation Michael' began at St Quentin on 21 March 1918. This was the German attempt to bring the war to an end before US forces arrived in Europe in numbers. The Allied forces were driven back 50 miles and by the end of May the Germans were only 37 miles from Paris. Their progress was halted in June by the French army supported by the US troops. The exhausted German soldiers were close to defeat.

After halting the German advance in June, US forces also played an important part in the second battle of the Marne in June and the subsequent battles in September and October. In total, about 1,250,000 US soldiers served in Europe; they showed immense bravery, but were not prepared for the dangers of modern warfare and their casualty rate was very high.

The commander of the US forces, General Pershing, allowed his troops to be used wherever they were needed. This gave Marshal Foch, the Allied commander, valuable reinforcements.

The defeat of Germany and the Peace Settlement

After Operation Michael the Germans were able to hold on to their gains until August 1918. Then on 8 August, the Allies attacked near Amiens. It was the 'Black Day', when the German army began to crumble. For three months the Allies advanced steadily, and it became more and more obvious that Germany was on the brink of disaster.

However, in October 1918, General Erich Ludendorff assumed command on the Western Front. He believed that the German army could hold out until spring 1919 and then resume the offensive. All that was needed, he said, was more reinforcements. Ludendorff's statements delayed the end of the war for a further three weeks.

In October and early November, a series of letters was exchanged between Berlin (Germany) and Washington (USA), discussing terms for an **armistice**. The Germans came to expect that any peace settlement would be based on the 'Fourteen Points' drawn up by President Wilson in January 1918. In Germany the situation became increasingly difficult. The people were starving and there was an attempted communist revolution on 7/8 November. Finally, on 9 November, Kaiser Wilhelm II stood down to allow his government to surrender. Germany surrendered unconditionally at 11 a.m. on 11 November 1918.

Terms of the Treaty of Versailles

- **Land** – Germany to lose about 10 per cent of its land, Alsace-Lorraine to be given back to France, the 'Polish Corridor' to be created to give the new country of Poland a way out to the Baltic. This would cut Germany into two. Germany was also to lose land to Belgium, Denmark and Czechoslovakia.

- **Colonies** – All German colonies to be taken away and handed to Britain and France to look after under League of Nations mandates until they would be ready for independence.

- **Armed Forces** – The German army to be reduced to 100,000 men and conscription banned, the Navy reduced to six ships and submarines banned, the Air Force to be completely destroyed.

- **The Rhineland** – To be demilitarised, no soldiers or military equipment to be kept within 30 miles of the east bank of the river. Allies to occupy it for 15 years.

- **The Saar** – To be occupied for 15 years. France would be able to mine coal in it for those years.

- **Reparations** – Germany to pay for the damage caused by the war, the full cost to be worked out by 1921; it eventually came to £6,600,000,000. This would be paid during the rest of the twentieth century.

- **War guilt** – Germany alone to accept blame for the war (Article 231).

In what ways were aircraft used during the First World War?

Why did the USA declare war on Germany in April 1917?

Why did Germany collapse so quickly in 1918?

Why were the German delegates horrified at the terms of the Treaty of Versailles?

The Treaty of Versailles was signed on 28 June 1919. The German delegates had not been allowed to attend any of the meetings at Versailles, but had been shown the terms of the Treaty in May. When they saw the terms, they were horrified. They had expected that the Treaty would be based on the Fourteen Points. But the Treaty was heavily influenced by Georges Clemenceau, the prime minister of France, who wanted to 'make Germany pay'. The German delegates considered restarting the war, but this was impossible.

The failure of the Schlieffen Plan

Source A

The Germans advanced in companies of 150 men five deep, and our rifle has a flat trajectory up to 600 yards. Guess the result. We could steady our rifles on the trench and take deliberate aim. The first company was simply blasted away to Heaven, and in their insane formation every bullet was bound to kill two men. The other companies kept advancing very slowly, using the bodies of their dead comrades as cover, but they had absolutely no chance.

▲ A British soldier describes the opening of the Battle of Mons on 23 August 1914.

Source B

One must face facts. Our Army Corps, in spite of the numerical superiority, which was assured to them, have not shown on the battlefield those offensive qualities, which we had hoped for ... We are therefore compelled to resort to the defensive ... Our object must be to last out as long as possible, trying to wear out the enemy, and to resume the offensive when the time comes.

▲ From a report written by the French General, Joffre, to the French Minister of War on 24 August 1914.

Source C

I had come to the conclusion that the great decisive battle in the West had been fought and decided in Germany's favour. I had intended to take these reinforcements from the Seventh Army, which had made as little progress towards the Moselle as the Sixth. Both these armies, however, consistently reported that they were opposed by superior numbers of the enemy, also that losses had been so heavy that no units of the Seventh Army were fit for employment elsewhere until they had been brought up to strength again. For these reasons, it was decided to send two Corps from the right wing ... to the Eastern Front. I admit that this was a mistake and one that was fully paid for on the Marne.

▲ From the memoirs of Von Moltke, describing his actions on 25–26 August 1914, when he sent reinforcements from the West to the Eastern Front.

Source D

Year	Right flank in Belgium	Left flank in Alsace-Lorraine
1905	54	8
1912	75	11
1914	54	17

▲ The numbers of German infantry divisions in the Schlieffen Plan.

Source E

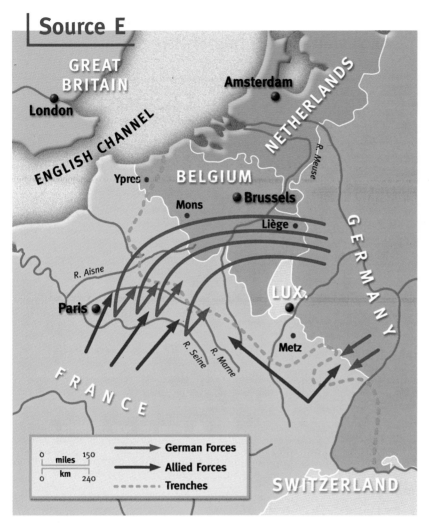

GREAT BRITAIN

London

Amsterdam

NETHERLANDS

ENGLISH CHANNEL

Ypres • BELGIUM

Mons • Brussels

Liège •

R. Meuse

GERMANY

R. Aisne

LUX.

Paris •

R. Seine

R. Marne

Metz

FRANCE

	German Forces
miles 150	Allied Forces
km 240	Trenches

SWITZERLAND

▲ The routes taken by the German armies in August and September 1914.

Source F

The numerically superior German units made deep inroads into the Allied lines, but never succeeded in breaking through. Their final defeat in the middle of November was principally a British victory. The English infantrymen, all professional soldiers, had mastered rapid rifle shooting to such an extent that the Germans suspected great numbers of British machine guns where there were hardly any. Many British marksmen could discharge 30 rounds a minute. The Allies were also helped by the determined stand of the Belgian King, Albert, who did not hesitate to have the lock gates of the canalised Yser River opened at Nieuport.

▲ From a modern history book.

Study Source A

a What can you learn from Source A about the German advance into Belgium in August 1914? (4)

Study Sources A and B

b i Does the evidence of Source B support the evidence of Source A about the German attacks in August 1914? (4)

b ii Use the sources and your own knowledge to explain the differences between Sources A and B. (6)

Study Sources C, D and E

c How useful are these sources in helping you to understand why the Schlieffen Plan failed? (6)

Study all of the sources

d 'The Schlieffen Plan failed because the Germans were outnumbered and made tactical errors.' Use the sources and your own knowledge to explain whether you agree with this view. (10)

Stalemate; the experience of trench warfare; the role of Haig

Source A

The three main objectives with which we had commenced our offensive in July had already been achieved ... Verdun had been relieved; the main German forces had been held on the Western Front; and the enemy's strength had been very considerably worn down.

▲ From the despatch written by Haig after the Battle of the Somme.

Source B

Far from the German loss being the greater, the British army was being worn down – numerically – more than twice as fast, and the loss is not just to be measured by bare numbers.
The troops who bore the brunt of the Somme fighting were the cream of the British population – the new volunteer army ...
A general who wears down 180,000 of his enemy by expending 400,000 men has something to answer for.

▲ From the *Official History of Australia in the War*, by C.E.W. Bean.

Source C

It is not too much to say that when the Great War broke out our Generals had the most important lessons to learn. They knew nothing except by hearsay about the actual fighting of a battle under modern conditions. Haig ordered many bloody battles in this war. He only took part in two. He never even saw the ground on which his greatest battles were fought, either before or during the fight.

▲ From the war memoirs of David Lloyd George.

Source D

▲ A photograph of the battlefield of the Somme.

Source E

Before going in to this next affair, at the same dreadful spot, I want to tell you, so that it may be on record, that I honestly believe Goldy [his brother] and many other officers were murdered on the night you know of, through the incompetence, callousness and personal vanity of those in high authority. I realise the seriousness of what I say, but I am so bitter, and the facts are so palpable that it must be said.

▲ From the last letter written by Lieutenant John Raws to his mother on 19 August 1916, during the Battle of the Somme. He was killed later in the same month.

Source F

	Haig's estimates	Actually available
Divisions	36	18
Guns	828	400
Roads	29	13
Railways	7	3

▲ A comparison of Haig's original estimates of men and equipment needed for the Battle of the Somme and what was actually available on 1 July 1916. Haig's estimates are taken from papers he wrote during 1915.

Study Source A

a   What can you learn from Source A about Haig's view of the Battle of the Somme? (4)

Study Sources A, B and C

Sources B and C give a different picture of the Battle of the Somme to that given in Source A.

b i In what ways do the sources differ? (4)

b ii Use the sources and your own knowledge to explain the differences between them. (6)

Study Sources D and E

c   How useful are these sources as evidence about Haig's role in the Battle of the Somme? (6)

Study all of the sources

d   'The failure of the Battle of the Somme was the result of bad planning by Haig.' Use the sources and your own knowledge to explain whether you agree with this view. (10)

The war at sea; the Gallipoli campaign

Source A

The departure from Mudros was to the accompaniment of wild cheering ... The troops were then told to rest; there was no wild excitement, but an air of quiet confidence. Very early on the morning of 25 April the men were roused and given a hearty meal before struggling into their kit ... Each man carried about 80 pounds, but instructions were to remove packs after landing and stack them in company piles ... Not a shot was to be fired ... Absolute silence was ordered until ashore, when only the bayonet was to be used.

▲ From a description of the landings at Anzac Cove written by Private Fred Fox.

Source B

The flotilla was nearly on shore when the senior naval officer realised a grave error had been made. The brigade was one full mile north of its intended landing place when at 4.25, with dawn clearly breaking ... they were only 50 yards from the beach, and at this moment the Turks saw them ... Instead of the gentle slope the troops had been led to expect, and the bank behind which they were going to form up and leave their packs, they were confronted by what appeared to be a steep cliff rising immediately off a narrow sandy beach.

▲ Another description of the landings on 25/26 April 1915, from a modern book on Gallipoli.

Source C

▲ A photograph of Anzac Cove.

Source D

'Y Beach', the Scottish Borderer cried

While panting up the steep hillside,

'Y Beach!

To call this thing a beach is stiff,

It's nothing but a b----- cliff.

Why beach?'

▲ A verse that appeared in the *Dardanelles Driveller*, a newspaper, on 17 May 1915.

Source E

How GHQ thought that to land the whole of the 11th Division in the dark on a strange shore and a few hours afterward land two brigades of the 10th Division on top of them could possibly be successful, passes the comprehension of even a junior officer ... At the actual landing my battalion lost the senior major, two captains and the adjutant killed and twelve officers wounded. I never saw my colonel for two days.

▲ A description of the landing at Suvla Bay in August 1915.

Source F

A week lost was about the same as a division. Three divisions in February would have occupied the Gallipoli peninsula with little fighting. Five would have captured it after 18 March. Seven were insufficient by the end of April, but nine might just have done it. Eleven might have sufficed at the beginning of July. Fourteen were to prove insufficient in August.

▲ From a book written by Winston Churchill after the war.

Study Source A

a What can you learn from Source A about the landings on Gallipoli in April 1915? (4)

Study Sources A, B and C

b Do Sources B and C support the evidence of Source A about the landings on Gallipoli? In your answer refer to all three sources. (4)

Study Sources B and C

c Use the sources and your own knowledge to explain why the landings did not go as planned. (6)

Study Sources D and E

d How useful are these sources in helping you to understand the problems faced by the Allied troops at Gallipoli? (6)

Study all of the sources

e 'The Gallipoli landings failed because the plans were badly carried out.' Use the sources and your own knowledge to explain whether you agree with this view. (10)

The impact of new technology: submarines, tanks, aircraft, gas

Source A

The monsters approached slowly. Nothing impeded them. Someone in the trenches said, 'The Devil is coming.' Tongues of flame leapt from the sides of the iron caterpillars. The English infantry came in waves behind.

▲ From a German description of the use of tanks at the Battle of Cambrai on 20 November 1917.

Source B

The news continues to be good, the tanks seem to have done good work and fairly put the wind up the Hun, who was seen to run like hell in front of them, shouting, 'This isn't war, it's murder.'

▲ From a letter written by a British officer in 1917.

Source C

▲ A painting of a tank crossing a trench.

Source D

Four hundred tanks in line of battle. Good going, firm ground, wheel to wheel and blazing brilliant weather. They crash through the barbed wire and bridge the trenches dealing death and retribution on the way.

The front line now, we swing her round, broadside on, a canister of shrapnel is poured into the huddling German troops. We trip merrily on, the six-pounder volleying shell after shell into the trench. The machine gunners firing as the Germans run for it.

▲ From an article in *The Fighting Forces Magazine*, describing a tank attack at the Battle of Amiens on 8 August 1918.

Source E

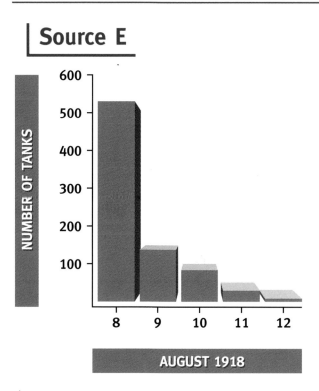

▲ The numbers of tanks in working order at the Battle of Amiens, 8–12 August 1918.

Source F

Their effect was largely on morale. They did a good service in crushing machine-gun posts and in village fighting. The infantry liked to see them, and as the enemy has invariably exaggerated the numbers employed, and has often reported their presence when there was none, he evidently stood in fear of them.

▲ A British general describing the impact of tanks in 1918.

Study Source A

a What can you learn from Source A about the impact of tanks on German troops in November 1917? (4)

Study Sources A, B and C

b Do Sources B and C support the evidence of Source A about the impact of tanks? (4)

Study Sources D and E

c i In what ways do these sources disagree about the impact of tanks in August 1918? (4)

c ii Use the sources and your own knowledge to explain why the sources differ. (6)

Study all of the sources

d 'Tanks were a decisive weapon in the final battles of the First World War.' Use the sources and your own knowledge to explain whether you agree with this view. (10)

The collapse of Russia: US intervention

Source A

We have no quarrel with the German people. We have no selfish ends to serve. We desire no conquest. We are but one of the champions of the rights of mankind. We shall fight for democracy, for the rights and liberties of small nations.

▲ From a speech made by Woodrow Wilson on 2 April 1917.

Source B

If this attempt is not successful, we propose an alliance on the following basis with Mexico: that we shall make war together and together make peace. We shall give general financial support, and it is understood that Mexico is to reconquer the lost territory in New Mexico, Texas and Arizona.

▲ From the Zimmermann Telegram, sent to the German Embassy in Mexico City in February 1917.

Source C

The rear was brought up by an enormous motor-bus load of the first American soldiers to pass through the streets of Paris. The crowds overflowed the sidewalks. From the crowded balconies and windows overlooking the route, women and children tossed down showers of flowers and bits of coloured paper.

Old grey-haired fathers of French fighting men bared their heads and with tears streaming down their cheeks shouted greetings to the tall, thin, grey-moustached American commander.

▲ From *And they thought we wouldn't fight*, a book written by a US soldier in the First World War.

Source D

▲ A photograph of US troops in 1918.

Source E

The sudden and dramatic entrance of the 2nd and 3rd Divisions into the shattered and broken fighting lines and their dash and courage in battle produced a favourable effect on the French soldiers. Although in battle for the first time, our men maintained their positions and effectively stopped the German advance on Paris. The Germans, who had been filled with propaganda about the poor quality of our training and war effort, must have been surprised at the strong resistance offered by the Americans.

▲ **From the war memoirs of General John J. Pershing, the commander of the US forces during the First World War. He is describing the first US actions in the spring of 1918.**

Source F

From the Allied point of view, the US entered the war just in time. France had fought herself to a standstill. Britain, reeling from the shock of losing virtually an entire generation of young men, was desperately short of both soldiers and munitions. Worse still, the Tsar's government had been overthrown by revolution in March 1917.

▲ **From a modern history textbook.**

Study Source A

a What can you learn from Source A about the reasons why the US declared war on Germany in 1917? (4)

Study Sources A and B

b In what ways does Source B add to the evidence of Source A about the reasons for the US declaration of war? (4)

Study Sources C and D

c How useful are Sources C and D as evidence about the impact of the US forces in France in 1918? (6)

Study Source E

d Use Source E and your own knowledge to explain why General Pershing believed the Americans played such an important role in saving Paris. (6)

Study all of the sources

e 'It was the entry of the USA into the First World War that brought about the final defeat of Germany.' Use the sources and your own knowledge to explain whether you agree with this view. (10)

The defeat of Germany and the Peace Settlement

Source A

July was a glorious month for the Allies, and August is even better. It began with the recovery of Soissons; a week later it was the turn of the British ... The 8th of August was a bad day for Germany for it showed that the counter-offensive was not to be confined to one sector, that from now on no respite would be allowed from hammer-blows.

▲ From an article in *Punch* August 1918.

Source B

As the sun set on 8 August on the battlefield, the greatest defeat which the German army had suffered since the beginning of the war was an accomplished fact. The positions between the Avre and the Somme, which had been struck by the enemy attack, were nearly completely annihilated.

▲ From the official German army report on 8 August 1918.

Source C

August was the black day of the German army in the history of this war. This was the worst experience that I had to go through, except for the events that, from 15 September onwards, took place on the Bulgarian Front.

We had to resign ourselves now to the prospect of a continuation of the enemy's offensive. Their success had been too easily gained. Their wireless was jubilant, and announced – and with truth – that the morale of the German army was no longer what it had been.

▲ From the war memoirs of General Erich Ludendorff.

Source D

These Armistice negotiations are having very bad consequences, since my soldiers can't see why they should continue fighting if they have to give up Belgium and Alsace-Lorraine. If we had battalions of full strength, the situation would be saved.

Yesterday we had a battle at Ypres. We were driven back, but came out well. It is true that gaps of four kilometres were broken in our line, but the enemy did not push through and we held the front. How much reinforcements from home would have meant to us.

▲ From a report by General Erich Ludendorff to the German cabinet in Berlin on 17 October 1918.

Source E

The morale of the troops has suffered considerably and their power of resistance is declining steadily. The men are surrendering in droves during enemy attacks ... We have no more dug-in positions and cannot build them any longer ... I want to emphasise that already at this moment our position is an extremely dangerous one, and according to circumstances, may turn into a catastrophe overnight. Ludendorff does not realise the seriousness of the situation.

▲ From a letter written by Prince Rupprecht of Bavaria, the commander of the German Sixth Army, to Prince Max von Baden, the German chancellor, on 18 October 1918.

Source F

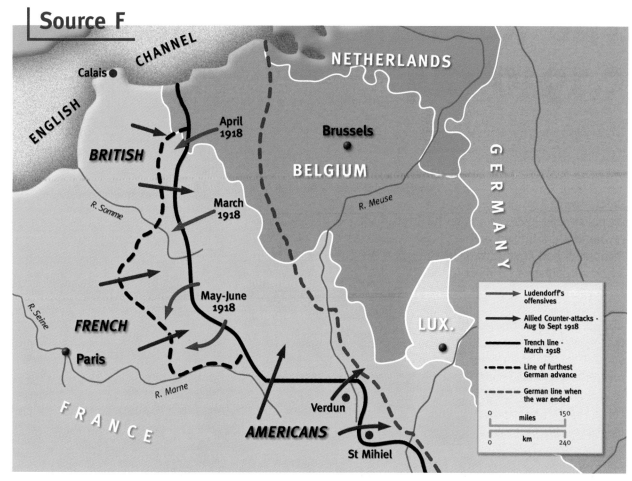

▲ A map showing the movements of the armies from August to November 1918.

Study Source A

a What can you learn from Source A about the Allied attacks on 8 August 1918? (4)

Study Sources B and C

b How useful are these sources in helping you to understand the impact of the Allied attacks upon the German army? (6)

Study Sources D and E

c i In what ways do these sources differ about the state of the German army in October 1918? (4)

c ii Use the sources and your own knowledge to explain why the sources differ. (6)

Study all of the sources

d 'The German army was defeated in 1918 through sheer weight of numbers.' Use the sources and your own knowledge to explain whether you agree with this view. (10)

CHAPTER 2

The Russian Revolution: c.1910~24

Essential Information

Russia before the First World War

Before the First World War, Russia was an autocracy. All power was in the hands of the Tsar. In 1905 revolution had broken out in St Petersburg and Nicholas II had been forced to set up the Duma, a sort of parliament. However, the Duma had little influence and no authority. As the years passed and the danger of further revolution seemed to disappear, Nicholas began to ignore it and regret that he had set it up at all. After 1911, it was of virtually no importance. This was typical of Nicholas, a kind, loving family man, who was totally unsuited to being the absolute ruler of 130,000,000 people. He lacked any real determination and was easily persuaded to do nothing.

The October Manifesto

In 1905 Nicholas II faced a revolution. The Russian army and navy were heavily defeated by Japan and there was widespread unrest in St Petersburg, which led to a general strike in October. Nicholas was only saved by the loyalty of the Russian army. Nicholas II agreed to issue the October Manifesto, which guaranteed freedom of speech, universal suffrage and a **Duma**, or parliament, which would have the power to make laws.

But Nicholas did have one very strong belief; he believed that it was his duty to pass on his **autocratic** power to his son, just as his father had passed it on to him. This belief made him even more determined to do as little as possible to change Russia.

In 1906, as well as having set up the Duma, Nicholas also appointed Peter Stolypin, a reformer, as prime minister. This seemed to suggest that Nicholas wanted to change Russia.

However, after Stolypin's murder in 1911, Nicholas gave up any real attempts at reform; Russia appeared to have recovered from the upheaval of 1905. Political power was once more in the hands of members of Nicholas's court. This maintained the extreme differences between rich and poor, which were greater in Russia than in any other European country.

On the face of it, Nicholas was right. In the years before the First World War, Russia appeared to be as strong and as secure as ever. More than 80 per cent of Russians were peasants, living in the countryside and working on the estates of wealthy landlords. Most were unable to read or write and used farming methods that were passed on from father to son. They were intensely loyal to the Tsar, who they addressed as 'Papa', and showed little interest in life beyond their village. When war broke out in 1914, vast numbers of peasants enrolled in the army, as they had often done before.

There were, however, important changes taking place in Russia. Although only 4 per cent of Russians worked in industry, the number was growing rapidly. In fact, between 1880 and 1900 the population of Moscow doubled. As more and more people swarmed in to the big cities, conditions deteriorated rapidly. Food shortages in St Petersburg and Moscow became common. In fact, Russia produced more than enough food to feed its population, but the railway network was unable to cope with the increased demands from the big cities. In 1917, the revolution would start in St Petersburg and the people of the city would decide the fate of Tsarist Russia. One of the most important factors influencing events would be shortages of food.

Opposition to Tsarist rule

In an autocracy opposition easily becomes violent. As there was no way of changing the government in Russia through a general election, terrorists used violence to try to force change. There were many assassinations in Russia. Nicholas II's own grandfather, Alexander II, had been killed by a terrorist bomb in 1881, and Nicholas had been shown the shattered body. Other members of the royal family suffered similar fates.

The Rule of the Tsar

All political power in Russia was in the hands of the Tsar, who was described as an 'autocrat'. This in effect made him a dictator. Tsars usually appointed prime ministers, but could just as easily dismiss them. There was nobody in Russia who could criticise or control the Tsar. This system could work as long as the Tsar was intelligent and competent, but Nicolas II was neither.

The largest and most violent of the terrorist groups was the Socialist Revolutionaries, led by Victor Chernov, which was supported by many peasants. Between 1901 and 1905 the group murdered more than 2,000 people. The next biggest was the Social Democrats, who split into two sections in 1903: the Mensheviks, led by Julius Martov; and the Bolsheviks, led by Vladimir Lenin. These two groups were only popular in the big cities, but it was here that most of the important events of 1917 would take place.

All three of these groups were Marxist. This means they based their beliefs on the writings of Karl Marx. They believed that the growth of industry would produce a working class, the proletariat, which would take power after a revolution and also take control of all industry and business. They believed that all property should be shared equally among the workers, and that each person should be paid what his or her work was actually worth. Both the Socialist Revolutionaries and the Mensheviks thought that this would not happen for many years, but Lenin, the leader of the Bolsheviks, believed that it was possible to force the pace. For this reason he was only prepared to allow committed revolutionaries to join the Bolsheviks. They became a small highly disciplined organisation.

The structure and organisation of the Bolsheviks made them the most important of the Marxist groups. They were the most committed and the most determined. When revolution broke out in 1917, Lenin was the only leader who tried to take full advantage of the situation. Both the Socialist Revolutionaries and the Mensheviks were prepared to let events take their course, this played into the hands of the Bolsheviks, who were able to seize power with little opposition. However, in 1914 most of the opposition groups had been broken up by the Okhrana, the Tsar's secret police, and their leaders were living abroad. Lenin was in Switzerland and the chances of a successful revolution appeared to be slight.

Inside Russia, the Constitutional Democrats, or Kadets, and the Octobrists were the most important opposition groups. The Kadets were formed in 1905 and were led by Paul Miliukov. They were mostly lawyers, teachers, doctors and civil servants. They believed in working within the **constitution** to bring about change. They attempted to make use of the Duma, which met for the first time in 1906, but Nicholas II closed the meeting after 72 days. Although it met on three more occasions, each time elections were more controlled and there was less opportunity for change. The Octobrists were also formed in 1906. They believed in change through the Tsar's October Manifesto, which the Tsar had issued in 1905. They dominated the Duma.

At the same time the Russian economy developed rapidly. From 1911 to 1914 exports and imports doubled, agricultural production increased and government debt fell. Not surprisingly, by 1914, the Kadets had achieved nothing.

How did the Tsar try to keep control of Russia?

Why were there very few changes to Russia from 1906, despite the 1905 Revolution?

List the main opposition groups in Russia before 1914. In what ways were they different from each other?

Why were the Bolsheviks the most dangerous of the opposition groups in Russia?

The impact of the First World War

On 1 August, Nicholas II was persuaded to declare war on Germany. Two weeks later the Russian army invaded Germany, taking the Germans completely by surprise. But their success was short-lived. The two Russian armies did not co-operate and actually competed with each other to be the first to gain victory. All messages were sent by wireless without any codes, and the maps used were years out of date. At the end of the month the Germans counter-attacked and defeated both armies one after another at the Masurian Lakes and Tannenberg. Some 230,000 Russian soldiers were either killed or taken prisoner. A succession of more heavy defeats followed in the next year.

Unfortunately, Russia was not equipped to fight a modern war. By the end of 1914 there were 6,500,000 men in the army, but they only had 4,600,000 rifles. The railway network was incapable of bringing fresh supplies of food and ammunition, and could not carry away the vast numbers of casualties. In September 1915, Nicholas II decided to assume command of the army himself and left for the Front. He was never to return to Petrograd (as St Petersburg was now known). His decision had two significant consequences: from this point onwards he was seen as being responsible for the failures of the army; and he was removed from the capital, which meant that he relied on others for information about the situation there.

By 1916, the situation had improved. The railway network had been extended, and supplies of food and ammunition were reaching the army; the Russian army was strong enough to go on the attack. It was able to take 300,000 Austrian prisoners, but failed to achieve a breakthrough against the Germans. Stalemate developed on the Eastern Front, just as it had in the West.

In Petrograd, the government became increasingly unpopular after Nicholas II left for the Front. The Tsarina Alexandra, who was German, was suspected of being a spy and her reliance on a holy man called Grigori Rasputin made her increasingly unpopular. He had gained influence over the Tsarina because he could apparently alleviate the haemophilia of her son, the heir to the throne.

From September 1915, ministers were replaced repeatedly, often at the whim of Alexandra and at the suggestion of Rasputin, with no thought for their ability or experience. Continuity in government became impossible. Most of the ministers responsible for the recovery of the Russian army in 1916 were sacked by the end of March. Rasputin and his relationship with Alexandra became more and more detested by the ruling classes and in December 1916 he was murdered by Prince Yusopov.

The population of Petrograd also began to suffer extreme shortages of food and severe inflation. One minister stated that 405 railway cars were needed to supply the city, but that on average it only received 116. There was plenty of food in Russia; the problem was transport – particularly as the railway network had been taken over by the army. As the war progressed and more and more workers were needed in industrial factories, more people crammed into the overcrowded capital. It was here that the very worst effects of the war were felt – the effects that were to lead to the downfall of the monarchy.

1917: the reasons for collapse

By early 1917 the situation in Petrograd was desperate. Food shortages, rapidly rising prices and rumours about the Tsarina led to widespread unrest in the overcrowded working class districts. Nicholas received regular reports from the President of the Duma, Mikhail Rodzianko, but tended to ignore them, preferring instead to believe the letters of his wife. He suspected that Rodzianko was trying to get more influence for himself. Rodzianko warned of severe unrest and the need for immediate action; the Tsarina described minor incidents, which she stated would soon pass. When the Tsar eventually realised the severity of the situation on 1 March, it was too late and he was forced to abdicate.

In fact the worst might have been avoided, but for a series of coincidences. International Women's Day was celebrated on 23 February and a series of marches were planned for the city centre. These became a focus for opposition to the Tsar and the number of strikers increased rapidly, urged on by

Russia and the First World War

August 1914
Battles of Tannenberg and the Masurian Lakes, 500,000 Russian soldiers killed or taken prisoner.

September 1915
Nicholas II appointed himself commander-in-chief. He now began to be blamed for the lack of success.

Severe shortages of food in the main cities, especially Petrograd. Mass desertions from the Russian army begin.

December 1916
Rasputin murdered by a cousin of the Tsar.

January 1917
Major unrest in Petrograd as a result of inflation and lack of bread.

their wives who were struggling to cope with the shortages. When troops were sent in to deal with the unrest, they began to side with the demonstrators. Within days royal authority in the city had collapsed. Immediately after the abdication a Provisional Government was set up by members of the Duma; the prime minister was Prince Lvov. The Provisional Government had no authority and very little power outside of Petrograd. Inside Petrograd it had a rival, the Petrograd **Soviet**, which virtually approved its decisions. The members of the Provisional Government believed that their main role was to prepare for a general election, which was planned for November and, in the meantime, to govern Russia as best they could. They did not feel able to bring the war with Germany to an end or to carry out any major reforms.

As a consequence, the Provisional Government was seen as little better than the Tsar's regime. It ordered a further offensive against the Germans in June, which failed, and although it did its best to solve the food shortages, these grew worse in the late summer and autumn.

Lenin arrived back in Petrograd in April 1917 and set about attracting as much support for the

Bolsheviks as possible. In the April Theses he promised 'Peace, bread, and land', although he did not explain how he would achieve any of those. When the Bolsheviks attempted to seize power in May and again in July they were crushed, and Lenin was forced to flee in disguise to Finland. In July a former Socialist Revolutionary, Alexander Kerensky, became prime minister. But in September the army Commander, General Kornilov, tried to overthrow him and Kerensky was forced to appeal to the Bolsheviks for help. He ordered the leaders to be let out of prison and party members to be given arms. Lenin realised the weakness of the Provisional Government and began to plan to seize power.

The failure of the Provisional Government
It was unelected and had no real power. Outside of Petrograd it was largely ignored.

Inside Petrograd the Provisional Government could do little without the approval of the Petrograd Soviet.

It decided to continue with the war against Germany. This increased the number of desertions and undermined the authority of the army commanders.

It did nothing to redistribute land, which the peasants had expected.

It did little to tackle the food shortages. Although bread rations rose from April to September 1917, they were still less than they had been in March.

Why was the Russian army unable to defeat the German army in 1914 and 1915?

What effects did Nicholas's decision to appoint himself commander-in-chief in 1915 have?

In what ways did the role of Rasputin make the Tsar even more unpopular?

Why did the Provisional Government find it hard to govern Russia?

The Bolshevik take-over

In September 1917, the Bolsheviks became the largest party in the Petrograd Soviet. They also controlled the Military Committee of the Soviet of which Leon Trotsky became the chairman. In September and October, when Lenin was still in hiding in Finland, Trotsky became the leading important Bolshevik in Petrograd. Lenin eventually returned on 16 October. On 6–7 November the Bolsheviks seized power, they cut telephone wires, seized control of the post office, railway stations and other key buildings, and isolated the Winter Palace, where the Provisional Government met. Military units loyal to the Provisional Government were ordered to defend Petrograd from an advance by the Germans.

According to later Bolshevik propaganda, the seizure was a triumph for the Red Guards organised and led by Trotsky. In fact, it now appears that Kerensky and the Provisional Government were so unpopular that few people were prepared to defend it. When the Bolsheviks attacked the Winter Palace, Kerensky sent repeated messages to the army appealing for help, but only a few hundred assorted troops turned up, including some students, 140 women and 40 soldiers who had been crippled by wounds. Even so it took the Bolsheviks the best part of two days to take over Petrograd.

The Petrograd Soviet

The Petrograd Soviet was a committee set up in March 1917 to represent the workers and soldiers of the city and became the basis for 'Soviets' set up in other parts of Russia. It was the only elected body in Petrograd. The Soviet was able to control the Provisional Government by preventing its decisions being carried out although few people took any notice of the Provisional Government in any case.

In September 1917 the Soviets came under Bolshevik control. This change was very important in the success of the Bolshevik seizure of power, as it enabled the Bolsheviks to move army units in and out of Petrograd.

While these events were unfolding in Petrograd, Lenin remained in hiding in disguise in the Bolshevik headquarters. Trotsky was the key to Bolshevik success. Once the seizure of power had been successful, Lenin emerged. He immediately announced the Peace and Land Decrees. The first stated that the war with Germany was over, the second allowed peasants to take over land for themselves. Further decrees banned other political parties and announced workers' control of industry. The general election on 12 November was won convincingly by the Socialist Revolutionaries. Lenin prevented the new Parliament, the Constituent Assembly, meeting until 5 January 1918, by which time he had set up his secret police force, the Cheka. When the Assembly finally met, Lenin closed it down. The Bolsheviks were now in control.

The events of 1917

2 March
Abdication of Nicholas II.
Formation of the Provisional Government.
Election of the Petrograd Soviet.

April
Lenin returns from Switzerland.
The April Theses.

May
Unsuccessful attempt by the Bolsheviks to seize power.

June
Provisional Government orders an offensive against the German army.

July
The 'July Days', a second failed attempt by the Bolsheviks to seize power. Lenin forced to escape to Finland, many Bolsheviks arrested. Kerensky becomes prime minister.

September
The Kornilov Revolt. Kerensky releases the Bolsheviks from prison and gives them arms to defend the Provisional Government.

The Bolsheviks take control of the Petrograd Soviet.

6/7 November
The Bolsheviks seize power in Petrograd.

Bolshevik rule and its impact

At first Lenin intended committees of workers to run factories and businesses. This happened all over Russia in the early months of 1918, sometimes with government backing, but more often without. But workers usually proved unable to run factories effectively and as the threat of civil war grew and food shortages increased, War Communism was introduced and this lasted from 1918 to 1921.

Civil war broke out in the summer of 1918. The Whites, the Bolsheviks' opponents, were made up of different groups, including the Tsarist army commanders, the Czech Legion, Poles, Cossacks, Ukrainians – all banded together. Britain, the USA and France all sent aid, partly because Lenin made peace with the Germans at the Treaty of Brest–Litovsk in March 1918. This allowed 1,000,000 German troops to be transferred to the Western Front. Lenin also cancelled all of the loans made to Russia before the seizure of power.

At first it appeared that the Whites held all the advantages. Their commanders were more experienced and they quickly closed in on the cities of Petrograd and Moscow, but the tide soon turned in the Bolsheviks favour. Trotsky organised the Red Army and provided inspirational leadership. His most important decision was recruiting thousands of ex-Tsarist officers who provided the backbone of the new army. He also introduced **conscription** in the areas controlled by the Bolsheviks, which were much more heavily populated than the outlying areas under White control. The Red Army rose to 2,000,000 men, against which the Whites could only raise 250,000. The Bolsheviks also controlled the main centres of industry as well as the railway and communications network.

The Whites made matters worse for themselves by not co-operating. They attacked at different times and the Bolsheviks were able to deal with one army after another. With the distances between Siberia, the Crimea and Poland being so vast, however, it is unlikely that they ever could have co-operated.

War Communism also played an important part in the Red victory. Everything and everybody came second to the needs of the Red Army: food, raw materials and industrial goods were confiscated and 'hoarders' were shot. The Cheka enforced Lenin's policy and 50,000 people were executed without trial. When the Whites approached Ekaterinburg, where the members of royal family were being held, in July 1918, the local Cheka commander executed them.

But victory was achieved at tremendous cost. By 1921 industrial production was 25 per cent of the 1913 level, and 5,000,000 people had died of famine since 1919. When the sailors of the Kronstadt Naval Base revolted in March 1921, Lenin decided to introduce what was called the New Economic Policy to allow Russia to recover. This was a step back to capitalism. Small businesses were allowed with up to 25 workers and instead of the government seizing produce, workers were allowed to pay taxes. By January 1924, when Lenin died, Russia was on the way to economic recovery.

Trotsky and the Civil War

In 1918 Trotsky took charge of the Red Army. His main contribution was as a leader and organiser. His most important action in the organisation of the Red Army was to recruit Tsarist officers. It was this that led to the Red Army becoming an efficient fighting force. To keep the officers under control, Trotsky appointed a Bolshevik official, a 'Commissar', to every army unit. These officials observed and reported the actions of the officers. He is also well known for his journeys to the front in his 'War Train' to encourage the Bolshevik soldiers.

Why did the Provisional Government receive so little support on 6 and 7 November?

Why did Civil War break out in 1918?

Why did the Bolsheviks win the Civil War?

What effects did the Civil War have on Russia?

Russia before the First World War: politics, society and the economy

Source A

His Majesty is an absolute monarch, who is not obliged to answer for his actions to anyone in the world but has the power and the authority to govern his states as a Christian sovereign, in accord with his desire and goodwill.

To the Emperor of All the Russias belongs the Supreme Autocratic power. God himself commands that he be obeyed, not only from fear of God's wrath, but also for the sake of one's conscience.

▲ From the Military Regulations of Peter the Great, 1716; this defined the power of the Tsar.

Source B

The Tsar's authority is unlimited – like a father's. This autocracy is only an extension of a father's authority. From the base to the summit, the Empire ... rests on one foundation: the authority of a father.

▲ A description of the power of the Tsar written in Russia in 1898.

Source C

The current attitude seemed to suggest that the government was a barrier between the people and the Tsar ... The Tsar's closest friends became convinced that the Sovereign could do anything by relying upon the unbounded love and utter loyalty of the people. The ministers of the government, on the other hand, did not hold to this sort of autocracy; nor did the Duma. Both were of the opinion that the Sovereign should recognise that conditions had changed since the day the Romanovs became Tsars of Moscow.

▲ A description of the Imperial Court of Nicholas II, written in 1913 by Count Kokovtsev, who succeeded Peter Stolypin as prime minister.

Source D

You are mistaken, my dear grandmama; Russia is not England. Here we do not need to earn the love of the people. The Russian people love their Tsars as divine beings, from whom all charity and fortune derive. As far as St Petersburg society is concerned, that can be completely disregarded.

▲ From a letter written by the Tsarina Alexandra to her grandmother, Queen Victoria.

Source E

From his youth he had been trained to believe that his welfare and the welfare of Russia were one and the same thing ... 'disloyal' workmen, peasants and students who were shot down, executed or exiled seemed to him mere monsters who must be destroyed for the sake of the country.

▲ From a description of Tsar Nicholas II written by Alexander Kerensky in 1917.

Source F

▲ A photograph of the Imperial Court.

Study Source A

a What can you learn from Source A about the power of the Tsar in Russia? (4)

Study Sources A and B

b Does Source B support the evidence about the power of the Tsar in Russia? In your answer refer to both sources. (4)

Study Sources A, B and C

c Source C gives a different impression of the position of the Tsar in Russia to that given in Sources A and B. Use the sources and your own knowledge to explain why they are different. (6)

Study Sources D and F

d How useful are these sources as evidence about the position of the Tsar in Russia? (6)

Study all of the sources

e 'It would have been difficult for the Tsar to have an understanding of the problems faced by the ordinary people of Russia, even if he did he would not have felt the need to act to solve them.' Use the sources and your own knowledge to explain whether you agree with this view. (10)

Opposition to Tsarist rule: Liberals, Socialists and Socialist Revolutionaries

Source A

The armies of the secret police are continuously growing in numbers. The prisons and penal colonies are overcrowded with thousands of convicts and political prisoners ... In all the cities ... the soldiers are employed and equipped with live ammunition ... yet this strenuous and terrible activity of the government results only in the growing impoverishment of the rural population ... A similar condition is the general dissatisfaction of all classes with the government and their open hostility to it.

▲ From an open address by the writer Leo Tolstoy to Tsar Nicholas II in 1902.

Source C

Let those in power make no mistake about the temper of the people; let them not take outward indications of prosperity as an excuse for lulling themselves into security. Never were the Russian people so profoundly revolutionised by the actions of the government, for day by day faith in the government is waning and with it is a waning faith in the possibility of a peaceful issue of the crisis.

▲ From a speech made at the Octobrist Party Conference in 1913.

Source D

There has never been so much tension. People can be heard speaking of the government in the sharpest ... tones. Many say that the shooting of the Lena workers recalls the shooting of the workers at the Winter Palace of January 1905 ... there have been references in the Duma to the necessity of calling a Constituent Assembly and to overthrow the present system by the united strength of the proletariat.

▲ From a report by a Moscow Okhrana agent in 1912.

Source B

Peasants burned the estates of the landowners, destroying everything they got their hands on ... Almost never did the peasants steal, but with a bright flame burned magnificent manors, cattle-sheds, barns and granaries ... And many landowners fled, without even having time to look back at their beloved homes, on which former generations had lavished so much labour and love.

▲ From an eyewitness account of events in 1905.

Source E

Date	Number of strikes
1910	222
1911	466
1912	2,032
1913	2,404

▲ Numbers of strikes in Russia; these figures were compiled by modern historians.

▲ A photograph of a demonstration against the government in 1913.

Study Source A

a What can you learn from Source A about the reasons why Nicholas II was unpopular in Russia? (4)

Study Sources A and B

b Does Source B support the evidence of Source A about the popularity of the government in Russia? Explain your answer by referring to both sources. (4)

Study Sources C and D

c How useful are Sources C and D as evidence about the opposition to the government in Russia? (6)

Study Sources D and F

d Use these sources and your own knowledge to explain how widespread the opposition to the Tsar's government was in the years leading up to the First World War. (6)

Study all of the sources

e 'The main reason for opposition to the Tsar in the period leading up to the First World War was the discontent of Russia's workers and peasants.' Use the sources and your own knowledge to explain whether you agree with this view. (10)

Impact of the First World War on Russian government and society

Source A

General Ruzsky complained to me of a lack of ammunition and the poor equipment of the men ... The soldiers fought barefooted. The war hospitals were disorganised. They were short of bandages and such things.

The Grand Duke stated that he was obliged to stop fighting, temporarily, for lack of ammunition and boots.

There was plenty of material and labour in Russia. But as it stood then, one region had leather, another nails, another soles, and still another cheap labour.

▲ From a report to the Duma by Mikhail Rodzianko in 1916.

Source B

Soldiers from the neighbouring barracks, who were looking over a low fence into the street, knocked down the fence, beating up and driving out the police. Cossacks were called out to arrest the soldiers and workers. But the Cossacks decided not to act and they were withdrawn. The soldiers' behaviour caused consternation among the military hierarchy ... 130 men were arrested and threatened with court-martial.

▲ An eyewitness account of unrest in Petrograd in 1916.

Source C

Date	Index of prices
1914	100
1915	130
1916	141
1917	398

▲ An index of prices in Russia; the figures were compiled by modern historians.

Source D

Date	Bread ration
January 1916	1.25 kilograms
December 1916	1.0 kilograms
March 1917	0.8 kilograms

▲ Bread rations in Petrograd; these figures come from official Russian sources.

Source E

There is a marked increase in hostile feelings among the peasants, not only against the government, but also against all other social groups. The proletariat of the capital is on the verge of despair. The mass of industrial workers are quite ready to let themselves go to the wildest excesses of a hunger riot ... the labour masses, led by the more advanced and already revolutionary-minded elements, assume an openly hostile attitude against the government.

▲ From an Okhrana report on events in Petrograd in January 1917.

Source F

▲ A photograph of a demonstration in Petrograd in 1916.

Study Source A

a What can you learn from Source A about the effects of the First World War on the Russian army? (4)

Study Sources B and C

b How useful are Sources B and C as evidence about unrest in Russia in 1916? (6)

Study Sources C, D and E

c In what ways do Sources C and D help explain the events described in Source E? Use your own knowledge and all of the sources in your answer. (6)

Study Source E

d How does Source E suggest that Russia was on the verge of revolution? (4)

Study all of the sources

e 'The most important effect of the war was to cut off food supplies to Petrograd.' Use the sources and your own knowledge to explain whether you agree with this view. (10)

1917: reasons for the fall of the Tsar and the collapse of the Provisional Government

Source A

It would be no exaggeration to say that Petrograd achieved the March Revolution. The rest of the country adhered to it. There was no struggle anywhere except in Petrograd. There was not to be found anywhere in the country any groups of the population ... or military units, which were ready to put up a fight for the old regime. Neither at the front nor at the rear was there a brigade or regiment prepared to do battle for Nicholas II.

▲ A description of the March Revolution written by Leon Trotsky.

Source B

The queues – well the queues haven't got smaller in the least; I think they're even bigger. You stand half the day, just as before ... They say 'It's all the same there's nothing to be had, the rich just keep fleecing the poor. The shopkeepers are the only ones making money.'

▲ An eyewitness describes queues in Petrograd in March 1917.

Source C

▲ A photograph of soldiers and workers fraternising in the streets of Petrograd in February 1917.

Source D

The Cossacks were firing on defenceless and unarmed crowds, striking people with whips, crushing the fallen with their horses. And then I saw a young girl trying to evade the galloping horse of a Cossack officer. She was too slow. A severe blow on the head brought her down under the horse's feet. She screamed. It was her inhuman, penetrating scream that caused something in me to snap. I jumped to the table and cried out wildly: 'Friends, friends! Long live the Revolution! To arms, to arms! They are killing innocent people our brothers and sisters.'

They all joined me in the attack against the Cossacks and the police. We killed a few of them. The rest retreated.

▲ From a letter written by a sergeant in the Russian army in March 1917, in which he describes how he persuaded his regiment to mutiny.

Source E

The Provisional Government has no real power of any kind and its orders are carried out only to the extent that is permitted by the Soviet of Workers' and Soldiers' deputies. The Soviet controls the most essential levers of power, insofar as the troops, the railways and the postal and telegraph services are in its hands. One can definitely say that the Provisional Government exists only as long as it is allowed to do so by the Soviet.

▲ From a letter written by the politician Alexander Guchkov on 9 March 1917.

Source F

Date	Number of members
1917 February	24,000
1917 April	100,000
1917 October	340,000

▲ Modern estimates of the numbers of members of the Bolshevik Party.

Study Source A

a What can you learn from Source A about why the Tsar was overthrown? (4)

Study Sources A, B and C

b Do Sources B and C support the evidence of Source A about why the Tsar was overthrown? In your answer refer to all three sources. (4)

Study Sources C and D

c How useful are these sources in helping you understand why the Tsar was overthrown? (6)

Study Source E

d Use the evidence of Source E and your own knowledge to explain why the Provisional Government had little authority in Russia. (6)

Study all of the sources

e 'The March Revolution succeeded because nobody was prepared to defend the monarchy.' Use the sources and your own knowledge to explain whether you agree with this view. (10)

The nature of the Bolshevik takeover; the roles of Lenin and Trotsky

Source A

In the cavernous dark hallways where here and there flickered a pale electric light, thousands and thousands of soldiers, sailors and factory workers tramped in their heavy boots every day ... Smolni worked 24 hours a day. For weeks Trotsky never left the building. He ate and slept and worked in his office on the third floor and many people came to see him.

▲ A description of the Bolshevik headquarters, the Smolni Institute, in November 1917 written by a British woman who was living in Petrograd.

Source B

There can be no doubt about it – Lenin is an extraordinary phenomenon, a man of absolutely exceptional intellectual power ... he represents an unusually happy combination of theoretician and popular politician, who had the ability not only to seduce the masses, who have no other teaching but that of the Tsarist whip, but also the Bolshevik Party itself.

▲ A description of Lenin written in 1917.

Source C

The entire Praesidium headed by Lenin were standing up singing with excited, exalted faces and blazing eyes ... while the mass of delegates were permeated by the faith that all would go well in the future too. They were beginning to be persuaded of the Communist Peace, Land and Bread.

▲ An eyewitness account of a meeting of the Bolshevik Party on 7 November 1917.

Source D

Party	Number of seats
Socialist Revolutionaries	370
Bolsheviks	175
National groups	99
Left SRs	40
Kadets	17
Mensheviks	16

▲ The results of the general election of November 1917.

Source E

The hall began to resemble a battlefield. Chairs and tables were overturned, pictures torn from the walls, in every row there were groups of soldiers trying to heckle speakers, their rifles cocked menacingly towards the platform. The sailors' faces were distorted with rage, they seemed almost inhuman. Their attitude was menacing; their impatient, feverish hands never left the trigger.

▲ A description of the opening of the Constituent Assembly on 5 January 1918, this was written by Olga Chernov, the wife of the leader of the Socialist Revolutionaries.

Source F

To hand over power to the Constituent Assembly would mean doing a deal with the bourgeoisie. The Russian Soviets place the interests of the toiling masses far above the interests of compromise ... Nothing in the world will induce us to surrender the Soviet power ... And by the will of the Soviet power, the Constituent Assembly, which has refused to recognise the power of the people, is dissolved. The Soviet Revolutionary Republic will triumph no matter what the cost.

▲ Lenin explains the closing the Constituent Assembly.

Study Source A

a What can you learn from this source about the role of Trotsky in the Bolshevik seizure of power? (4)

Study Sources B and C

b Use Sources B and C and your own knowledge to explain the part played by Lenin in November 1917. (6)

Study Sources C and D

c Sources C and D give different accounts of the popularity of the Bolsheviks in late 1917. How do you explain the differences between the two sources? (6)

Study Source E

d Why was the meeting of the Constituent Assembly so chaotic? (4)

Study all of the sources

e 'Lenin played a more significant part than Trotsky in the Bolshevik takeover of Russia.' Use the sources and your own knowledge to explain whether you agree with this view. (10)

Bolshevik rule and its impact, 1918–24: the Civil War

Source A

Private ownership of all land shall be abolished forever; land shall not be sold, purchased, leased ... All land, whether state crown, monastery, church, factory, private, public ... shall be confiscated without compensation and become the property of the whole people.

▲ From the Decree on Land, November 1917.

Source B

In order to provide planned regulation of the national economy, workers' control over the manufacture, purchase, sale and storage of produce and raw materials and over the financial activity of enterprise is introduced in all industrial, commercial, banking, agricultural co-operative and other enterprises, which employed hired labour.

▲ From the Decree on Workers' Control, November 1917.

Source C

Force is necessary for the transition from capitalism to socialism. The type of force is determined by the development of the revolutionary class and also by special circumstances. For example, the heritage of a long and reactionary war and the forms of resistance put up by the bourgeoisie. There is absolutely no contradiction between Soviet democracy and the exercise of dictatorial powers.

▲ From an article written by Lenin in 1918, in which he is explaining why force must be used in Russia.

Source D

Our revolution is in danger. Do not concern yourselves with the forms of revolutionary justice. We have no need for justice now. Now we have need of a battle to the death. I demand the use of the revolutionary sword, which will put an end to all counter-revolutionaries.

▲ From a directive issued in 1918 by Felix Dzerzhinsky, head of the Cheka from its formation.

Source E

В БОРЬБЕ
с ЭКОНОМИЧЕСКОЙ РАЗРУХОЙ
МЫ НЕ ЗНАЕМ ОГРАНИЧЕНИЯ РАБОЧЕГО
ВРЕМЕНИ

▲ A photograph of the Cheka in action.

Source F

The troops of the army of the south blotted their reputation by pogroms against the Jews ... The pogroms brought suffering to the Russian people, but they also affected the morale of the troops, warped their minds and destroyed discipline.

▲ **From the memoirs of General Denikin, the leader of the White Armies in Southern Russia, in which he is describing the White forces.**

Study Source A

a What can you learn from Source A about the changes the Bolsheviks made in Russia? (4)

Study Sources A, B and C

b Do Sources B and C support the evidence of Source A about the way the Bolsheviks governed Russia? Explain your answer by referring to all three sources. (4)

Study Sources C and D

c How useful are these sources as evidence about the impact of Bolshevik rule on Russia? (6)

Study Sources D and E

d Use the sources and your own knowledge to explain why Lenin set up the Cheka. (6)

Study all of the sources

e 'The Bolsheviks succeeded because they used a mixture of terror and popular reforms.' Use the sources and your own knowledge to explain whether you agree with this view. (10)

Depression and the New Deal The USA: 1929~41

Essential Information

Introduction: the USA in the 1920s

The First World War ended on 11 November 1918 and during the next ten years the USA became one of the strongest economic powers in the world. The war had had a great effect on America, whose economy had improved as the need for food, raw materials and manufactured goods of all kinds increased. The USA had made loans of US$10.3 billion during the war to its allies, and 90 per cent of this money had been used to buy American goods. American farmers were sending three times as much food to Europe in 1918 as they had in 1914.

Between 1921 and 1933 all three American Presidents were Republicans.

- Harding: in power from 1921–23.

- Coolidge: in power from 1923–29.

- Hoover: in power from 1929–33.

Under Harding and Coolidge, the USA enjoyed a period of great prosperity. Most Republicans believed that governments should be involved as little as possible in the day-to-day running of the economy. If business people were left alone to make their own decisions, it was thought that high profits, more jobs and good wages would be the result. This policy is often known as *laissez-faire*. The only role for the government was to help business when requested. With the coming of peace in 1918, the Republicans were determined to 'return to normality' – that is, peace and continued prosperity.

But the government did make one significant intervention. In 1922 it introduced the Fordney–McCumber **Tariff**, which raised import duties on goods coming into the USA to the highest level ever. This made imports dearer and so encouraged Americans to buy home-produced goods.

As profits increased, so did some people's wages. Between 1923 and 1929, the average wage rose by 8 per cent – enough for some workers to buy the new consumer luxuries that many people were hearing about through advertisements and radio commercials.

An industrial revolution

In the 1920s there was a wave of increased productivity as a result of the use of electrical power. In 1912 only 16 per cent of American people lived in electrically lighted homes. By 1927 the number had risen to 63 per cent. The growth of electric power meant that electrical items such as irons, ovens, washing machines, vacuum cleaners, refrigerators, radios and telephones became very popular with people. During this period other energy sources also had similar rises. For example, twice as much oil was used and four times as much gas.

One product that had a phenomenal impact on American life was the automobile. Henry Ford developed a system of mass production whereby large numbers of vehicles could be made by a standardised mechanical process.

The industry used so much steel, glass, wood,

The consumer boom

For those Americans who had jobs, life in the 1920s was enjoyable. Unemployment remained low for most of the 1920s and wages increased, permitting workers to participate in the consumer boom. There were more than 26 million cars in the USA in 1929 and 20 million telephones. There were more than 10 million radios by the end of the decade and food sales increased threefold and clothing four-fold.

petrol, rubber and leather that it provided jobs for five million people. It transformed American buying habits, making hire purchase a way of life for most Americans.

It promoted highway construction and travel which, in turn, produced hotels and restaurants in what had once been considered remote and out-of-the-way places. The production of automobiles rose from 1.9 million in 1920 to 4.5 million in 1929, manufactured mainly by the three giant firms of Ford, Chrysler and General Motors.

Poverty in the midst of plenty

Many people did not share in the country's increasing wealth. There were people in urban **ghettos** and in rural areas who were easily overlooked as they struggled to make ends meet. Very real poverty continued to exist among unskilled immigrants in the big cities and among African-Americans in the Deep South and the north. They were treated as second-class citizens who were low paid, undernourished and lived in poor housing conditions. In 1929, the average wage in the north-east was US$881 a year but in the south-east it was US$365 a year.

American farmers had an especially difficult time during the 1920s; during the First World War they had cultivated more and more land to meet the government's request for food. After 1920, Europe began to produce its own food and as US food exports dropped so did prices. Many of the American farmers had bought extra land on credit in order to meet the new food demands and as prices fell they started to encounter difficulties in paying their mortgages.

People actually ate less in the 1920s than in the pre-war years, and demand for cotton and wool fell because of the competition from synthetic fibres such as rayon. Farmers were also severely hit by **prohibition** (the ban on the sale of alcohol introduced in 1919) because half the market for barley and much of the grape market were no longer needed.

The income of the farm labourer even in the most affluent years of the 1920s was generally only about half that of coal miners, and not much more than one-quarter of clerical workers.

Causes and consequences of the Wall Street Crash

The Share Boom

> **Wall Street**
> Wall Street is in New York and is the home of the American Stock Exchange where stocks and shares are bought and sold daily.

During the 1920s investing in shares became a regular feature of the lives of many Americans. The number of shares bought and sold rose from 451 million in 1926 to 1.1 billion in 1929. In the same three years the average top price for the 25 leading companies rose from US$186 to US$469 per share. Many ordinary people made good profits from their shares.

The upsurge in the stock market relied on confidence – confidence that US industry would continue to expand and make high profits. People often bought shares 'on the margin', which means they paid only a 10 per cent or 20 per cent down payment on their shares and relied on selling the shares at a high profit to cover the 80 per cent or 90 per cent when they paid the **stockbroker** what they owed him. This system seemed to work.

For example, an investor who bought shares in Hershey Chocolate in August 1928 and sold in September 1929 made over 100 per cent profit.

But such rises could not last. They were based on the confidence that prosperity would continue. However, by 1929, there were signs that it was coming to an end.

Overproduction

We have already seen that farmers were having a bad time in the 1920s. By 1929 other industries were also beginning to suffer.

> What was Laissez-faire?
>
> How rich was America in the 1920s?
>
> Why did so many Americans buy shares in the 1920s?

Chapter 3 *Depression and the New Deal. The USA: 1929–41*

45

The construction boom began to slow and by 1929, construction was at a standstill. Car manufacturers found that they had more cars to sell than there were customers because most families who could afford a car already owned one. By August 1929, automobile factories had to lay off thousands of workers because of reduced demand. The problem grew serious because industries such as textiles, lumber, mining and railroad were also experiencing severe difficulties. Radios, telephones, washing machines, refrigerators and other goods were piling up in warehouses across the country. The USA was experiencing the very serious problem of overproduction. But it could not increase sales abroad because other countries had reacted to the Fordney–McCumber Tariff by imposing high duties on American goods.

As companies' sales slumped, so did their profits and their shares. Share buying ceased to be a guaranteed way of making money.

The Crash
During the summer of 1929, share prices in New York began to fall and despite assurances from the financial community, panic began when prices continued to fall.

This led to the situation where shares became almost worthless and people who had bought 'on the margin' could not pay their debts. Americans who had known prosperity now joined the great numbers of existing poor as a result of the Wall Street Crash.

But it was not just investors in shares who lost their money. Many banks had loaned money to investors to buy shares, or had invested large amounts on Wall Street themselves. Now those banks lost their money, too. In desperation they recalled loans they had made to companies, causing those companies to fail and leading to more unemployment.

The Great Depression
The Crash was the beginning of what came to be known as the Great Depression, which lasted through the 1930s and was the worst economic decline in the history of the USA. It happened at a time when millions of Americans could not find work, thousands were turned out of their homes and many roamed the land in freight cars. Banks failed and people lost their life's savings.

The impact of the Depression on people's lives throughout US society

Herbert Hoover did not believe that it was the role of government to deal with the consequences of the Wall Street Crash. **Laissez-faire** had helped create wealth, and Hoover believed in '**rugged individualism**', meaning that people should look after themselves.

America was rapidly becoming a land of unemployment, tramps, bread queues and soup kitchens. But within a short time many Americans found themselves homeless, living at the edge of cities in shacks made of tin and old crates. These became known as '**Hoovervilles**' as an insult to Hoover for his lack of action.

However, Hoover did take some action. He reduced taxes on the wealthy, expecting the money saved to build new plants and hire more workers. He also gave aid to the farmers through the Agricultural Marketing Act but it was not enough. The farmers wanted help paying their mortgages and because they could not afford to pay, the result was bankruptcy.

With the number of unemployed growing every month, charity funds proved completely inadequate. Toledo (in Ohio), could only afford to spend 2 cents per relief meal per day. New York City gave only US$2.39 per week to each family on relief.

Effects of the Crash
Following the 'Crash', there were large-scale bankruptcies in the USA. The number of businesses that collapsed in 1929 was about 20,000 and reached a peak of some 30,000 in 1932. This naturally had an impact on the number out of work and there were about 12 million unemployed in 1932. Moreover, the average family's income dropped from US$2,300 to US$1,600 in 1932.

President Hoover

Herbert Hoover has had an extremely bad press in American history. He was the president who stated in 1928 that America would soon 'be in sight of the day when poverty will be banished from this nation'. When the Crash came just twelve weeks later angry Americans named their shacks 'Hoovervilles' and wrapped themselves in 'Hoover blankets' (newspapers) to keep warm. But Hoover was unfortunate. He had not caused the Crash and there was little he could do to lessen its impact.

President Hoover set up the Reconstruction Finance Corporation (RFC) which distributed US$300 million to state governments for unemployment relief. But this did no more than scratch the surface.

Resentment among the people

With wages falling and unemployment rising, resentment grew among people affected by the Depression. Hoover became more unpopular when he ordered the army to disband a group of ex-servicemen who had marched to Washington to ask for a monetary bonus, due in 1945, to be paid early, to help them through the Depression. More than 100 people were injured and the incident left a bitter taste in the mouths of many Americans.

It seemed as though it was time for a change, and in November 1932, Franklin Delano Roosevelt, a Democrat, was elected president of the USA.

The nature of the New Deal; policies to deal with agriculture, industry, unemployment and welfare: the role of Roosevelt in recovery

In his inaugural speech to the USA in March 1933, President Roosevelt said: 'The only thing we have to fear is fear itself.' He felt that it was his task to restore the faith that most Americans had lost in their country. He promised a 'New Deal' for the American people.

He began by promoting a feeling of friendliness and informality in frequent radio broadcasts, known as 'fireside chats'. In these chats, Roosevelt explained the legislation of the New Deal in simple and straightforward terms. People came to feel that at last they had a president who understood their problems.

President Roosevelt once said, 'In order to preserve we had to reform', and it was with this in mind that he introduced a series of proposals that tackled the problems of the Depression in a way that was, for the USA, quite revolutionary. For the first time the federal government began to take responsibility for its citizens; the USA had to accept that it would only emerge from its troubles if *laissez-faire* and 'rugged individualism' were abandoned.

The day that Roosevelt took office a flurry of activity began that did not let up for over three months. This time of intensive activity became known as the Hundred Days. The various bodies that were set up during it have acquired the term 'Alphabet Agencies'.

Roosevelt and the banking system

Before and during 1933 the USA had experienced the collapse of many banks; people's savings had been lost and there was little confidence in the banking system. On his first day in office, President Roosevelt closed all banks for three days. Congress passed the Emergency Banking Relief Act. This act stated that only banks in sound financial shape would be reopened. People's faith in the banks was immediately restored and within a few days, deposits exceeded withdrawals and the banking crisis was over. Banks were also forbidden to invest their funds in the stock market.

Why was there a Great Depression after 1929?

What effect did the Depression have on the American people?

What do you think Roosevelt meant when he said, 'The only thing we have to fear is fear itself'?

Relief for the unemployed

President Roosevelt persuaded **Congress** to provide money for public works projects and set up a programme to put young people without jobs to work.

The Civilian Conservation Corps (CCC) was set up to improve the country's natural resources. By early summer 1933, about 1,300 CCC camps had been set up and were providing work for young men between the ages of 18 and 25. The work involved reforestation, prevention of soil erosion, flood control, fire prevention, road building, and park and recreational area development. By the time that the CCC was closed down in the 1940s, it had given work to 2.5 million young Americans.

The Federal Emergency Relief Act (FERA) was authorised to distribute US$500 million through grants to state and local agencies for employment relief. Later this was replaced with the Civil Works Administration (CWA) to create public jobs. By January 1934, about 4 million Americans, mostly unskilled workers, were on the CWA's payroll. (In 1935, the CWA was replaced by the Works Project Administration and over the years it employed more than 8 million people.)

In April 1933, President Roosevelt set up the Tennessee Valley Authority (TVA). This organisation was to be responsible for flood and erosion control, the development of navigation, the generation and sale of electric power, and the manufacture and distribution of fertiliser. The activities of the TVA covered seven states, 40,000 square miles and affected the lives of seven million people.

The Public Works Administration stimulated the economy by means of huge public works projects such as dams, port facilities, sewage plants, bridges, roads, airports and hospitals.

To help factories recover, Roosevelt set up the National Industry Recovery Act (NIRA). NIRA tried to establish a co-operative relationship between government, business and labour. One section of the Act set codes of fair practice for working conditions, wages and business practices. The codes were to be enforced by the National Recovery Administration. NIRA also declared that workers should be allowed to organise trades unions and to bargain collectively. Shortening individual worker's hours forced businesses to hire more people, which in turn created two million additional jobs.

The Agricultural Adjustment Act (AAA) proved to be quite controversial. It paid farmers a subsidy to reduce the production of crops and the number of animals they raised. Such cutbacks would help to bring the supply of agricultural products more in line with the demand for them, causing prices to rise.

Farmers had to plough under portions of their crops and kill animals at a time when thousands of people were suffering from malnutrition. Farm prices rose, but there was a great deal of criticism.

In January 1935, in his annual message to Congress, President Roosevelt introduced his second New Deal. This included the Works Progress Administration (WPA). Its work consisted of projects such as building hospitals, schools and airports. The WPA also put unemployed teachers back to work. Additionally, there were schemes whereby artists, writers and actors were employed. The National Labour Relations Act, or Wagner Act, protected the rights of workers to join unions.

How Roosevelt helped some areas of society

President Roosevelt was particularly concerned with providing security for the unemployed, the aged and the handicapped. In the Social Security Act of 1935 the government introduced pensions for those over 65, unemployment benefits and aid to the handicapped and dependent children.

In the presidential election of 1936, Roosevelt received 60.7 per cent of the vote and won 523 out of 531 electoral college votes. Nevertheless, this election was especially bitter, and Roosevelt had to endure personal attacks on his family and himself. The Republican candidate, Senator Alfred Landon, claimed that the New Deal was undermining traditional American initiative and self-reliance. There were many in big business who supported Landon because they saw the recent legislation limiting their own power.

Opposition to the New Deal

Although Roosevelt won a landslide victory in the 1936 elections, there was much opposition to the New Deal and the way in which Roosevelt carried out his policies.

Between 1933 and 1938, dozens of government agencies were created, the number of civil servants rose from 500,000 to over 850,000 and many new federal buildings appeared in Washington DC.

This vast extension of federal government activity horrified the Republicans, big businesses and the Supreme Court, which declared several acts of the New Deal unconstitutional. The New Deal with its enormous extension of federal power seemed to undermine the whole American tradition of individualism. To many the New Deal was **socialism**.

The New Deal permitted workers to join and form unions. One major result was that there was a large number of strikes in 1934. Because unionisation tended to increase strikes, business leaders and factory owners generally tried to stop workers from joining unions. Although it was illegal, many employers sacked or intimidated workers who tried to start unions.

Opposition to Roosevelt

The most famous individual who opposed President Roosevelt was Senator Huey Long of Louisiana. He claimed that there should have been a redistribution of wealth in the USA and he began to develop his own plan to do so. His 'Share Our Wealth' plan called for the federal government to guarantee every family in the USA a minimum annual income of US$5,000. To pay for this, Long planned to tax the property, inheritance and income of wealthy people. By 1935, Long claimed to have about 27,000 'Share Our Wealth' clubs and a mailing list of 7.5 million people.

Roosevelt encountered most opposition from the Supreme Court. In 1935, the Supreme Court stated that NIRA was unconstitutional and in 1936, the Court said that the AAA was unconstitutional.

In 1937, President Roosevelt put forward a plan to reorganise the Supreme Court. He stated that the nine existing judges were too old to keep up with their heavy judicial workload. He would create another six judges.

The plan aroused bitter opposition. It was viewed as an attempt to 'pack' (fill) the Supreme Court with pro-New Deal judges, which would destroy the independence of the judiciary and gain more power for the president. Roosevelt was forced to back down.

The extent of recovery and success of the New Deal to 1941

The aim of President Roosevelt was to revive the US economy by massive government spending. The theory was that jobs would be created. There would be greater confidence in business and industry, and greater investment would follow.

The New Deal certainly did help to restore the US's broken economy. The TVA proved to be very successful and the New Deal did bring relief, employment and hope back to millions of Americans. Most Americans were better off by the end of 1938 than they had been in 1932.

The New Deal also strengthened democracy in the USA. President Roosevelt gave the American people renewed faith in their country's way of life. But the New Deal was not totally successful. By 1937 unemployment began to rise again. No new measures were introduced after 1938 to fight rising unemployment. Moreover, as tension grew in Asia and Europe, Roosevelt started to concentrate on international issues. The New Deal slowly ground to a halt. Only when war broke out in 1939 did the USA begin to emerge from recession.

How did Roosevelt help the unemployed of America?

Why was there opposition to Roosevelt's measures?

How successful was the New Deal?

Causes and consequences of the Wall Street Crash

Source A

Company	August 31 1928	September 3 1929	October 29 1929
American and Foreign Power	$38.00	$167.75	$73.00
AT and T	$182.00	$304.00	$230.00
Hershey Chocolate	$53.25	$128.00	$108.00
IBM	$130.86	$241.75	–
People's Gas, Chicago	$182.86	$182.86	–
Detroit, Edison	$205.00	$350.00	–

▲ Selected share prices, Wall Street, 1929.

Source B

The New York Times

"All the News That's Fit to Print"

VOL. XVI   NEW YORK, THURSDAY, OCTOBER 24, 1929

PRICES OF STOCKS CRASH IN HEAVY LIQUIDATION, TOTAL DROP OF BILLIONS

2,600,000 Shares sold in the final hour in record deadline

PAPER LOSS $4,000,000,000

ORGANISED BACKING ABSENT

MANY ACCOUNTS WIPED OUT!

No Brokerage House in difficulty, as margins kept high

Bankers confer on steps to support market – highest break is 96 points

▲ From the *New York Times* report on the Wall Street Crash, October 1929.

Source C

I knew something was terribly wrong because I heard everybody talking about the stock market. Six weeks before the Crash I wanted to sell shares which had been left to me by my father. My family adviser persuaded me to keep hold of the shares, even though I could have got $160,000. Four years later I sold them for $4,000.

▲ From an interview in 1970 with an American who was in New York in October 1929.

Source D

We in America are nearer to the final triumph over poverty than ever before in the history of any land. The poorhouse is vanishing from among us.

▲ From a speech by Herbert Hoover in the autumn of 1928.

Source E

The Hoover administration encouraged overproduction through its false policies. It refused to recognise problems at home; moreover, it not only delayed reform but forgot reform.

▲ From a speech by Franklin Roosevelt during his first presidential campaign, 1932.

Source F

We've got more wheat, more corn, more food, more everything in the world than any nation ever had, yet we are starving to death. We are the first nation in the history of the world to go to the poorhouse in an automobile.

▲ Will Rogers, an American humourist, speaking in 1931.

Study Source A

a What can you learn from Source A about the American stock market in the 1920s? (4)

Study Sources A, B and C

b Do Sources B and C support the evidence of Source A? Explain your answer by referring to all three sources. (4)

Study Sources A, B and C

c Use the sources and your own knowledge to explain why many people bought shares in the USA in the 1920s. (6)

Study Sources D and E

d How useful are these sources in helping you to understand why there was a 'Crash' in 1929? (6)

Study all of the sources

e 'The Crash in stockmarket prices on 29 October 1929 took America completely by surprise.' Use the sources and your own knowledge to explain whether you agree with this view. (10)

Chapter 3 *Depression and the New Deal. The USA: 1929~41*

51

Government reaction and attempts at recovery, 1929–33

Source A

We have been passing through one of those great economic storms which periodically bring hardship and suffering on our people. I am convinced we have now passed the worst and we shall recover. There is one certainty in the future of a people such as ourselves and that is, prosperity.

▲ From a speech by President Hoover, May 1930.

Source B

	Failed businesses	Farm income in $billions	Average weekly earnings in manufacturing
1930	26,355	4.1	$24.77
1931	28,285	3.2	Not available
1932	31,822	1.9	$16.21

▲ Economic statistics from Hoover's presidency.

Source C

I see nothing in the present situation that is either menacing or pessimistic. I have every confidence there will be a revival of activity in the spring and that during the coming year the country will make steady progress.

▲ From a speech by Andrew Mellon, President Hoover's Secretary of the Treasury, January 1930.

Source D

Economic depression cannot be cured by simply making laws or intervention by the president. The economy can only be healed by the producers and consumers themselves.

▲ Adapted from a speech by President Hoover in 1930.

Source E

Hoover failed ... He first coldly assured the people that the Depression was an illusion which it was their patriotic duty to ignore. When economic collapse occurred in Europe, he denounced the Depression as something un-American from which we should isolate and insulate ourselves.

▲ From a book written in 1948 by Robert Sherwood. Sherwood was a speech writer for President Roosevelt.

Source F

Everybody wanted to have somebody to blame the Depression on. Hoover had the misfortune to be inaugurated in March 1929, just in time to get the blame for the Crash. When the collapse came, Hoover did not sit still – he brought business and union leaders to the White House where they promised to try to keep wages up and keep factories going. He actually cut his own presidential salary by one-fifth.

▲ From an American history textbook written in 1987 by D. Boorstin.

Study Source A

a What can you learn from Source A about President Hoover's attitude to the Depression? (4)

Study Sources A, B and C

b Do Sources B and C support the evidence of Source A? Explain your answer. (4)

Study Sources A, B and C

c Use the sources and your own knowledge to explain why unemployment continued to rise in the years 1930–32. (6)

Study Sources D and E

d How useful are these sources in helping you to understand the economic problems of the USA in the early 1930s? (6)

Study all of the sources

e 'President Hoover did not bring the USA out of the Depression because he did too little too late.' Use the sources and your own knowledge to explain whether you agree with this view. (10)

The impact of the Depression on people's lives throughout US society

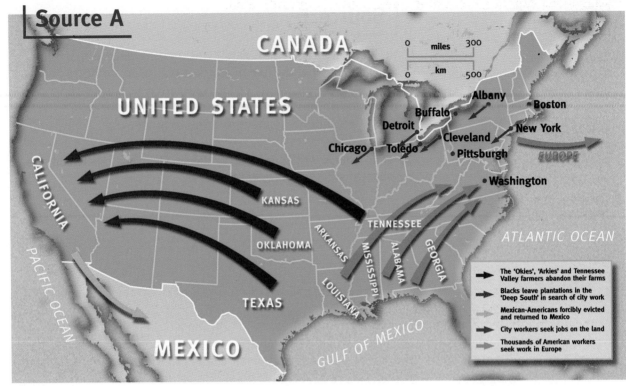

Source A

▲ The movement of population throughout the USA during the 1930s.

Source B

Year	Unemployed (approximate)
March 1930	3.5 million
March 1931	7.75 million
March 1932	11.75 million
March 1933	14.0 million

▲ Chart showing how unemployment increased from 1930 to 1933.

Source C

▲ Unemployed people in New York in 1931. The men are queuing for Christmas dinner. It is Christmas day.

Source D

The average man won't really do a day's work unless he is caught and cannot get out of it. There is plenty of work to do, if people would do it.

▲ From a speech made in 1931 by Henry Ford, who ran a successful business manufacturing motor cars.

Source E

Here were all those people living in old, rusted-out car bodies. I mean that was their home. There were people living in shacks made of orange crates. One family with a whole lot of kids were living in a piano box. This wasn't just a little section, this was maybe ten miles wide and ten miles long. People living in whatever junk they could put together.

▲ From an interview with Peggy Terry in 1970. Peggy Terry had lived in a Hooverville in the 1930s.

Source F

People who were wealthy before the Depression had much greater chances of weathering the economic storm and coming out with minimal financial damage. A handful of people took advantage of the rock bottom prices brought on by the Depression in order to increase their wealth.

▲ From an American history textbook written in 1991.

Study Source A

a What can you learn from Source A about the impact of the Depression on the people of the USA? (4)

Study Sources A, B and C

b Do Sources B and C support the evidence of Source A? Explain your answer. (4)

Study Sources A, B and C

c Use the sources and your own knowledge to explain why the number of homeless people in the USA increased in the early 1930s. (6)

Study Sources D and E

d How useful are these sources as evidence of the plight of the unemployed in the 1930s? Explain your answer. (6)

Study all of the sources

e 'The Depression affected only the working classes in the early 1930s.' Use the sources and your own knowledge to explain whether you agree with this view. (10)

The nature of the New Deal; policies to deal with agriculture, industry, unemployment and welfare: the role of Roosevelt in recovery

Source A

Unemployed citizens face the grim problem of existence and an equally great number toil with little return. Our greatest ... task is to put people to work. This is no unsolvable problem if we face it wisely and courageously. It can be accomplished by direct recruiting by the government itself, treating the task as we would treat the emergency of war, but at the same time, through this employment, accomplishing greatly needed projects. [We must] raise the values of agricultural products. There must be a strict supervision of all banking.

▲ From President Roosevelt's statement to Congress when he became president in 1933.

Source B

There was a problem with the price of cotton. Prices were down to 4 cents a pound and the cost of producing was 10 cents. So the government set up a programme to plough up the cotton. A third of the crop was ploughed up. Cotton prices went up 10 cents, maybe 11.

▲ From an interview in 1970 with C. R. Baldwin. Baldwin had been the Assistant to the Secretary of Agriculture in the New Deal.

Source C

▲ Workers in the Civilian Conservation Corps with President Roosevelt in 1933.

Source D

... the migrants streamed in on the highways and their hunger was in their eyes ... When there was work for a man, ten men fought for it ... if that fella'll work for 30 cents, I'll work for 25 ... I'll do it for 20. No, me, I'm hungry. I'll work for 15 cents. I'll work for food ... The kids ... I'll work for a little piece of meat.

▲ From the novel *The Grapes of Wrath* by John Steinbeck, written in 1939.

Source E

Any jackass can spend the people's money. Any crackpot with money at his disposal can build himself a dictatorial crown. It is time for the American people to perform a sit-down strike – on politicians. The politicians are sitting down on you waiting for the Supreme Court to put its head on the chopping block.

▲ From a speech in 1937 by the radio priest, Father Charles Coughlin, an opponent to Roosevelt.

Source F

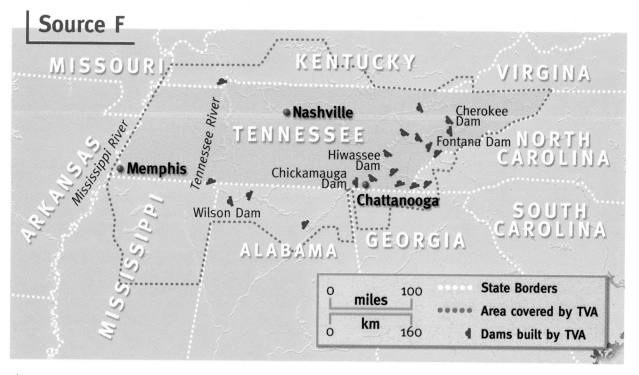

▲ The Tennessee Valley area and the states affected by the work of the TVA.

Study Source A

a What can you learn from Source A about the situation in the USA and 1933? (4)

Study Sources A, B and C

b Do Sources B and C support the evidence of Source A? Explain your answer. (4)

Study Sources A, B and C

c Use the sources and your own knowledge to explain why President Roosevelt was carrying out policies of intervention. (6)

Study Sources D, E and F

d How useful are these sources in helping you to understand the work of President Roosevelt? (6)

Study all of the sources

e 'President Roosevelt's measures to improve agriculture were popular and effective.' Use the sources and your own knowledge to explain whether you agree with this view. (10)

Chapter 3 *Depression and the New Deal. The USA: 1929~41*

57

Opposition to the New Deal

Source A

Roosevelt did not get everything his own way. In 1936 the Supreme Court ruled against the Agricultural Adjustment Act. Roosevelt was disturbed that this court could overrule laws which the elected President and Congress had passed. He thought this was because they were old men who lived in the past.

▲ From a British textbook, 1989.

Source B

Our president evidently has noted the apparent success of Adolf Hitler and is aiming at the same dominance.

▲ A US political commentator writing in 1937 about President Roosevelt's decision to reform the Supreme Court.

Source C

By bringing into the Supreme Court a steady stream of new and younger blood, I hope to make justice speedier and less costly. Also I intend to bring in younger men who have had personal experience and contact with today's circumstances and know how average men have to live and work.

▲ From a radio broadcast by President Roosevelt, 1937.

Source D

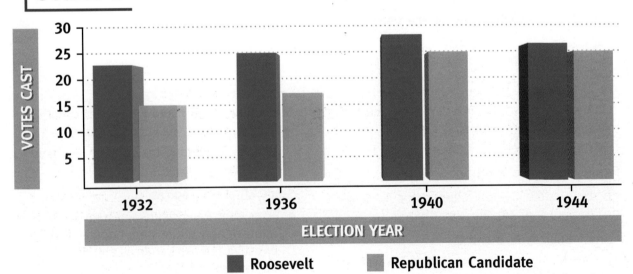

▲ This graph shows the number of votes, in millions, cast in the presidential elections between 1932 and 1944.

Source E

Roosevelt's proposals would not banish older judges from the courts. They would not reduce expense nor speed decisions. They would place the courts under the will of Congress and the President and would destroy the independence of the courts.

▲ From the Senate Judiciary Committee's rejection of President Roosevelt's proposals to bring in more judges, 1937.

Source F

Dear Mr President,

This is just to tell you everything is all right now. The man you sent found our house all right and we went down the bank with him and the mortgage can go a while longer. You remember I wrote you about losing the furniture too. Well, your man got it back for us. I never heard of a president like you, Mr Roosevelt. Mrs _____ and I are old folks and don't amount to much, but we are joined with those millions of others in praying for you every night. God bless you, Mr Roosevelt.

▲ A letter, sent to President Roosevelt by a grateful voter in 1934.

Study Source A

a What can you learn from Source A about the conflict between Roosevelt and the Supreme Court? (4)

Study Sources A, B and C

b Do Sources B and C support the evidence of Source A? Explain your answer. (4)

Study Sources A, B and C

c Use the sources and your own knowledge to explain why Roosevelt wished to reform the Supreme Court. (6)

Study Sources D and E

d How useful are these sources for showing the popularity of the changes Roosevelt wished to make to the Supreme Court? (6)

Study all of the sources

e 'Roosevelt attempt to reform the Supreme Court was an unwise move which seriously undermined his popularity.' Use the sources and your own knowledge to explain whether you agree with this view. (10)

Chapter 3 Depression and the New Deal. The USA: 1929–41

59

The extent of recovery and success of the New Deal to 1941

Source A

Mrs Roosevelt,

I suppose from your point of view the work relief, old age pensions, slum clearance and all the rest seems like a perfect remedy for all the ills of this country, but I would like for you to see the results, as the other half see them. We have always had a shiftless, never-do-well class of people whose one and only aim in life is to live without work ... There has never been any necessity for any one who is able to work, being on relief in this locality, but there have been many eating the bread of charity and they have lived better than ever before. I have had taxpayers tell me that their children come home from school and asked why they couldn't have nice lunches like the children on relief.

▲ A letter sent to President Roosevelt's wife, Eleanor.

Source B

The New Deal is encouraging the unfit to be more unfit. Even such a measure as old-age insurance removes one of the points of pressure which has kept many persons up to the strife and struggle of life.

▲ An extract from a pamphlet written by the American Liberty League in 1935.

Source C

I've been dealing with unemployed people for years and they want to 'get off' poor relief – but they can't – where can they turn to if they can't turn to their government?

▲ From a speech in 1933 by Harry Hopkins, a member of President Roosevelt's administration.

Source D

There were three reasons why Roosevelt wanted war. One: you had 10 million Americans unemployed after six years of the New Deal. Two: to be a war president because then you become a great man overnight. Three: he hoped to put through a United Nations, of which he would be the author and be like the uncrowned ruler of the world.

▲ From an interview in 1970 with a Republican Congressman.

Source E

Before Roosevelt became President, there was one person to take care of all the letters the White House received. Under Roosevelt, there are fifty and they handled the thousands of letters written to the President each week.

▲ **From an American history book about Roosevelt and the New Deal, written in 1963.**

Source F

My name is William Edwards, I live down Cove Creek way,
I'm working on a project they call the TVA.

The government began it when I was but a child,
But now they are in earnest and Tennessee's gone wild.

Oh, see them boys a-comin' – their government they trust;
Just hear their hammers ringin' – they'll build that dam or bust.

I meant to marry Sally, but work I could not find;
The TVA was started and surely eased my mind.

I'm writing her a letter, these words I'll surely say:
'The Government has saved us, just name our wedding day.'

Oh, things looked blue and lonely until this come along;
Now hear the crew a-singing and listen to their song.

'The Government employs us, short hours and certain pay;
Oh, things are up and comin', God bless the TVA.'

▲ **A popular song at the time of the New Deal.**

Study Source A

a What can you learn from Source A about attitudes to helping the needy under the New Deal? (4)

Study Sources A, B and C

b Do Sources B and C support the evidence of Source A? Explain your answer. (4)

Study Sources A, B and C

c Use the sources and your own knowledge to explain why many Americans did not want to help the poor. (6)

Study Sources D, E and F

d How useful are Sources D, E and F in helping you to understand whether the New Deal was a success? (6)

Study all of the sources

e 'By 1941, Roosevelt got America working again and had given the people hope.' Use the sources and your own knowledge to explain whether you agree with this view. (10)

Chapter 3 *Depression and the New Deal. The USA: 1929~41*

61

CHAPTER 4

Nazi Germany: 1930~39

Essential Information

Hitler, Nazism and Nazi beliefs

Adolf Hitler was born in 1889 in Braunau, Austria. After an unsettled childhood – both his parents died while he was young – he moved to Vienna where he tried to enrol as an art student. Unfortunately, he was rejected and ended up living in poverty for several years, earning money from giving art lessons and painting postcards.

When the First World War broke out in 1914, Hitler volunteered for the German army and enlisted in a Bavarian regiment. He was a good soldier and was awarded medals for bravery. He later said that this was the happiest period of his life and the first time that he made real friends.

In October 1918, Hitler was caught in a gas attack and temporarily blinded. While he was recovering in hospital, the Armistice was signed. Hitler came to believe that the Army had never been defeated, but had been 'stabbed in the back' by the 'November Criminals', the politicians who had signed the Armistice.

The Treaty of Versailles
- Took away 14% of Germany's territory and split the country in two.
- Placed severe restrictions on Germany's armed forces.
- Made Germany accept blame for starting the war and agree to pay **reparations** to the Allies.

After the war Hitler joined the German Workers' Party. The leader of the party, Anton Drexler, was fanatically **anti-Semitic**. He believed that there had been an international Jewish conspiracy to betray Germany in 1918. Hitler joined the Party Committee and then became the leader in 1921,

changing its name to the National Socialist German Workers' Party – 'National' to attract right-wing nationalists, and 'Socialist' to attract working men.

The Nazis, as their opponents called them, were just one of a number of extreme right- and left-wing parties in Germany in the early 1920s. At first they were little more than a rabble, but after Hitler's attempt to seize power in Munich in November 1923, which led to his arrest and imprisonment for treason in 1924, he set about reorganising the party. He made it into a national organisation and tried to win seats in the Reichstag, the lower house of the German parliament. In 1924 Hitler published his ideas in a book called *Mein Kampf*, which he had written while in prison. This set out his views on how Germany should be governed.

Like all extreme right-wing parties, the Nazis believed that individuals did not count and that what mattered was the state. All Germans must be prepared to sacrifice their own personal freedom for the good of Germany as a whole. Men and women had their own distinct roles to play; women were to be housewives and mothers, and men were to be soldiers and workers.

What made the Nazis different, however, was their belief in the **Herrenvolk**, the Master race. They believed that Germans were born to rule, and that all other races were inferior to a greater or lesser extent. At the bottom of the pile were the **Untermenschen**, the sub-humans – Jews, Blacks, Slavs and Gypsies – some of whom they blamed for Germany's defeat in the First World War. If Germany was to become great again, these peoples would have to be removed from the German race.

There was, of course, no evidence whatsoever for any of Hitler's claims or beliefs, but in a country still suffering from the effects of defeat in the First World War, there were always people who were ready to listen to him.

The Nazi rise to power

Despite Hitler's reorganisation of the Nazi Party, from 1924 to 1928 they had very little election success. In the 1928 general election the Nazis won just twelve seats. Gustav Stresemann, who had become chancellor of Germany in 1923 and then foreign minister the following year, had enabled Germany to recover from the **hyperinflation** of 1923. So successful was he, that by 1926 Germany was admitted to the League of Nations and given a permanent seat on the Council. But everything changed in three weeks in October 1929. On 3 October Gustav Stresemann died and on 24 October, the Wall Street Crash in the USA began. Of all European countries, Germany was the worst hit by the Crash. Stresemann had borrowed huge sums of money from the USA to help with reparations, but as the Depression grew worse, the German government had to rearrange loans and unemployment rose. In 1931, a number of leading banks collapsed and the situation deteriorated.

This exactly suited Hitler; as people became desperate, they would be more likely to listen to his radical ideas. He toured Germany by aeroplane, and car to town halls and told Germans what they wanted to hear, not offering policies, only promises and scapegoats. His message was simple: the Germans were not to blame and he, Hitler, would sort matters out. Hitler found a valuable ally in Alfred Hugenberg, leader of the German National Party. Hugenberg was the millionaire owner of 53 German newspapers. He helped to pay Hitler's expenses and spread his message. Hitler's message came in two forms: hatred and abuse for his opponents, in particular communists and Jews; and promises of immediate action. His power as a public speaker won over millions of Germans and concealed the real terror behind his words.

In 1930, the Nazis won 107 seats in the Reichstag, and in July 1932 they won 230, making them the largest single party. Democratic government was almost impossible. Bruning, the chancellor from 1930–32, was forced to govern using the emergency power of President Paul von Hindenburg. The success of the Nazis led Hitler to stand for president in 1932, but he lost to Hindenburg, who was re-elected by 19,000,000 votes to 11,000,000. In a second general election in November 1932 the Nazis won only 196 seats and it seemed that Hitler had missed his chance.

One politician who believed that Hitler was finished was Franz von Papen, chancellor from June to November 1932. In January 1933 he persuaded Hindenburg to appoint Hitler as chancellor, with himself as vice-chancellor. Hindenburg despised Hitler, but gave in to von Papen, who assured him that Hitler would be kept under control. Hitler agreed that there would be only three other Nazis in the cabinet and on 30 January 1933, Adolf Hitler was appointed German chancellor.

Creation of the totalitarian state

When von Papen took his place in Hitler's cabinet for a photograph on 30 January 1933, he expected to be controlling the government. But he was wrong. Hitler had no intention of allowing von Papen to manipulate him and immediately called for another general election for 5 March 1933. His aim was to win an overall majority so that he would no longer need to be part of a coalition government.

The Weimar Republic
Was founded after the Kaiser abdicated at the end of the First World War.

- Germany was now a democracy with an elected Reichstag (Parliament).
- Germans could vote for Deputies elected by proportional representation.
- The chancellor led the government.
- The president was Head of State. Elected every seven years, the president could suspend Parliament and rule by himself in times of emergency.

Why was the Wall Street Crash so important in the rise of the Nazi Party to power in 1933?

Six days before the general election, on 27 February 1933, the **Reichstag** building burnt down. The Nazis immediately blamed the communists. Almost certainly they were not to blame, as it seems possible that the fire was started by the Nazis in an attempt to blacken the reputation of their opponents. When a subsequent trial was held in November 1933, all of the accused were found 'not guilty' except for Marinus van der Lubbe, who was executed.

At the general election the Nazis won 288 seats – not an overall majority, but more than enough to dominate the Reichstag as most of the socialists and communists stayed away when it met. Hitler filled the building with the SA – the Sturm Abteilung, or Stormtroopers – and forced through the Enabling Act, which gave him the power to rule for four years without the Reichstag. He had legally become dictator.

Hitler now set about removing opposition to himself and his ideas in Germany. All political parties except for the Nazis were banned. Concentration camps were set up and the leaders of the communists and socialists were rounded up and imprisoned. The SA were used to run the camps and to intimidate Hitler's opponents. Trades unions were abolished and replaced by the Labour Front.

Most Germans accepted the changes that Hitler introduced, but anyone who opposed them was dealt with ruthlessly. The Gestapo, the secret state police, could arrest people on sight and they could be tried in secret courts. Children were encouraged to spy on their parents and report their actions. In every village, street or neighbourhood there were Nazi spies. Each block of flats had a 'warden' who recorded all movements in and out, and all visitors.

The most dangerous opposition, however, came from within the Nazi Party itself. When Hitler added the words 'National Socialist' to the name of the German Workers Party, he had wanted to attract as many people as possible. In 1933–34 this began to prove something of the problem. The Nationalists wanted a strong centralised state, in which individual people came second to the needs of Germany; the Socialists wanted to change Germany so that working men had more power.

The leader of the Socialist section of the Nazi Party was Ernst Röhm, the head of the SA. He tried to force Hitler to amalgamate the SA and the army and appoint him as Commander in Chief. Hitler did not dare to do this as he knew that the army generals would never agree to take orders from Röhm, who they disliked.

The Reichstag Fire

The Reichstag, the lower house of the German parliament, caught fire on the evening of 27 February 1933. This was just six days before the general election that Hitler had announced. Marinus van der Lubbe was found inside and arrested. He was carrying matches and had apparently set fire to the building using his shirt. Van der Lubbe was Dutch, mentally retarded and a former member of the Communist Party.

The blaze may have been started by the Nazis themselves. Subsequently, Hermann Goering claimed that he was responsible, but the probable culprit was Josef Goebbels, Hitler's propaganda chief. Some historians think he ordered Karl Ernst, a SA leader to carry out the deed along with other SA members. But the event gave Hitler the chance to persuade the German people that this represented a communist threat.

The Enabling Act

The Enabling Act was passed by the Reichstag on 23 March 1933, eighteen days after the general election. The meeting was held in the Kroll Opera House and was presided over by Hermann Goering, the president of the Reichstag. In theory the Nazis did not have a majority in the Reichstag, but all the socialist and communist members stayed away, and only one member spoke out against Hitler's proposals. The Act gave Hitler the power to govern Germany without consulting the Reichstag until 1937.

The solution came on 29 June 1934, when Hitler had Röhm and about 400 other SA members murdered in 'The Night of the Long Knives', whereby everybody who was any sort of risk to Hitler was removed within 48 hours.

Five weeks later President Hindenburg died. Hitler did not bother with an election; he appointed himself President and gave himself the new title of **'Führer'**. Now he had complete control.

The Nazi state

Between 1933 and 1938 every aspect of life in Germany was taken over by Nazism. The Nazis controlled radio and censored books and newspapers. All forms of entertainment, art and music were strictly controlled. Teachers were forced to become members of the Nazi Party and textbooks were rewritten to pass on the Nazi message New subjects, such as 'race studies', were introduced into every school to emphasise the Nazi message. In girls' schools there were lessons on health biology and domestic science with mathematics. This meant that the only mathematics that girls learnt was to do with cooking and shopping. Girls were being educated to look after their families and to bring up children. Only boys were encouraged to study science, foreign languages and mathematics as a separate subject.

Sport was encouraged for both boys and girls, as it would increase fitness for mothers and soldiers. When the Olympic Games were held in Berlin in 1936, Hitler hoped that it would show the superiority of the German Master race, but instead the greatest athlete of the Games was the black American, Jesse Owens.

When children went home from school they were expected to attend the youth movements. Boys joined the Pimpfen at the age of five; then the German Youth at ten and Hitler Youth at fourteen. At the age of eighteen, they went into the Labour Service for six months and were then conscripted into the army. Girls joined the League of German Maidens at the age of ten and stayed in it until they were twenty one.

The youth organisations met every evening and at weekends. Hitler's aim was simple: he wanted to saturate children's minds with the Nazi message so that they would never question it. In Nazi

The 1936 Olympic Games

Hitler wanted the Berlin Olympics to show Germany's superiority. He was pleased that Germany won the most gold medals at the Games. The 100 metres was won by Jesse Owens, a black American, who also won the 200 metres, the long jump and a relay gold medal. Immediately after Owens' victory, Hitler stormed out of the stadium in fury.

Germany children had no spare time to develop their own ideas, and the plan worked. In 1945, fourteen year old boys were prepared to defend Hitler as the Soviet army closed in on Berlin.

The greatest threat to Hitler was religion, a belief even stronger than Nazism. Hitler attempted to come to an agreement with the Christian churches, often claiming that he was a Roman Catholic. Many Christians refused to accept Nazi ideas and some like Martin Bonhoeffer, a Protestant minister, died for their beliefs. Others were prepared to accept Nazi ideas, especially when Hitler set up a Reich Church, in which the **swastika** and the cross were put side by side.

What Hitler was really trying to do was to stop people thinking for themselves. If he controlled education, the press, literature and every form of creative art, he could control the information that people used to form their own opinions, then they would accept his ideas without question. It is true, however, that Nazi rule did bring benefits such as political stability and employment, so people might have supported Hitler anyway.

Why was Hitler appointed chancellor in January 1933?

How did Hitler try to take advantage of the Reichstag Fire?

Racism and the treatment of minorities

The Nazis wanted to create a pure German race. They talked about the supremacy of **Aryans**, the original Germans, and even produced pictures of eight different Aryan types. All of this was nonsense, but it gave some sort of scientific backing to the attacks that the Nazis made on other racial groups. They claimed that Jews and others had polluted the blood of Germans and, therefore, had to be eliminated. Many Jews had fought in the German army during the First World War. What Hitler was doing was taking advantage of the extreme prejudice that had existed against Jews for nearly 2,000 years and using them as a scapegoat.

Persecution of the Jews

As soon as Hitler was in power in Germany, he began to persecute the people who he believed were responsible for weakening Germany – in other words, Jews, Gypsies, Slavs, the disabled and the mentally ill. Schoolchildren were taught to hate Jews, and Jewish children were ridiculed in front of their classmates. Mathematical problems involved working out how much money could be saved by killing disabled people, or how difficult it would be to bomb cities in eastern Europe. School textbooks included blatant **anti-Semitic** pictures and stories, and pupils had lessons in Race Study, which taught them to hate Jews. The process began as early as possible, and even nursery rhymes were written to encourage anti-Semitism.

The persecution of Jews began in 1933 with boycotts of Jewish shops and Jews being banned from some occupations, such as the medical and legal professions. In 1935 the Nuremberg Laws made Jews second-class citizens. They were not allowed to marry 'pure' Germans and were forced to use separate seats in public places. Anyone who had one Jewish grandparent was declared to be Jewish.

In November 1938 Jewish businesses, property and synagogues all over Germany were attacked and destroyed in **Kristallnacht**. This followed the murder of a Nazi official in Paris by a Jew. The Jewish community was forced to pay for the cost of repair and fined DM1 billion. Around 30,000 Jews were arrested, but almost all were released within a week after international protests. All of the actions against Jews were intended to force them to leave the country. When they tried to do so, however, they found that they had to leave most of their property and savings behind. Nevertheless, many Jews fled abroad to the USA, Britain and France.

The majority of Germans appear to have accepted Hitler's rule. Until 1939 the worst aspects of Nazi policy remained hidden. There were no mass killings, but there was falling unemployment and a genuine economic recovery. There was opposition from the Lutheran Church and from students, such as the 'White Rose' and other groups, who objected to being forced to join the youth organisations. To many people, however, both inside and outside Germany, Hitler appeared to be a change for the better.

Opposition to Nazi Rule

There was little opposition to the Nazis in the mid-1930s. At that time Hitler appeared to be working a miracle in Germany and the real nature of his regime was still hidden. Opposition grew when membership of the Nazi youth organisation became compulsory in 1939 and when the persecution of the Jews and other groups became more significant.

The strongest opposition to the Nazis came from young people. There were a number of student groups who distributed leaflets and organised meetings. One group, at Munich University, called the 'White Rose', centred around Hans and Sophie Scholl. They were arrested and executed in 1944. Some young people simply rejected the Nazis. 'Swing' groups listened to American jazz and openly admired American fashions. 'Edelweiss Pirates' were working-class groups who mocked the self-righteous Nazis and refused to join the Hitler Youth.

The social impact of Nazism

By 1934 the Nazi Party completely dominated life in Germany. All government officials and civil servants had to be party members and promotion was only possible through loyalty. However, after 'The Night of the Long Knives' in June 1934 there were no mass executions and there were often major disagreements within the party about policy. This was partly because Hitler actually encouraged rivalry between the senior party members, such as Goering and Himmler, and partly because the party was not nearly as well organised as it could have been.

The rivalry and disorganisation meant that there were plenty of opportunities for ambitious individuals to make names for themselves; that usually involved being more violent and extreme than their superiors. In this way, the Nazi Party did create a new social framework. The old aristocratic families who had governed Germany before 1919 generally remained aloof from this. Most army generals carried out their duties faithfully, but did not join the Nazi Party.

The changes in everyday life
For ordinary Germans, however, there were major changes in everyday life. Nazis believed that men and women had separate roles in society. Women were expected to give up work when they got married and spend all of their time at home. They were encouraged to wear traditional peasant dress, use no make-up and wear their hair in plaits. These fashions were not followed, however, by the wives of many of the Nazi leaders, particularly Magda Goebbels, who refused point blank to follow these conventions.

The exclusion of women from the workforce was one method used by the Nazis to reduce unemployment. Another was the Labour Service, which had actually been planned before Hitler came to power. This involved six months' work for very low pay at the age of eighteen. The Labour Service built the **Autobahns**, often using hand tools, because this meant that more workers were needed. The creation of the Autobahn network employed hundreds of thousands of workers, but also led to work in other industries, such as engineering, and iron and steel.

In 1935, conscription was introduced and this reduced unemployment still further. Most men went into the army after they had completed their Labour Service. This meant that they would be members of Nazi-controlled organisations from the ages of five to twenty-one. Rearmament also began in 1935 and this led to a reduction in unemployment. In 1933 there had been more than 6,000,000 people out of work; by 1938 the Nazis claimed that the number had fallen to 500,000. At one point Hitler claimed that 126,000 jobs were being created every week.

Many of the jobs created were temporary. The Nazis could not go on building Autobahns forever, but the overall impact was of great success, especially when compared with the effects of the Depression in other European countries. Hitler appeared to be performing a miracle.

The Nazis and the Arts
The Nazis attempted to control all forms of art. Many films were produced covering events in German history, such as the *Teutonic Knights* and *Frederick the Great*. Examples of non-German art were destroyed. Jazz was forbidden, as were the works of all Jewish composers, painters and writers. Any anti-war novels, such as *All Quiet on the Western Front* were banned. Hitler claimed to be an expert on painting and ordered that all impressionist and post-impressionist paintings should be removed from art galleries. The Nazis only approved of realist art and demanded that it should carry a message supporting Nazi beliefs and values.

In what ways did the treatment of Jews change from 1933 to 1939?

In what ways were the lives of women changed in Nazi Germany?

Why do you think the Nazis were so concerned about controlling the Arts?

Hitler, Nazism and Nazi beliefs

Source A

I knew all was lost. Only fools, liars and criminals could hope on the mercy of the enemy. In the nights hatred grew inside me, hatred for those responsible for this deed. In the days that followed, my own fate became known to me. I decided to go into politics.

▲ From an article written by Hitler describing the moment he heard about the Armistice in November 1918.

Source B

It is ridiculous to attempt to liberate ourselves from the chains of Versailles unless we take our destiny in our own hands and unless we work ... at our science of war. For there can be no doubt for anyone – between our present misery and our future happiness, there is war. This is why everybody, man, woman and child must know what war is.

▲ From the *Science of Military Defence*, a book written by a Nazi, Leipzig, 1932.

Source C

It is necessary, then, for better or for worse, to resort to war if one wishes seriously to arrive at pacifism. The pacifist idea will perhaps work on that day when the man superior to all others will have conquered the world and become the sole master of the earth. First, then, the battle, and afterwards – perhaps – pacifism.

▲ From *Mein Kampf*, written by Adolf Hitler in 1924.

Source D

Germany has a right to greater living space (*lebensraum*) than other nations. Our foreign policy is to unfold, enlarge and protect the entire German racial community, no matter where Germans might live in other countries. Space is paramount. Britain and France are both inspired by hate and will oppose Germany. They will have to be fought.

▲ From a speech made by Hitler in November 1937.

Source E

▲ A poster published by the Nazi Party in the 1930s.

Source F

Hitler invaded Austria in 1938 to complete the Anschluss, or union with Germany. Although this was a deliberate breach of the Treaty of Versailles there were many who were prepared to accept Hitler's claim that he was simply righting a serious wrong. If the Treaty of Versailles had recognised the right of other people of the same nationality and language to rule themselves, then, said Hitler, it was only proper that this right should also apply to Germans.

▲ A comment on support for Hitler's policy of reversing Versailles in a modern school textbook.

Study Source A

a What can you learn from Source A about Hitler's aims? (4)

Study Sources A, B and C

b Do Sources B and C support the evidence of Source A about the aims of the Nazis? Explain your answer by referring to all three sources. (4)

Study Sources B and C

c Use the sources and your own knowledge to explain why the Nazis believed that war was necessary. (6)

Study Sources D and E

d How useful are these sources in helping you to understand the beliefs of the Nazis? (6)

Study all of the sources

e 'Nazi beliefs meant that war was inevitable.' Use the sources and your own knowledge to explain whether you agree with this view. (10)

The Nazi rise to power: the role of Hitler

Source A

Hitler himself spoke at sixteen major rallies. Columns of SS troops shouting slogans marched through the villages and towns from morning till night. In every market square an SA band or Nazi minstrels played marches for hours on end.

▲ From an eyewitness account of the part played by Hitler in election campaigns in February 1933.

Source B

Here it seemed to me was hope. Here were new ideals ... The perils of communism ... could be checked. Hitler persuaded us, and instead of hopeless unemployment, Germany could move towards economic recovery. He had mentioned the Jewish problem only in passing. But his remarks did not worry me ... It was during these months that my mother saw an SA parade in the streets of Heidelberg. The sight of discipline in a time of chaos ... seems to have won her over.

▲ From *Inside the Third Reich,* by Albert Speer, a German architect and former Nazi minister during the Second World War, in which he describes a meeting that Hitler addressed in 1931.

Source C

▲ A photograph of an SA rally at Nuremberg in 1933.

Source D

There stood Hitler in a simple black coat and looked over the crowd, waiting – a forest of black swastika pennants swished up, the jubilation of the moment was given vent in a roaring salute. His main theme – out of parties shall grow a nation, the German nation. He laid into the system – 'I want to know what there is left to be ruined by this state!' When the speech was over, there was roaring enthusiasm and applause.

▲ An eyewitness account of a speech made by Hitler at a Nazi Party rally in 1932.

Source E

What had Hitler provided to persuade the Germans to give up their freedom so happily? Well, there was something for everyone in his political stewpot. Work for the unemployed, an army for the generals, a phoney religion for the gullible, a strident manner in foreign affairs for those who still smarted under the indignity of a lost war. Hitler knew he needed the support of the middle class, so he threw up a smoke screen of respectability around everything he did.

▲ Christabel Bielenberg, a British woman living in Germany, describes events in 1934.

Source F

They call me a stateless corporal and a housepainter. Is there anything improper in earning one's daily bread by manual labour? ... the day of reckoning is not far off. An increasing number of industrialists, financiers, intellectuals and army officers are now looking for a man who will at last bring some order into affairs at home, who will draw the farmers, the workers and the officials into the German community once more.

▲ From an interview with Hitler in a German daily newspaper in May 1931.

Study Source A

a What can you learn from Source A about the methods used by the Nazis in election campaigns? (4)

Study Sources B and C

b How useful are these sources in helping you to understand why people were attracted to the Nazis? (6)

Study Sources B, D and E

c Do Sources D and E support the evidence of Source B about Hitler's role in Nazi election campaigns? Explain your answer by referring to all three sources. (4)

Study Source D and E

d Use these sources and your own knowledge to explain why the Nazis became so much more popular in the years from 1930 to 1932. (6)

Study all of the sources

e 'It was solely the brilliance of Hitler's leadership which brought the Nazis to power.' Use the sources and your own knowledge to explain whether you agree with this view. (10)

Creation of the totalitarian state: the elimination of the opposition

Source A

Adolf is a swine. He will give us all away. He's getting matey with the generals – they are his cronies now ... the generals are a lot of old fogeys. They've never had a new idea ... I'm the nucleus of a new army don't you see that? Don't you understand that what's coming must be new, fresh and unused? You only get the opportunity once to make something new and big that will help lift the world off its hinges.

▲ From a reported conversation between Ernst Röhm and other members of the SA.

Source B

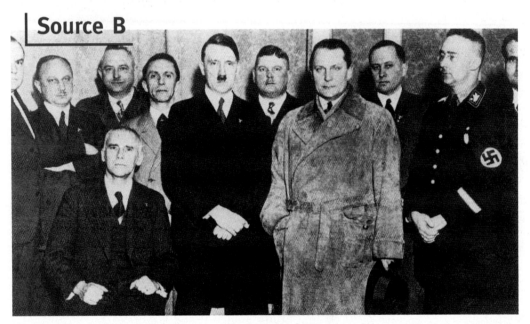

▲ A photograph of leading members of the Nazi Party, taken on 31 January 1933.

Source C

▲ The same photograph as published in late 1934. The missing figure is Ernst Röhm.

Source D

Rearmament is too serious a business to be carried out by swindlers, drunkards and homosexuals.

◀ **A comment made by General Walther von Brauchitsch, the Commander in Chief of the German Army in 1934.**

Source E

The Führer with soldierly decision and exemplary courage has himself attacked and crushed the traitors and murderers. The army as the bearer of arms of the entire people, far removed from the conflicts of domestic politics, will show its gratitude through devotion and loyalty.

▲ **A statement made by the German defence minister, General von Blomberg, in July 1934, after 'The Night of the Long Knives'.**

Source F

I swear by God this holy oath, that I will render to Adolf Hitler, Führer of the German Reich and people, Supreme Commander of the armed forces, unconditional obedience, and I am ready, as a brave soldier, to risk my life at any time for this oath.

▲ **The oath sworn by members of the German armed forces after the death of President Hindenburg in August 1934.**

Study Source A

a What can you learn from Source A about relations between Hitler and Ernst Röhm in 1934? (4)

Study Sources B and C

b Use your own knowledge to help you explain the differences between these two sources. (4)

Study Sources A, B, C and D

c In what ways does the evidence of Sources A and D help you to understand the differences between Sources B and C? (6)

Study Sources D and E

d How useful are these sources in helping you to understand why 'The Night of the Long Knives' took place? (6)

Study all of the sources

e '"The Night of the Long Knives' gave Hitler complete control of Germany.' Use the sources and your own knowledge to explain whether you agree with this view. (10)

The Nazi state: propaganda, education, youth movements, the arts, sport and entertainment

Source A

What puffs and patters?

What clicks and clatters?

I know what, oh what fun

It's a lovely Gatling gun.

▲ A Nazi nursery rhyme.

Source B

This Archangel is leading the column of comrades, a column formed by warriors of the Reich. They have only one enemy – the opponents of the Reich and its rulers. We do not want to speak the warm words of peace here. Our words are dictated by the terrible appeal of war. Young people, raise your hands and swear an oath before this monument, which is dedicated to bloodshed.

▲ From a speech made by a Hitler Youth leader on 31 October 1933 at the unveiling of a monument to the Archangel Michael.

Source C

So stand the Storm Battalions,

Ready for the racial fight.

Only when Jews lie bleeding

Can we be really free.

▲ A verse from the National Socialist *Little Song Book*.

Source D

Adolf Hitler gave us back our faith. He showed us the true meaning of religion. He came to take us from the faith of our fathers? No, he has come to renew for us the faith of our fathers and to make us new and better things ...

Just as Christ made his twelve disciples into a band faithful to the martyr's death whose faith shook the Roman Empire, so now we witness the same spectacle again: Adolf Hitler is the true Holy Ghost.

▲ From a speech made by the Reich Minister for Church Affairs in 1935.

Source E

Adolf Hitler to thee alone we are bound. In this hour we would renew our solemn vow; in this world we believe in Adolf Hitler alone. We believe that National Socialism is the sole faith to make our people blessed. We believe that there is Lord God in heaven, who has made us, who, leads us, who guides us and who visibly blesses us. And we believe that the Lord God has sent us Adolf Hitler that Germany might be established for all eternity.

▲ A prayer published by the Nazis for use in Roman Catholic churches.

KOMM ZU UNS!

DEUTSCHES JUNGVOLK
IN DER HITLER-JUGEND

▲ A poster advertising the Nazi Youth movement.

Study Source A

a What can you learn from Source A about Nazis' attitudes to education? (4)

Study Sources A, B and C

b i Do Sources B and C support the evidence of Source A about Nazi policies towards the young? Explain your answer by referring to all three sources. (4)

b ii Use the sources and your own knowledge to explain why the Nazis put so much effort into controlling children and young people. (6)

Study Sources D and E

c How useful are these sources as evidence about Nazi policies towards religion? (6)

Study all of the sources

d 'The Nazis believed that they could use young children to control their parents.' Use the sources and your own knowledge to explain whether you agree with this view. (10)

Racism, citizenship and treatment of minorities, persecution of the Jews: opposition to Nazi rule

Source A

On the evening of 9 November 1938, Dr Goebbels told the Party leaders that there had been anti-Jewish riots during which shops and synagogues had been set on fire. The Führer had decided that such actions were not to be prepared or organised by the Party, but neither were they to be discouraged. The Reich propaganda director said that the Party should not appear in public to have started the disturbances, but that in reality it should organise them and carry them out in secret.

▲ From a secret report of the Nazi Supreme Court on the events of Kristallnacht.

Source B

In one of the Jewish sections an eighteen year old boy was hurled from a three-storey window to land with both legs broken on a street of broken glass littered with burning beds. The main streets of the city were a positive litter of shattered glass. All of the synagogues were completely gutted by fire. One of the largest clothing stores was destroyed. The fire brigade made no attempts to put out the fire. It is very difficult to believe, but the owners of the clothing store were actually charged with setting fire to their own store, and were dragged from their beds at 6 a.m. and thrown into prison. Many male Jews have been sent to concentration camps.

▲ From a report on the events of Kristallnacht, 9 November 1938. This was written by the American Consul in Leipzig on 21 November 1938.

Source D

Two SS men came to my house to fetch me. When about 20 people had been collected we were put into a lorry and taken to police headquarters. On the way I saw Jewish shops which had been destroyed. The big synagogue was in flames.

At the police station we were lined up in the yard. There were already hundreds there. Some had been there since early morning. About six o'clock we were formed into a procession of about 2,000 and began to march to the railway station. Crowds lined the streets, some shouted abuse, but the majority remained silent.

▲ From a letter written by a Jew in February 1939. This was smuggled out of Germany and published by the German Freedom Party.

Source C

▲ A photograph of the damage caused by Kristallnacht. This is the interior of a synagogue in Munich.

Source E

HEUTE prima (trefo) Hackfleisch sehr billig

▲ A poster encouraging anti-Semitism in 1939. It suggests that Jewish butchers used rats to make sausages.

Source F

All damage to Jewish businesses or dwellings on 8, 9 and 10 November 1938 must be repaired by the Jewish occupant or by Jewish businessmen.

A fine of 1,000,000,000 Reich marks has been imposed on the Jews of German nationality.

From 1 January 1939, a Jew cannot be a businessman any longer. If any Jews are leading employees in businesses, they will be dismissed after six months' notice.

Jews are not permitted to employ female citizens of German blood under 45 years of age as domestic help.

▲ Decrees issued by Hermann Goering 12 November 1938.

Study Source A

a What can you learn from Source A about the effects of Kristallnacht? (4)

Study Sources A and B

b Does Source B support the evidence of Source A about the effects of Kristallnacht? Explain your answer with reference to both sources. (4)

Study Sources A, B and C

c Use the sources and your own knowledge to explain why Kristallnacht took place. (6)

Study Sources D and E

d How useful are these sources as evidence of Nazi policies towards the Jews? (10)

Study all the Sources

e 'Kristallnacht was organised and planned by the Nazis.' Use the sources and your knowledge to explain whether you agree with this view. (10)

The social impact of Nazism on social classes; the role and status of women: employment opportunities in the economy

Source A

Every Aryan hero must marry a blonde Aryan woman with blue, wide open eyes, a long oval face, a pink and white skin, a narrow nose and who is under all circumstances a virgin. The Aryan hero must only marry his equal Aryan woman, but not one who goes out too much or likes theatres, entertainment or sport, or who cares to be seen outside her house.

▲ From *The Knowledge of the Nation*, a book published in Germany in 1934.

Source B

We want our women tried and true
Not as decorated toys
The German wife and mother too
Bears riches no foreign woman enjoys.

The German woman is noble wine
She loves and enriches the earth.
The German woman is bright sunshine
To home and hearth.

Worthy of respect she must always be seen;
Not of strange races the passion and game
The Volk must remain pure and clean.
That is the Führer's highest aim.

▲ From *The ABC of National Socialism*, a book published in Germany in the 1930s.

Source C

Fifty-two year old pure Aryan doctor, veteran of the Battle of Tannenberg, who intends to settle on the land, desires male progeny through a registry-office marriage with a healthy Aryan, virginal, young, unassuming, economy-minded woman, adapted to hard work, broad-hipped, flat-heeled and earring-less.

▲ An advert that appeared in a German newspaper in the 1930s.

Source D

A German woman does not use make up!
A German woman does not smoke!
A German woman has a duty to keep herself fit and healthy!

▲ From the rule book of the League of German Maidens.

Source E

There is no room for political women in the world of National Socialism. All that this movement has ever said and thought on the subject goes against political women. Woman is relegated to her ordained family circles and to her business as a wife. The German revolution is an event made by, and supremely concerned with, the male.

▲ **From an article published in Germany in 1933.**

Source F

▲ **A poster published in Germany in the 1930s showing the ideal Nazi family.**

Study Source A

a   What can you learn from Source A about Nazi beliefs about the role of women? (4)

Study Sources B and C

b i In what ways do Sources B and C support the evidence of Source A about Nazi attitudes towards women? (4)

b ii Use the sources and your own knowledge to explain why the Nazis had strong views about the role of women in German society. (6)

Study Source D and E

c   How useful are these sources as evidence of the ways that women were treated in Nazi Germany? (6)

Study all of the sources

d   'The Nazis believed that the role of women was to serve men.' Use the sources and your own knowledge to explain whether you agree with this view. (10)

CHAPTER 5

The world at war: 1938~45

Appeasement, Chamberlain and the outbreak of war

Neville Chamberlain became prime minister of Britain in 1937. He already had a long career as a government minister behind him, but no experience of foreign affairs. When Hitler united Germany and Austria in March 1938, Chamberlain protested, but took no action. He immediately made up his mind that if Hitler attacked Czechoslovakia, Britain would be able to do nothing about it. He decided to follow the policy of **appeasement** (1938–39), giving in to Hitler's demands in the belief that the dictator would be satisfied. He decided that when the crisis came, he would meet Hitler face to face to sort out the problems. This became known as Plan Z. Chamberlain was convinced that he would be able to deal with Hitler.

Many people in Britain agreed with Chamberlain for different reasons. Some believed that Hitler was, indeed, a reasonable man and admired his successes in Germany. Others saw Hitler as an ally against communism. The Soviet Union was seen as a threat and Hitler openly stated his hatred of communism. Most people were too horrified at their memories of the First World War even to consider another war.

Chamberlain did not see appeasement simply as giving in to Hitler; he appears to have tried to give way to Hitler only until the British armed forces were strong enough to face him. Unfortunately, Chamberlain's behaviour failed to make this clear to Hitler. He came to see the British prime minister as a weak leader who could be ignored.

On 15 September, Hitler demanded self-government for the Sudeten Germans – the German-speaking inhabitants of western Czechoslovakia. Chamberlain flew to meet him and agreed to his demands. He then persuaded the French to support him and told the Czech government that it would have to agree. But when Chamberlain returned to Germany, Hitler had changed his demands; he now wanted the Sudetenland handed over to Germany. Chamberlain returned to Britain in despair.

However, at the last moment, Benito Mussolini, the Italian **dictator**, suggested a four power conference to settle the matter. France, Britain, Germany and Italy agreed to hand over the Sudetenland to Hitler. Chamberlain and Hitler signed an agreement the following day stating that their countries would never go to war again. When Chamberlain returned from Munich he was given a hero's welcome. He appeared on the balcony of Buckingham Palace between the king and queen. But there was a substantial, and growing, body of opinion that criticised his actions.

In March 1939, Hitler occupied western Czechoslovakia and Chamberlain realised that appeasement had failed. In April he guaranteed to defend Poland and Romania if they were attacked and in June conscription began. These were intended to be warnings to Germany, but they were ignored.

In August, Hitler signed the Nazi–Soviet Pact with Stalin. This came as a major shock as the two leaders had appeared to be bitter enemies. On the face of it this was a **non-aggression** pact, but secretly the two leaders agreed to invade Poland and divide it between them. Hitler also agreed to allow Stalin to occupy the Baltic states and Finland, and Stalin agreed to let Hitler have a free hand in western Europe. The Pact made war inevitable.

On 1 September 1939 the German army invaded Poland. After a day's delay, Chamberlain sent an ultimatum to Berlin, threatening war if Hitler did not withdraw by 11 am on 3 September. Hitler took no notice, so Britain declared war on Germany.

Reasons for early German success

The German invasion of Poland in September 1939 was a complete success, and within three weeks the Polish army had been destroyed. In April and May 1940 the invasions of Denmark, Norway, Belgium, Holland and France went just as smoothly.

Hitler at first appeared to be following the Schlieffen Plan as in 1914, but after driving through the Allied forces, the German armies turned north and south, separating the French and the British. The British Expeditionary Force, which had taken up position in Belgium in 1939, was forced back to Calais and Dunkirk and had to be evacuated in the first two weeks of June 1940. Almost all of its equipment was lost, but 310,000 men were rescued. British forces were also sent to Norway in April, but proved completely ineffective and had to be rescued after six weeks. By mid-June Hitler appeared to have won the war.

One reason for Hitler's success was the scale of rearmament. Germany had started rearming first. The German army was much larger than any other European army, except for the French. Denmark, Holland and Belgium were all neutral countries and only had small armed forces. They could put up very little resistance.

A second reason was the new tactics developed by the Germans. **Blitzkrieg** involved sudden attacks using massed tank formations, dive-bombers and paratroops. The Germans had also developed new weapons. Their tanks were more mobile and the Stuka dive-bomber was very effective in Poland. The Allied armies were taken by surprise at the mobility and speed of the German army.

Blitzkrieg had already been tried out during the Spanish Civil War. Hitler had sent about 10,000 men to support General Franco of Spain, and their experience proved invaluable. Many people throughout Europe had seen newsreel film of the bombing of the Spanish town of Guernica; there seemed to be no way of stopping the German armed forces.

The French government had pinned its hopes on a massive line of fortifications along the Franco–German border. It was called the Maginot Line after the general who designed it. It was believed to be **impregnable**, and it probably was, but it ended at the Belgian border. It was a series of underground forts, linked by railway, that was designed to prevent an invasion of France.

Although the French tried to extend the Line from 1936 onwards, they failed and in 1940 the Germans simply went round it, sending their tanks through the Ardennes, a wooded hilly area. The French commanders had believed that it would be impossible for the Germans to get through the Ardennes and across the River Meuse, so no French forces were stationed there. The French army was taken completely by surprise and found itself outflanked.

Although the French army outnumbered the German army and much of its equipment was superior, the French appeared to lack the determination to fight. There was a strong defeatist attitude in both the French government and army. Once the German army had got round the Maginot Line and reached the English Channel, there were few attempts to carry on the fight. Some people seem to have believed that Hitler would cure some of the problems that France had suffered from during the 1930s, especially communist influence, and many Frenchmen were to **collaborate** with the Nazis during the four years of occupation.

Why did Chamberlain agree to the Munich Agreement?

Why did war break out in September 1939?

Why were the Germans able to overrun western Europe so easily in 1940?

Falls and survivals

The French government surrendered to Germany on 22 June 1940. Hitler accepted the surrender at exactly the same spot near Compiegne where the Germans had signed the Armistice in November 1918. All of northern and western France was occupied by Germany; the remainder was governed from Vichy by a new French government headed by Marshal Petain. He was given almost dictatorial powers by the deputies to the assembly and appointed Pierre Laval as his prime minister. The Vichy government collaborated with the German occupying forces in many ways during the rest of the war.

From July 1940, the German armed forces began to attack Britain. It is unlikely that Hitler ever planned an invasion of Britain, but at the time one was expected almost daily. The first attacks were on shipping in the English Channel and the ports on the south coast. These were followed by bombing raids on radar stations and then airfields. Finally, from mid-August came attacks on Fighter Command. This was the Battle of Britain. At first the Royal Air Force (RAF) was able to defeat the **Luftwaffe**, but by the first week of September the tide was beginning to turn. Fortunately, Hitler lost patience and ordered night attacks on London instead. When daylight attacks were renewed on 15 September the RAF regained the initiative and the Luftwaffe turned to night bombing London and other British cities in what became known as the **Blitz**.

There were major attacks on many British cities from September to November 1940 and again in the spring of 1941. These were intended to break the morale of the British people by destroying their homes and possessions. Although the official government line was that 'Britain could take it', there is plenty of evidence that the bombing had very serious effects. The worst of the attacks came to an end when the bombers of the Luftwaffe were sent east to begin the attack on the Soviet Union in June 1941; this was known as Operation Barbarossa.

Hitler's invasion of the Soviet Union was the turning point of the war. At first, however, the German army was very successful. The Red Army was caught unaware because Stalin had not believed reports sent to him by his spies in Berlin that the Germans were about to attack. The Red Army had also lost most of its senior officers in the purges of 1937–38. Within months the Germans had swept east in a massive three-pronged attack. But the Germans failed to capture Moscow, falling just 20 miles short in December 1941.

Hitler had made two fateful mistakes. The invasion had been delayed for two months from April to June because German troops had been sent to the Balkans to support Hitler's ally Mussolini. This delay meant that the invasion was not completed before the onset of winter. Instead of reaching Moscow in September, the German army arrived on the outskirts of the Soviet capital just as the temperatures dropped way below zero, and Hitler had not supplied winter clothing. The three-pronged attack weakened the German advance, and a single thrust might well have succeeded.

The Eastern Front proved a nightmare for the German army. The vastness of the country, the extremes of temperature and the reserves available to the Red Army slowly turned the tide in Stalin's favour. In February 1943, the German Sixth Army was surrounded at Stalingrad and was forced to surrender. It was the first major defeat of the German armed forces.

Operation Barbarossa
A Russian proverb states, 'When all our other generals have been defeated, we still have Generals January and February'. In the sub-zero temperatures of December and January – down to minus 40° celsius – the fuel and oil in German tanks and lorries froze and guns became unusable. But the German troops had little winter clothing. At this very moment, Red army units from Siberia counter-attacked. They were used to such temperatures and were fully equipped for the cold weather.

The causes of war in the Pacific

On 7 December 1941 the Japanese armed forces launched a surprise attack on the main US base in the Pacific Ocean, Pearl Harbor in Hawaii. Eight battleships were destroyed and 2,600 Americans were killed. The following day, President Roosevelt declared war on Japan.

Japan wanted to create an empire in the Far East. The main obstacle to Japanese expansion was the USA. The attack on Pearl Harbor was an attempt to knock the USA out of the war before it had even started. The military government believed that Japan would have to fight the USA sooner or later and so decided to strike while the USA was unprepared.

The Japanese already occupied large areas of Asia in 1941. In 1931 the Japanese army had invaded Manchuria, which was part of China, and set up a **puppet government**. In July 1937 the Japanese army invaded northern China. Shanghai and other Chinese cities were bombed into submission. Within a year Nanking, the capital, Tsingtao, Canton and Hankow had all been taken. Britain and the USA gave large loans to the Guomingdang government of China, but the Japanese government began to demand that Britain and the other Western countries should give up supporting China and co-operate with Japan in establishing a 'new order' in the Far East.

The new order was the 'Greater East Asia Co-prosperity Sphere'. In fact, this was to be nothing more than a Japanese Empire, intended to provide living space for Japan's growing population. Japan also needed raw materials – especially oil. The main supplier of oil to Japan was the USA, but in July 1941 the USA cut off all supplies of oil to Japan in protest against Japan's actions in China.

The attack on Pearl Harbor was a daring raid because it involved the Japanese force sailing more than 3,000 miles before launching its attack. US intelligence discovered the force's movements and decoded its messages, but failed to warn Pearl Harbor in time. So when the Japanese planes attacked at 8 a.m., they achieved total surprise. There is some suggestion that President Roosevelt deliberately withheld information of the attack so that he would have an excuse to declare war.

In fact, the effects of Pearl Harbor were not as disastrous as they seemed at first. The main aim of the Japanese had been to destroy the three US aircraft carriers, but these were at sea on manoeuvres at the time and all escaped unharmed. Even so, Japanese forces were able to follow up their success by over-running much of South-East Asia and the South-West Pacific. All of Indo-China, Malaya and Indonesia were occupied, as well as the Philippines and parts of Borneo and New Guinea. To the west Burma was overrun and India was invaded. By June 1942 they appeared to be unstoppable.

What effects did the Blitz have on Britain?

Why did Operation Barbarossa fail?

Why did the Japanese attack Pearl Harbor?

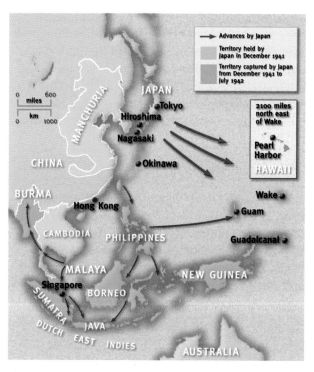

▲ Japanese conquests and the war in the Pacific.

Reasons for German defeat

In 1940 and 1941 the German armed forces appeared to be invincible. Yet by this time, Hitler had laid the seeds of his own destruction. On too many occasions he interfered in military matters – unlike Stalin, who left everything to his commanders. Hitler had ordered the German tanks to stop on the outskirts of Dunkirk in May and June 1940. Hitler also stopped attacks on Fighter Command on 7 September 1940, just when the Luftwaffe was on the verge of winning the Battle of Britain. Hitler held back production of U-boats in 1939 and 1940, so that when the Battle of the Atlantic began in 1941 the German Navy only had 37 submarines.

The determination of the British people in holding on alone from June 1940 until June 1941, when Germany invaded the Soviet Union, set an example to the rest of the world and showed that the British people were not prepared to give in. Prime Minister Churchill again played a key role in maintaining morale by his speeches and visits to bombed areas.

Britain also received invaluable aid from President Roosevelt of the USA. In 1940 he signed the Destroyers for Bases agreement, and in March 1941 he signed the Lend Lease Act. But Roosevelt was not able to declare war until the Japanese attack on Pearl Harbor on 7 December 1941. Hitler declared war on the USA on 11 December 1941 and aid to Britain was immediately stepped up. By 1943, US war production was in full swing, producing four times as much each month as Germany. In the end the military and economic might of the USA was to be a key factor in victory.

From 1942 the RAF began to bomb Germany every night. When the US airforce arrived in the UK it began to bomb during the day. By 1943, 1,000 bomber raids were organised, which saturated German cities with **incendiaries** and heavy explosives.

Hitler made the mistake of believing that Germany was invincible and allowed his armed forces to take on too much. In 1941 German forces were sent to North Africa to attack Egypt, and in 1943 German troops occupied Italy after the Allied invasion threatened to bring about the downfall of Mussolini.

But the real body blows to Germany were struck on the Eastern Front, where the German armed forces suffered 90 per cent of their total war casualties. The surrender of the Sixth Army at Stalingrad in February 1943 was followed by the Battle of Kursk in July 1943 when the Soviet army destroyed 1,500 German tanks. This effectively marked the end of German attempts to conquer the Soviet Union. The war in the East dragged on for another two years, but in the end the enormous manpower advantage of the Red Army was too much.

In the West, British, US and Canadian forces landed in Normandy on 6 June 1944. This 'D-Day' landing was the result of meticulous planning by the Allies. The biggest naval fleet ever assembled escorted the invasion force and bombarded the German defences; 10,000 aircraft provided air cover. Paratroopers were landed the night before the invasion to knock out enemy positions. Gliders carrying 40 soldiers each were towed across to France to land behind the German defences. The Germans had expected the invasion to take place at Calais on the French coast, and even after the Allied troops landed went on believing that this was a feint. Hitler also refused to allow Field Marshal Rommel to take control of the **Panzer divisions** in Normandy. This weakened the German army when it tried to counterattack the Allies after they had landed.

Although the war lasted another eleven months, the superiority of the Allies, in men and supplies, was overwhelming. By 1945, Germany was on its knees, having been bombed around the clock and starved by the Allied blockade. The surrender was signed in northern Germany on 8 May 1945.

Germany in 1945
Although most factories were working, the effects of the Allied blockade were everywhere. Fuel, food and most raw materials were in very short supply. When Hitler committed suicide on 30 April, there was little will to continue the fight.

Reasons for the defeat of Japan

Some Japanese commanders believed that the war was lost when the attack on Pearl Harbor failed to destroy the three US aircraft carriers, because air power was to be the key to the naval war in the Pacific. They may well have been right and the significance of the failure was revealed six months later when the Japanese tried to occupy Midway Island in June 1942. US intelligence was able to break the Japanese military code and intercept its fleet. Four Japanese aircraft carriers were sunk. This convinced the Japanese High Command that the war would be lost. News of the losses was never published during the war.

The war in the Pacific lasted for another three years; in the end US manpower, oil and war production made all the difference. However, Japanese forces often refused to surrender and fought to a finish on almost every island. On Leyte, in the Philippines, the Japanese garrison of 80,000 fought to the last man. US forces adopted the policy of 'island-hopping', leaving Japanese units isolated on islands without supplies and selecting targets carefully. However, when the first two Japanese islands – Okinawa and Iwo Jima – were attacked, the Japanese defenders cemented themselves into bunkers in the hillsides and refused to come out. Some 28,000 US marines were killed capturing the islands.

To the west of Japan, the British held up the Japanese advance in the jungles of Burma. Raids were sent behind enemy lines to cut the Japanese supply routes, but the first real success did not come until June 1944, when Allied forces began to recapture the areas occupied by the Japanese. In August 1944 Japanese forces were driven out of India and began to retreat.

By summer 1945 almost all Japanese conquests in the Pacific had been recaptured and Japanese forces were retreating in South-East Asia, but there still remained the prospect of an invasion of Japan itself. The losses suffered in the landings on Iwo Jima and Okinawa convinced the new US President, Harry S. Truman, that an invasion of Japan would result in massive Allied casualties. His chiefs of staff estimated them to be as high as 500,000, with the possibility of the war lasting another two years. Truman decided to use the atomic bomb as a means of bringing the war to an end as soon as possible.

On 6 and 9 August 1945, atomic bombs were dropped on the Japanese cities of Hiroshima and Nagasaki. Within a week the Japanese government had surrendered. It is still not clear whether the dropping of the bombs forced the Japanese government to surrender, or whether it was about to surrender anyway. What is certain is that it began a new period in world history.

Island-hopping

The US army developed the strategy of island-hopping as it tried to re-occupy the chains of island captured by the Japanese. Instead of attempting to invade every island, they left some alone, leaving the Japanese garrison isolated. Even so, the US forces suffered appalling losses.

The effects of the atomic bomb

When the Americans dropped the atomic bomb on Hiroshima on 6 August 1945, at the very centre of the explosion the heat was so great that anything caught in it turned from a solid to a gas. Further out, people were burnt alive. The explosion created a wind of 800 kilometres an hour which crushed many people. But in many ways the worst damage was caused by radiation. It caused flesh to dissolve and hang down in strips. Soldiers in an anti-aircraft battery were found with their eyes melted.

How did the Allies prepare for the invasion of Normandy?

Why did the US forces adopt the strategy of island-hopping?

Why did Truman decide to use the atomic bomb in August 1945?

Appeasement, 1938–39: the role of Neville Chamberlain; the outbreak of the Second World War

Source A

We are in no position to enter into a war with such a formidable power as Germany, much less if Germany were aided by Italian attacks on our Mediterranean bases. Therefore, until we have rearmed we must adjust our foreign policy to our circumstances. I do not myself take too pessimistic a view of the situation. The dictators (Hitler and Mussolini) are too often regarded as though they were inhuman.

▲ From a letter written by Neville Chamberlain to a friend in the USA on 16 January 1938.

Source B

You only have to look at the map to see that nothing that France or we could do could possibly save Czechoslovakia from being overrun by the Germans if they wanted to do it. The Austrian frontier is practically open; the great Skoda munition works are within easy bombing distance of the German aerodromes, the railways all pass through German territory. Therefore we could not help Czechoslovakia, it would simply be an excuse for going to war with Germany. I have therefore abandoned any idea of giving guarantees to Czechoslovakia.

▲ From Neville Chamberlain's diary, 20 March 1938.

Source C

I had established a certain confidence, which was my aim. In spite of the hardness and ruthlessness I thought I saw in his face, I got the impression that here was a man who could be relied upon when he had given his word.

▲ From a letter written by Neville Chamberlain to his sister after meeting Hitler at Berchtesgaden in September 1938.

Source D

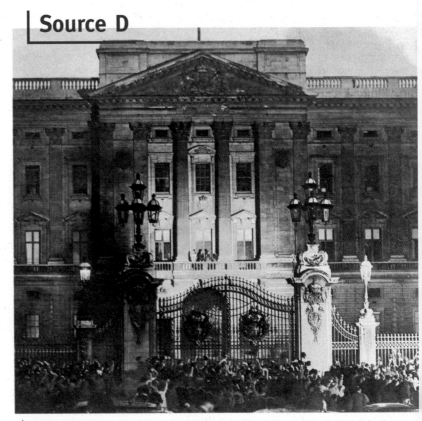

▲ Photograph of Neville Chamberlain who was greeted by cheering crowds after he had returned from Munich on 30 September 1938.

Source E

Be Glad in your hearts. Give thanks to your God.

The wings of peace settle about us and the peoples of Europe. People of Britain your children are safe. Your husbands and your sons will not march to battle.

If we must have a victor, let us choose Chamberlain. For the prime minister's conquests are mighty and enduring – millions of happy homes and hearts relieved of their burden. To him the laurels.

▲ From the *Daily Express,* 30 September 1938.

Source F

In 1938 Czechoslovakia was the one country ready for war. The Czechoslovak army of 35 divisions faced a German army which was slightly larger, but the Czechs were better equipped than the Germans in a number of ways, notably artillery. In military terms, Hitler's aggression was lunacy, as his generals knew. The avoidance of war in 1938 was not only a shameful act, but a foolish one.

▲ A comment on Chamberlain's policy of appeasement from a modern history book.

Study Source A

a   What can you learn from Source A about Neville Chamberlain's policy towards Hitler in early 1938? (4)

Study Sources A, B and C

b i Do Sources B and C support the evidence of Source A about Chamberlain's policy? Explain your answer by referring to both sources. (4)

b ii Use the sources and your own knowledge to explain why Chamberlain decided to sign the Munich Agreement. (6)

Study Sources D and E

c   How useful are these sources in helping you to understand the reaction to the Munich Agreement in Britain? (6)

Study all of the sources

d   The writer of Source F described Chamberlain's actions in September 1938 as 'shameful' and 'foolish'. Use the sources and your own knowledge to explain whether you agree with this view. (10)

Reasons for early German successes

Source A

Our strength lies in our quickness and brutality. I have given the command and I will shoot everyone who utters one word of criticism. The aim in war is not to reach a certain point, but of completely destroying the enemy. I met those poor worms Daladier and Chamberlain in Munich. They will be too cowardly to attack. I shall attack France and England at the most favourable and earliest moment. Breaking the neutrality of Belgium and Holland is of no importance. No one will question what .we have done.

▲ From speeches made by Hitler to his generals in late 1939.

Source C

Three months before the collapse, I made a tour of the French front. When we reached the ill-fated section of Sedan, the French commander had taken us to the River Meuse and shown us the wooded banks and rushing waters. 'Look at the terrain,' he had said to us. 'No German army can get through here.'

▲ From the memoirs of a British politician, written after the Second World War.

Source B

In 1940 the Germans devised a plan to cut off British and French armies in northern France. First they invaded Belgium and Holland, intending to draw British and French armies to help those countries. Then from 12 May, they struck in the area of Sedan, at the top of the Maginot Line. Fierce strokes launched by tanks and Stuka dive-bombers soon cracked a way through the defences. By using fast-moving Panzer divisions the Germans advanced swiftly.

▲ From a modern history textbook.

Source D

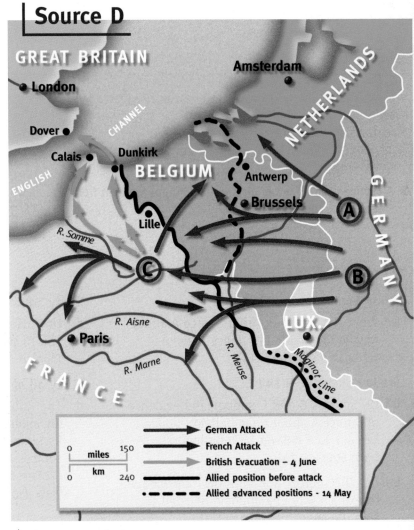

▲ German attacks in 1940.

Source E

On we went at a steady speed. Every so often a quick glance at the map by a shaded light and a short wireless message to Divisional Headquarters to report the position and this was the success of the 25th Panzer division. We were through the Maginot Line! It was hardly believable. Twenty-two years before we had stood for four and a half years before this self-same enemy.

▲ From a description of the German advance in 1940 written by General Rommel.

Source F

▲ Germans troops advancing in the Ardennes in May 1940.

Study Source A

a What can you learn from Source A about Hitler's plans for war? (4)

Study Sources A and B

b Does Source B support the evidence of Source A about Hitler's military strategy? Explain your answer referring to each of the sources. (4)

Study Sources B and C

c How useful are these sources in helping you to understand the successes of the German army in May 1940? (6)

Study Sources D and E

d Use these sources and your own knowledge to explain why the Allies were unable to stop the German advance in May and June 1940. (6)

Study all of the sources

e 'The main reason for the defeat of the Allies in 1940 was the French belief that the Maginot Line would stop the German advance.' Use the sources and your own knowledge to explain whether you agree with this view. (10)

The fall of France: the survival of Britain: Barbarossa and the Eastern Front

Source A

Conflicting orders started coming in to erect barriers or lay mines or so on. Then another order would cancel this and then another order would arrive saying that it had to be done at once. I personally received an order from the Chief of Staff on the evening of 22 June telling me to withdraw my troops from the border. I could sense the nervousness and lack of agreement. The troops and the staff were below strength, and they had inadequate communications and transport. They were not ready for battle.

▲ From the memoirs of the Commander of the Soviet Eighth Army, describing the events of 22 June 1941.

Source B

The Germans were vastly outnumbered by Soviet forces. But they had the priceless advantage of excellent organisation and of surprise. The Soviet master spy Richard Sorge, a German newspaper correspondent working in Tokyo, had warned Stalin in April of the German plan. But Stalin simply did not expect the Führer to turn east when he had not yet defeated Britain.

▲ From a modern history textbook

Source C

The enemy is cruel and implacable. He is out to seize our lands, which have been watered by the sweat of our brows, to seize our grain and oil, which have been obtained by the labour of our hands. He is out to restore the rule of landlords, to restore Tsarism, to destroy the national culture and national existence as states of the Russians, Ukrainians, Belorussians, Lithuanians, Latvians, Estonians, Uzbeks, Tartars, Moldavians, Georgians, Armenians, Azerbaijanians and the other free peoples of the Soviet Union. The enemy wants to Germanise them and convert them into slaves.

▲ From the first speech made by Stalin after the German invasion, made on 3 July 1941.

Source D

Those Arctic blasts that had taken us by surprise in our protected positions cut through our attacking troops. In a couple of days there were 100,000 casualties from frostbite alone. A few days later our winter clothing arrived. There was just enough for each company to be issued with four heavy fur-lined greatcoats and four pairs of felt-lined boots. Four sets of winter clothing for each company. Sixteen greatcoats and sixteen pairs of winter boots to be shared among a battalion of 800 men.

▲ From the diary of a German soldier in the USSR written in late 1941.

Source E

▲ A photograph of Soviet troops in December 1941.

Source F

Map key:
- → German Advance
- Countries occupied or allied with Germany
- Area of Soviet Union taken by Germany
- Neutral countries
- .... Furthest extent of German advances

miles 0–150
km 0–240

FINLAND, SWEDEN, Leningrad, BALTIC SEA, GERMANY, POLAND, Smolensk, Moscow, SOVIET UNION, Kiev, Stalingrad, UKRAINE, CZECHOSLOVAKIA, AUSTRIA, HUNGARY, ROMANIA, CAUCASUS, CASPIAN SEA, YUGOSLAVIA, BULGARIA, BLACK SEA, ALBANIA, GREECE, TURKEY

▲ German attacks on the Soviet Union in 1941.

Study Source A

a What can you learn from Source A about the reasons for the successes of the German army at the beginning of Operation Barbarossa? (4)

Study Sources A and B

b Does Source B support the evidence of Source A about the reasons for German successes in 1941? Explain your answer by referring to both sources. (4)

Study Sources C and D

c Use these sources and your own knowledge to explain the problems faced by the German army in late 1941. (6)

Study Sources C, D and E

d How useful are these sources in helping you to understand the Soviet reaction to the German advance in 1941? (6)

Study all of the sources

e 'The weather was the main reason for the failure of Operation Barbarossa in 1941.' Use the sources and your own knowledge to explain whether you agree with this view. (10)

The causes of the outbreak of the war in the Pacific

Source A

If the Japanese government takes any further steps in pursuance of its policy of military domination by force or threat of force of neighbouring countries, the government of the United States will be compelled to take immediately any steps which it may consider necessary to safeguard the security of the United States.

▲ From a note sent by the US government to the Japanese government on 17 August 1941.

Source B

In the first few months of war it is very likely that we would achieve total victory. I am convinced that we should take advantage of this opportunity. We should use the high morale of the Japanese people and their determination to overcome the crisis facing our country, even at the risk of losing their lives. It would be better to attack now than to sit and wait while the enemy puts more and more pressure upon us.

▲ From a speech made at a meeting of the Japanese government and the Japanese military commanders on 5 November 1941.

Source C

▲ A photograph of US warships being attacked at Pearl Harbor.

Source D

	Destroyed or damaged
Battleships	8
Cruisers and other warships	11
Aircraft	188
Casualties	dead or missing 3,219 wounded 1,272

▲ The damage inflicted by the Japanese attack on Pearl Harbor.

Source E

I lunched with the President today at his desk in the Oval Office. We were talking about things far removed from war when at about 1.40 the Secretary of the Navy Knox called and said that they had picked up a radio call from Honolulu advising that an air raid attack was on and that it was 'no drill'.

I said that there must be some mistake. The President thought the report was probably true and thought it was just the kind of unexpected thing the Japanese would do.

▲ From the diary of Harry Hopkins, one of Roosevelt's advisers, 7 December 1941.

Source F

Yesterday, December 7 1941 – a date which will live in infamy – the United States of America was suddenly and deliberately attacked by naval and air forces of the Empire of Japan. The United States was at peace with that nation and was still in conversation with its government and its Emperor, looking forward to the maintenance of peace in the Pacific.

▲ From a speech made by President Roosevelt on 8 December 1941.

Study Source A

a What can you learn from Source A about relations between the USA and Japan in 1941? (4)

Study Sources A, B and C

b In what ways does Source A help you to understand the evidence of Sources B and C? (6)

Study Sources C and D

c How useful are these sources as evidence about the aims of the Japanese attack on Pearl Harbor? (6)

Study Sources B, C and E

d Does Source E support the evidence of Sources B and C? Explain your answer by referring to all three sources. (4)

Study all of the sources

e 'The attack on Pearl Harbor was a failure.' Use the sources and your own knowledge to explain whether you agree with this view. (10)

Reasons for the defeat of Germany

Source A

On 24 May the German Air Force reported no sudden concentration of shipping in the ports of Dover, Folkestone and along the Thames. On 2 June it became obvious that the weather along the Channel was going to worsen. Rommel, who had expected an attack in early June, if the reports that Allied training had been taking place during low tide were true, chose now to go and see Hitler. His wife's birthday was on 6 June, so he could combine business with pleasure.

▲ From a modern history textbook.

Source B

If I know the British, they'll go to church next Sunday one last time and then sail on Monday. Army group B says they are not going to come yet and when they do it'll be at Calais. So I think that we'll be welcoming them on Tuesday, right here.

▲ From a reported conversation between General Erich Marcks and another German officer on 1 June 1944.

Source C

For various reasons, almost all of the senior commanders of the German forces were absent from their stations during the early morning of 6 June. General Friedrich Dollman, commanding the German 7th Army, was on his way to Rennes in Brittany, with most of the divisional commanders. The German High Command had studied earlier Allied landings in the Mediterranean, all of which had taken place in fine, calm weather. The Germans therefore saw this period as a respite, during which they could stage exercises.

▲ From a modern history textbook.

Source D

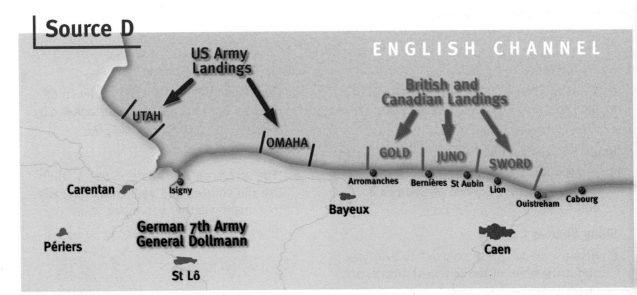

▲ The D-Day landings, 6 June 1944.

Modern World History

Source E

▲ A photograph of the D-Day landings at Omaha beach in June 1944.

Source F

There was often disagreement between Hitler and his generals, as he was always suspicious of them. He refused to delegate authority to them and preferred to play off one against the other. There was little agreement between the generals themselves and Hitler preferred to keep it that way. Despite Rommel's pleas, Hitler refused to hand over control of the crack Panzer divisions in Normandy.

▲ From a modern history textbook.

Study Source A

a   What can you learn from Source A about German preparations for D-Day? (4)

Study Sources A, B and C

b i Do Sources B and C support the evidence of Source A about German preparations for D-Day? Explain your answer by referring to all three sources. (4)

b ii Use the sources and your own knowledge to explain why the Germans were taken by surprise on 6 June 1944. (6)

Study Source D and E

c   How useful are these sources in helping you to understand why the D-Day landings succeeded? (6)

Study all of the sources

d   'The main reason for the success of the D-Day landings was the careful planning of the Allies.' Use the sources and your own knowledge to explain whether you agree with this view. (10)

Reasons for the defeat of Japan

Source A

The total strength of the Japanese army was estimated at about 5,000,000 men. The air force Kamikaze attacks had already inflicted serious damage on our seagoing forces. There was a very strong possibility that the Japanese government might decide upon resistance to the end. We estimated that the major fighting would not end until the latter part of 1946 at the earliest.

▲ **From an article written by Henry Stimson, the US Secretary for War in 1945.**

Source B

I was a 21 year old lieutenant leading a rifle platoon. When the bombs dropped and news began to circulate that the invasion of Japan would not take place, after all, that we would not be obliged to run up the beaches near Tokyo assault-firing while we were shelled and mortared, we cried with relief and joy. We were going to live. We were going to grow up to manhood after all.

▲ **From an interview with a US army officer.**

Source C

It was my reaction that the scientists and others wanted to make this test because of the vast sums that had been spent on the project. My own feeling was that in being the first to use it we had adopted the ethical standards common to barbarians in the Dark Ages. I was not taught to make war in that fashion.

The use of this barbarous weapon at Hiroshima and Nagasaki was of no material assistance in our war against Japan. The Japanese were already defeated and were ready to surrender because of the effective sea blockade and the successful bombing with conventional weapons.

▲ **From the memoirs of Admiral William Leahy, the US Chief of Staff in 1945.**

Source D

The war situation has developed not to Japan's advantage. Moreover the enemy has begun to employ a new and most cruel bomb, the power of which to do damage is incalculable, taking the toll of many innocent lives. We have resolved to pave the way for a grand peace for all generations.

▲ **From the radio broadcast made by the Emperor of Japan announcing the surrender.**

Source E

The Americans dropped atom bombs on the Japanese cities of Hiroshima and Nagasaki killing hundreds of thousands of civilians. Officially Washington 'claimed' that the bombings were aimed at bringing the end of the war nearer and avoiding unnecessary casualties. But they had entirely different objectives. Neither strategy nor tactics required the use of the atom bomb. The purpose of the bombings was to intimidate other countries, above all the Soviet Union.

▲ **From a history book published in the Soviet Union in 1984.**

Source F

We feared that, if the Japanese were told that the bomb would be used on a given locality, they might bring our boys who were prisoners of war to that area. Also if we were to warn the Japanese and if the bomb then failed to explode, we would have given aid and comfort to the Japanese military.

▲ **From evidence given to a committee by the US Secretary of State; the committee was discussing the possibility of warning the Japanese about the use of the bomb.**

Study Source A

a What can you learn from Source A about the use of the atom bomb in August 1945? (4)

Study Sources B and C

b Sources B and C give very different reasons for the use of the bomb. In what ways do the sources differ? Explain your answer by referring to both sources. (4)

Study Sources C and D

c How useful are these sources as evidence about the reasons why the bomb was used? (6)

Study Sources D and E

d How far do these two sources agree about the need to drop atomic bombs on Japan. Use the sources and your own knowledge to to explain your views. (6)

Study all of the sources

e The writer of Source F believed that there was no alternative to dropping the atom bomb on a Japanese city. Use the sources and your own knowledge to explain whether you agree with this view. (10)

CHAPTER 6

Conflict in Vietnam: c.1963~75

Essential Information

The Vietnam conflict was a very humiliating experience for the USA. In the space of twelve years a superpower lost a war against a developing nation.

Reasons for US involvement in Vietnam

American involvement in Vietnam goes back to the end of the Second World War. When Japan surrendered to the USA in 1945, it was decided that the territories of Indo-China (Laos, Cambodia, and Vietnam) would be returned to the French empire, which they had been a part of before the war.

However, many Vietnamese people had no wish to remain a part of the French empire and formed the league for Vietnamese Independence (Vietminh). The communist leader of the Vietminh, Ho Chi Minh, declared Vietnam's independence on 2 September 1945. As the French wished to keep Vietnam – it was rich in minerals – fighting broke out. Soon, the French had about 500,000 soldiers (this number was made up of French and Vietnamese troops) involved in the fight against the Vietminh. However, by 1952, 90,000 soldiers had been killed, wounded or captured and several hundred million francs had been spent on the war.

The French asked the USA for financial help and President Truman gave almost US$3 billion. This was the USA's first intervention in Vietnam – initially it had been against the French re-creating their empire. The USA became involved because it feared the spread of communism and so was keen to prevent Ho Chi Minh and communism from taking over Vietnam. Despite the American aid, the French suffered a major

defeat at Dien Bien Phu in May 1954. This persuaded them that the time had come to withdraw from Vietnam. A peace conference was held at Geneva to discuss the future of Vietnam. The following was decided.

- Vietnam would be divided in two. The north would be controlled by the communist regime of Ho Chi Minh, and the south would be controlled by Ngo Dinh Diem, an anti-communist Catholic politician.

- There would be a general election in 1956 for the whole of Vietnam.

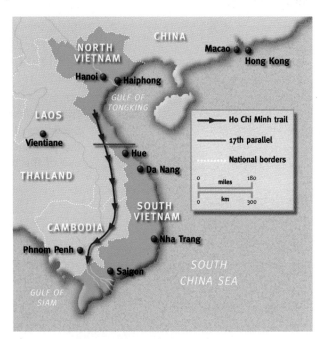

▲ **The division of Vietnam.**

However, the USA did not take note of the Geneva agreement. President Eisenhower was concerned that communist aggression in Asia must be stopped. The Korean War had just ended and the communist takeover in China was still fresh in the minds of many Americans.

The domino theory?

The USA feared that one by one each country in Asia would fall to communism, like a row of dominoes, and felt that South Vietnam would be the next 'domino' to fall.

So it was in support of the domino theory that in the 1950s US involvement in Vietnam began to grow. From 1954–61 the USA gave more than US$1 billion to South Vietnam – most of which went on military spending.

A small team of US military advisers was sent out in 1954 to help 'prepare' for the 1956 elections in Vietnam, as set out in the Geneva peace conference. However, in South Vietnam, the leadership of President Diem became more and more dictatorial and corrupt. The 1956 election was not held and Diem's corrupt rule meant that socialists, communists, journalists, trade unionists and religious leaders were thrown into jail.

Diem's actions caused some of the opposition groups to fight against him and they formed the National Liberation Front (NLF). Ho Chi Minh agreed to send military supplies to the NLF, which promised to:

- re-unite Vietnam
- promote economic and land reform
- represent all classes and religions.

The Kennedy years

In 1960, John F. Kennedy was elected president of America. He wanted to be tough on communism but at the same time, he did not like to be linked with the corruption of the Diem regime. Kennedy was a firm believer in the domino theory and convinced many in the USA of the need to oppose communism.

Kennedy felt he could increase US involvement in Vietnam and at the same time put pressure on Diem to introduce domestic reforms. By the time of Kennedy's death, there were more than 16,000 American advisers training the South Vietnamese Army (ARVN). At the same time, the number of NLF forces fighting against South Vietnam (now called **Vietcong** – VC – by the USA) had grown to approximately 16,000.

Kennedy introduced 'strategic hamlets' to try to prevent the Vietcong's influence spreading. The purpose of these hamlets was to move villages away from the VC, then defend the new ones with barbed wire and ARVN guards. The '**strategic hamlets**' policy was a failure. Many South Vietnamese could not understand what was happening and did not like being forced to leave their villages, so they became resentful in their dealings with the USA. In fact, many of these ordinary people became members of the Vietcong.

At the same time, the position of Diem as leader of South Vietnam became less secure in 1963. Diem's regime campaigned against the Buddhist religion, so Buddhist monks protested against the lack of religious tolerance in the country. Although South Vietnam was predominantly Buddhist (approximately 70 per cent of the population), President Diem and his colleagues were Roman Catholic. Following a series of Buddhist demonstrations, and to draw attention to their campaign, some Buddhists publicised their discontent by burning themselves to death. As a result, opposition to the corrupt Diem regime intensified across the world. At the height of the Buddhist crisis, President Kennedy imposed a freeze on loans to South Vietnam and threatened to withdraw military aid.

President Diem's corrupt regime became so unpopular that he was overthrown by a military coup at the beginning of November 1963. This coup was supported by President Kennedy who took no action to protect Diem.

Lyndon Johnson

Kennedy's successor, Lyndon Johnson, also believed in the domino theory, but he was reluctant to pour money into South Vietnam.

However, the overthrow of Diem did not bring

Why did the Americans become involved in Vietnam?

What were the aims of the NLF?

Why was President Diem so unpopular in South Vietnam?

stability to South Vietnam, nor did it bring a defeat of the communists. Johnson's military advisers in the USA suggested he ought to send in combat troops to defeat the Vietcong. It was suggested that the USA should bomb North Vietnam to prevent the VC being supplied, but Johnson was unsure that he could count on the support of Congress and public opinion if he took this action. However, the situation changed in August 1964 with the Gulf of Tonkin incident. North Vietnamese gunboats attacked USS *Maddox*, a surveillance ship, in the Gulf of Tonkin. Two days later the *Maddox* was allegedly attacked again. President Johnson said the two attacks were 'unprovoked'. He asked Congress to give him authority to 'take all necessary measures to repel any armed attack against the forces of the US and to prevent further aggression'.

Congress passed the Gulf of Tonkin Resolution, which gave Johnson the power to increase US involvement in Vietnam.

Nature of the conflict: United States and South Vietnam

On 8 March 1965, 3,500 US marines arrived in South Vietnam. They were the first combat troops to arrive. Three weeks before their arrival, 'Operation Rolling Thunder' had begun – this was the code name used for the US bombing of North Vietnam. The bombing lasted three and a half years, and by 1967 the American air force had dropped more bombs on North Vietnam than the Allies did on Germany in the whole of the Second World War.

The aims of Operation Rolling Thunder were to bomb railways, roads and bases in North Vietnam and also to destroy the Ho Chi Minh Trail.

The Ho Chi Minh Trail was the supply route from North Vietnam to the Vietcong in the south. By bombing this supply route, President Johnson hoped to starve the Vietcong of weapons and equipment, and he was confident that because the USA had access to the latest military technology, victory would be assured. However, victory did not come as President Johnson hoped. By the end of 1965 there were about 150,000 US

troops in Vietnam and the Vietcong were still fighting strongly. The US therefore needed to adopt new strategies to defeat the VC.

The first change in the US strategy was the introduction of 'search and destroy' operations. US troops went deep into the countryside to flush out the Vietcong. Trying to capture the VC was not easy. The US soldiers found it difficult to cope with the climate and conditions – heat, mosquitoes, leeches, razor-sharp jungle grasses. Moreover, it was difficult to know who was the enemy and who were innocent villagers.

The Americans tried to win the 'hearts and minds' of the South Vietnamese peasants, who they hoped would help them in their fight against the VC. There were special development projects whereby medical care was brought to villages and assistance with farming was also offered, but these attempts failed to guarantee the support of the peasants, who resented the Americans coming to their country to tell them how it should be run.

American military tactics were also unlikely to win the support of the local population. The US government felt that the way to win the conflict was to increase the number of combat soldiers and to use all available conventional technology.

The Vietcong hid in the jungle and in order to destroy the jungle hideouts of the Vietcong, the US air force dropped chemicals to defoliate trees. The most infamous of these chemicals was 'Agent Orange' (42 million litres were dropped on Vietnam), which destroyed hundreds of thousands of hectares of land. 'Agent Blue' was sprayed on crops to prevent the VC from growing food. Neither of these 'agents' deterred the VC. As well as saturation bombing, the US used incendiary weapons – especially napalm. Napalm contained petrol, chemicals and phosphorous, and when it came in contact with human skin it could burn straight through to the bone.

North Vietnam and the War

The North Vietnamese had no hesitation in deciding to support the VC. The USA could not be tackled head on, so **guerrilla** tactics were adopted. The aim of the VC was not only to wear down the US forces, but also to win over the peasants in South Vietnam. Sometimes the VC terrorised villagers into supporting them.

The VC was supplied by the Ho Chi Minh Trail from North Vietnam, but also used weapons captured from the ARVN and US troops. Other communist countries, like the USSR and China, gave at least 6,000 tons of supplies per day to North Vietnam to fight the USA. Much of this material was then sent down the Ho Chi Minh Trail. The VC forces became experts at making **booby traps** – using mines, mantraps, trip wires with punji sticks, pits with sharpened bamboo canes. These created constant fear in the American soldiers' minds, which meant that the soldiers could never relax. The VC also built thousands of miles of tunnels to avoid capture – often US soldiers were killed by booby traps when they pursued VC in them.

The North Vietnamese also built underground shelters to avoid the US air raids and to minimise casualties. However, the bombing campaigns resulted in the deaths of approximately 100,000 North Vietnamese civilians. But the deaths seem to have made the north more determined to resist the Americans.

In addition to guerrilla tactics, the Vietcong also made conventional attacks on the US forces. In the Tet offensive at the beginning of January 1968 almost 60,000 Vietcong troops drove deep into South Vietnam. They even reached the US Embassy in Saigon.

Guerrilla warfare
The VC fought using guerrilla tactics and used the jungle to their advantage. They made booby traps, carried out ambushes and sabotaged US property. Following attacks, the VC would simply disappear back into the jungle. As most of the local population supported the VC, they were easily absorbed back into village life. This made it almost impossible for soldiers to find the culprits.

The VC attack was eventually repulsed with heavy losses, but it had a major impact on feelings in the USA to see their embassy under attack.

After the Tet offensive, President Johnson refused to send more troops to Vietnam. He began to seek an end to the war: 'talks about peace talks' were started.

In 1968 Republican Richard Nixon was elected president. The US now had more than half a million troops in Vietnam. The war was costing US$500 million a week with 300 American casualties each week. But victory seemed no nearer. Nixon promised to reduce the number of US troops in Vietnam and 'Vietnamise' the war – that is, ensure the South Vietnamese army could fight the war on its own. Then US troops could gradually withdraw.

Nixon also started peace talks to discuss ways of ending the conflict in Vietnam. During the peace talks US bombing of Vietcong bases in North Vietnam increased. The new president, Nixon, began a policy of Vietnamisation – this was to encourage the South Vietnamese to defend themselves. Nixon also gave orders for the neighbouring countries of Laos and Cambodia to be bombed. He wanted to destroy the VC bases there. US troops were sent into those countries the following year. The operation failed. But Nixon and the North Vietnamese leaders finally agreed on a settlement in October 1972, though at first it was rejected by President Thieu of South Vietnam. The Paris Peace Agreement was signed on 27 January 1973. South Vietnam eventually signed because the USA promised them US$1 billion of military equipment. It was agreed that the US would withdraw and elections would be held in the South to choose a new government.

The impact of the war on the peoples of Vietnam and USA during the 1960s and 1970s

The Vietnam War became the most important issue in US life in the late 1960s and early 1970s. It was the main focus of the 1968 and 1972 elections, and even seemed to overtake civil rights and the space programme in importance.

The US soldiers

US soldiers were drafted (conscripted) into the army and their tour of duty was one year. The average age of the **GI** was nineteen and he was most likely to be working class. There was a disproportionate number of African American soldiers – they made up one-fifth of the soldiers yet they were only one-tenth of the population.

As the war progressed, enthusiasm for it waned. Many young men became 'draft dodgers', refusing to join when called up to fight, and fled to Canada or were imprisoned. At the same time, many soldiers in Vietnam could not understand what they were fighting for and, when victory did not come quickly, frustration set in. Many turned to drugs. In 1970 it was estimated that 58 per cent of US soldiers smoked marijuana and 22 per cent used heroin. In 1971, 5,000 soldiers needed treatment for wounds sustained in combat, yet more than 20,000 were treated for serious drug abuse.

Often soldiers killed officers whom the soldiers thought had risked their lives on pointless missions. Officers were shot in the back or were 'fragged' (had a fragmentation grenade thrown in their tent). Between 1969–71, 83 officers were killed by fraggings and 730 'fragging' incidents were reported. More than 500,000 US soldiers deserted in the period 1960–73 at a time when about 10 million men were drafted.

US civilians

Protests against the war began in 1964 but the vast majority of the population in the USA and importantly, Congress, were still in favour of the war. However, opposition to the war grew. When newspaper and television reporters went to cover the war in 1965 the US public were able to watch the action from their living rooms. Seeing the pictures of the war on television shocked many Americans and by 1967 there were protests against the war across the USA. Martin Luther King opposed the war raising the issue of the disproportionate number of African American casualties in the war. Many civil rights leaders felt that money used to fight the war could have been better used on improving the welfare system in the USA. When US taxes went up in 1967, so did US taxpayers' hostility to the war. Public opinion had begun to change.

Many historians now consider that the Tet offensive was the turning point in changing US public opinion against involvement in Vietnam. Within weeks, President Johnson's approval rating fell from 48 per cent to 36 per cent. The Tet offensive was shown on television and scenes of the US Embassy being attacked led many Americans to think the war was being lost.

When news of the My Lai (Son My) massacre emerged in 1969 public opinion hardened against the war even further.

Students continued to be at the forefront of the demonstrations. There was widespread trouble and demonstrations at universities across the USA. Four students were shot by the National Guard on 5 May 1970 at Kent State University – some of the dead were demonstrators, some were merely moving between classes. The war had created much division within the country.

My Lai

My Lai was a South Vietnamese village suspected of housing Vietcong troops. US forces led by Lt. William Calley entered the village on 16 March 1968. They found no suspects. On Calley's orders, the US soldiers killed 347 unarmed civilians. Old men, children, babies were shot and the women were raped and shot.

The peoples of Vietnam

The peoples of North Vietnam were bombed, shelled and attacked with chemicals. Places such as Hanoi and Haiphong endured some of the heaviest air raids in history. Conscription was introduced and soldiers were sent to South Vietnam to assist the Vietcong.

In the south, the people were faced with the arrival of several hundred thousand US soldiers, the ARVN and the rival Vietcong and North Vietnamese forces. Often the people would be terrorised by both sides. Villages were destroyed by both American and Vietcong forces – but frequently Americans destroyed villages because they were unsure of the loyalty of the peasants. They were not sure who were VC and so they took no chances.

It is difficult to estimate the impact of the war on Vietnam. More than eight million tons of bombs were dropped, millions of gallons of defoliants and other chemicals were dropped on the jungle and farming land. Large numbers of children have since been born deformed as a result of the chemicals from bombing raids entering the water supply and the food chain. Land mines planted in the war continue to kill and maim today.

The reunification of Vietnam

After the Paris Peace Agreement in 1973, it seemed as if South Vietnam would be able to resist the Vietcong and the forces of the north. There were more than one million men in the South Vietnamese army and it controlled the bulk of the people and territory. However, corruption in the south and rapidly dwindling morale enabled the Vietcong and North Vietnam to defeat the forces of the south. In 1976 Vietnam was reunited.

The consequences of the war

Altogether about 2.5 million Vietnamese soldiers and civilians were killed, and approximately 1.5 million wounded, out of a population of 32 million. In addition, it is thought that about 100,000 US soldiers who served in Vietnam have committed suicide since the end of the war.

After reunification, Vietnam followed communist economic policies but they were unable to feed a growing population. Many people of the south were unwilling to stay in the newly re-united country and the phenomenon of the 'boat people' occurred. People simply fled in any kind of vessel possible – more than one million did so in the years 1975–90. It has been estimated that well over two million people fled South Vietnam after the communist takeover. There were about 50,000 children who were 'American-Asian', the children of GIs who served in Vietnam, and most were treated as outcasts by the Vietnamese people. Many have now gone to live in the USA.

The USA was certainly weakened by the Vietnam war. At home, it prevented President Johnson building his 'Great Society'. This was his programme of domestic policies for improving education, healthcare, and air and water quality; for promoting voting rights and preventing crime and delinquency. Abroad, the world saw a superpower humbled by a developing nation. As a result of the defeat suffered by the USA, it became unwilling to involve itself in any international conflict.

Numbers of soldiers killed during the Vietnam War	
58,000	US soldiers
137,000	South Vietnamese soldiers
c700,000	North Vietnamese soldiers
c1 million	Vietcong

Why did the Americans lose the war in Vietnam?

Reasons for US involvement in Vietnam

Source A

President Kennedy saw Vietnam as President Eisenhower had – part of the fight against communism. Kennedy wanted to help the South Vietnamese army with US technology. He also wanted to give economic aid to South Vietnam.

▲ From an American textbook published in 1991.

Source B

If we quit Vietnam, tomorrow we'll be fighting in Hawaii and next week we'll have to fight in San Francisco.

▲ From a speech made by President Johnson in 1964.

Source C

▲ A photograph of a buddhist monk who had set fire to himself. The photograph was taken in 1963.

Source D

We seek an independent, non-communist South Vietnam. We do not require South Vietnam to serve as a western base or become a member of the western alliance. South Vietnam must be free to accept outside assistance in order to maintain its security.

▲ From a report written in 1964, by Robert McNamara, the US Secretary of Defence.

Source E

I have dedicated my life to serving the revolution and I am proud to see the growth of international communism. My ultimate wish is that the communist party and my people will stay together for the building of a peaceful, united and independent Vietnam.

▲ An excerpt from Ho Chi Minh's will, read in May 1969.

Source F

Let every nation know, whether it wishes us well or ill, that we shall pay any price, bear any burden, meet any hardship, support any friend, oppose any foe to assure the survival and success of liberty.

▲ From President Kennedy's inaugural speech in 1961.

Study Source A

a What can you learn from Source A about why the USA became involved in Vietnam? (4)

Study Sources A, B and C

b Do Sources B and C support the evidence of Source A about US involvement in Vietnam? Explain your answer. (4)

Study Sources A, B and D

c Use the sources and your own knowledge to explain why the USA was concerned about the activities of South Vietnam in the early 1960s. (6)

Study Sources D and E

d How useful are these sources in helping you to understand the reasons for US involvement in Vietnam? (6)

Study all of the sources

e 'The US sent combat troops to Vietnam solely to protect its advisers and the South Vietnamese Government from attacks by Vietcong and North Vietnam forces.' Use the sources and your own knowledge to explain whether you agree with this view. (10)

The nature of the conflict: Operation Rolling Thunder; the Tet offensive

Source A

It was explained to us that anything alive in that area was supposed to be dead. We were told that if we saw a 'gook' (slang for Vietnamese person) or thought we saw one, no matter how big or small, shoot first. No need for permission to fire. It was just a turkey shoot – men, women and children, no matter what their ages, all went into the body count. This was a regular 'search and destroy' mission in which we destroyed everything we found.

▲ Sergeant James Weeks, a US soldier fighting in Vietnam, describes the orders he was given in 1967.

Source B

▲ A photograph of dead civilians, massacred at My Lai by US soldiers in 1968.

Source C

We didn't look at the Vietnamese as human beings. They were sub-human. To kill them would be easy for you. If you continued this process you didn't have any bad feelings about it because they were a sub-human species. We used terms like 'gooks' and 'zipperheads' and we had to kill different insects every day and they would say 'There's a gook, step on it and squash it.'

▲ A US marine speaking about his training in the 1960s.

Source D

A question posed to the Americans surveyed was:

In view of the developments since we entered the fighting in Vietnam, do you think the United States made a mistake sending troops to fight in Vietnam?

The results were:

Yes	52%
No	39%
No opinion	9%

▲ An opinion poll conducted by Gallup in January 1969.

Source F

The Vietcong adopted the military tactics of Mao Zedong, the Chinese Communist leader. Mao said, 'The enemy advances, we retreat, the enemy camps, we harass, the enemy tires, we attack, the enemy retreats, we pursue.'

▲ A description of Vietcong military tactics, from a British school textbook published in 1996.

Source E

WE WILL FIGHT AND FIGHT FROM THIS GENERATION TO THE NEXT

▲ A North Vietnamese woodcut from the 1960s.

Study Source A

a What can you learn from Source A about US methods of warfare in Vietnam? (4)

Study Sources A, B and C

b Do Sources B and C support the evidence of Source A? Explain your answer. (4)

Study Sources A, B and C

c Use the sources and your own knowledge to explain why the US found it difficult to win the support of the South Vietnamese peasants. (6)

Study Sources D and E

d How useful are these sources as evidence of the Vietnam War? (6)

Study all of the sources

e 'The US lost the war because American public opinion forced the politicians to withdraw from South Vietnam.' Use the sources and your own knowledge to explain whether you agree with this view. (10)

The impact of the war on the peoples of Vietnam and the USA during the 1960s and 1970s

Source A

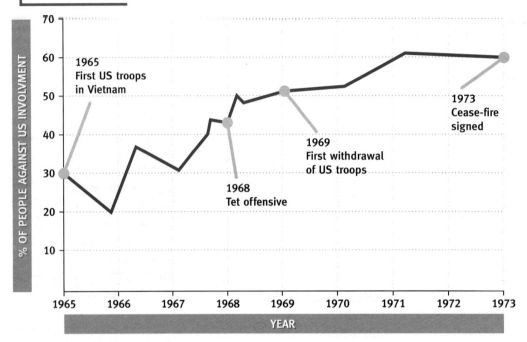

▲ A graph showing the US public's opposition to the Vietnam War, 1965–73. It is taken from a high school textbook published in the USA.

Source B

In 1967, tens of thousands Americans protested across America. Congressmen put more pressure on President Johnson. The churches and black civil rights leader Martin Luther King led the opposition. Black Americans resented the high number of black casualties in the war.

▲ From a study of the Vietnam conflict by a British historian written in 1998.

Source C

▲ Pro-war demonstrators in Florida in 1967.

Source D

We huddled the villagers up. We made them squat down. I fired about four clips-worth of bullets into the group ... The mothers was hugging their children. Well, we kept on firing.

▲ Paul Meadlo, a soldier at My Lai in 1968, giving evidence at the trial of Lt. William Calley.

Source E

Officer: When you go into My Lai you assume the worst ... you assume they're all VC.

Soldier: But sir, the law says killing civilians is wrong. We're taught that, even by the army.

Officer: Of course killing civilians is wrong. But these so-called civilians are killers. Female warriors out in the rice fields spying.

Soldier: But how do you know that this peasant or that peasant is VC? They look alike ...

▲ From *If I die in a combat zone* by Tim O'Brien. O'Brien was an American soldier who served two years in Vietnam and won seven medals.

Source F

By 1971, the morale of the American army had plummeted. In that year, President Nixon warned the new graduates of the West Point Military Academy that they would be leading troops guilty of drug abuse and insubordination.

▲ From a study of the Vietnam War written in 1998 by a British historian.

Study Source A

a What can you learn from Source A about opposition to the Vietnam War in America? (4)

Study Sources A, B and C

b Do Sources B and C support the evidence of Source A? Explain your answer. (4)

Study Sources A, B and C

c Use the sources and your own knowledge to explain why there was growing opposition to the war by 1968. (6)

Study Sources D and E

d How useful are these sources in helping you to understand why some Americans opposed involvement in the war? (6)

Study all the sources

e 'The US government withdrew from the war because it could not rely on its soldiers.' Use the sources and your own knowledge to explain whether you agree with this view. (10)

Reasons for the US defeat

Source A

▲ A Vietcong patrol in South Vietnam in 1966.

Source B

On the evening of 31 January 1968, about 70,000 Vietcong troops launched surprise attacks on more than 100 cities and towns in Vietnam. The boldest stroke was an attack on the US embassy in Saigon.

▲ From a study of the Vietnam War written in 1992 by a British historian.

Source C

If we spread out too thin and our soldiers moved out of the village we pacified, the Vietcong came right back in again. The guy who might have been your cook during the day that night he put on his black pyjamas and took out his AK47 from under his mattress and went out to your camp to shoot at you.

▲ From an interview in 1980 with Dan Pitzer, an American soldier who was a prisoner of the Vietcong for four years.

Source D

The US can go on increasing aid to South Vietnam. It can increase its own army. But it will do no good. I hate to see the war go on and intensify. Yet our people are determined to struggle. It is impossible for westerners to understand the force of the people's will to resist and to continue.

▲ Pham Van Dong, a leading North Vietnamese politician, speaking in 1964.

Source E

In sending US troops to South Vietnam, the US invaders and land grabbers have met a people's war. The people's war has succeeded in gathering all the people to fight their attackers in all ways and with all kinds of weapons.

▲ Vo Nguyen Giap, a North Vietnamese army general speaking in 1967.

Source F

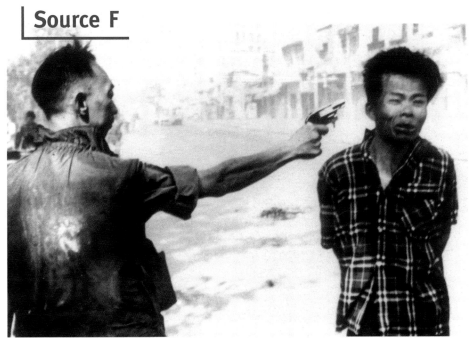

▲ South Vietnam's police chief executing a Vietcong in the Tet Offensive in 1968.

Study Source A

a What can you learn from Source A about Vietcong methods of warfare in South Vietnam? (4)

Study Sources A, B and C

b Do Sources B and C support the evidence of Source A about VC methods of warfare? Explain your answer. (4)

Study Sources A, B and C

c Use the sources and your own knowledge to explain why the Vietcong adopted guerrilla tactics. (6)

Study Sources D and E

d How useful are Sources D and E as evidence of the Vietnam War? (6)

Study all of the sources

e 'The Vietcong and North Vietnamese forces were successful because they used guerrilla tactics.' Use the sources and your own knowledge to explain whether you agree with this view. (10)

The reunification of Vietnam

Source A

In October 1972, peace talks re-opened in Paris. For the first time in nearly ten years of war, peace seemed within reach. The US offered concessions – the Vietcong would play a part in the final negotiations. With the 1972 presidential election approaching, the White House was eager to reach a firm agreement of peace.

▲ From an American history textbook written in 1990.

Source B

When we read the drafts of the agreement – what we were prepared to give as concessions to the North Vietnamese – it was clear that there was no way the government of South Vietnam was going to be able to withstand Vietcong infiltration and propaganda before the election. Once I saw the concessions, I knew that we were prepared to sell South Vietnam down the river.

▲ Edward Brady, a US intelligence adviser, who was present at the Paris Peace talks, speaking in 1978.

Source C

Rather than explore the differences that existed between the US and North Vietnam, President Nixon gave the signal for a new operation – Linebacker Two. Starting on 18 December 1972, B-52 bombers and other aircraft flew nearly 3,000 missions over Hanoi and Haiphong. They dropped 40,000 tons of bombs in eleven days.

▲ From a book about the Vietnam conflict written in 1983 by an American journalist.

Source D

In 1973, President Nixon secretly promised to intervene, if need be, to protect South Vietnam. Is an American's word reliable these days?

▲ President Thieu of South Vietnam, in his resignation speech of April 1975.

Source E

It was clear that the South Vietnamese forces were spread pretty thin in the Central Highlands. The South Vietnamese complained of a lack of hand grenades and ammunition. They were not operating aggressively ... One company of troops had been hit hard by a North Vietnamese regiment. The South Vietnamese forces had not been properly equipped to defend the camp.

▲ From an interview in 1980 with K. Moorefield, special adviser to the US Ambassador to South Vietnam in 1975.

Source F

The army of South Vietnam was beginning to fall apart and morale was very poor. An American investigation in the summer of 1974 reported that 90 per cent of the South Vietnamese troops were not being paid enough to support their families. Corrupt government officials were stealing the soldiers' pay.

▲ From a British history textbook about Vietnam written in 1997.

Study Source A

a What can you learn from Source A about the Paris Peace talks? (4)

Study Sources A, B and C

b Do Sources B and C support the evidence of Source A? (4)

Study Sources A, B and C

c Use the sources and your own knowledge to explain why peace talks were successful in January 1973. (6)

Study Sources D and E

d How useful are these sources for understanding the military problems faced by South Vietnam after 1973? (6)

Study all of the sources

e 'Vietnam was re-united because the US had given too many concessions to the North Vietnamese at Paris.' Use the sources and your own knowledge to explain whether you agree with this view. (10)

Consequences for the USA of its failure in Vietnam

Source A

On returning home, American soldiers did not expect to be treated as criminals or child murderers as they sometimes were. Many veterans found it difficult to get jobs or get their own jobs back. More American veterans have committed suicide since the war than were killed in the war itself. They felt betrayed by a country which was embarrassed by them.

▲ From a British history textbook about Vietnam written in 1995.

Source B

▲ Photograph of the Vietnam War Memorial Wall in Washington DC. The wall was paid for by subscriptions from Vietnam veterans.

Source C

'How do you feel about killing all of those innocent people?' The woman asked me. I didn't know what to say. The bartender got a little uptight.

'Excuse me,' I called the bartender over. 'Could I buy these people a drink?' I felt guilty. I did kill. I tried to make up for it somehow.

'We don't accept any drinks from killers,' the girl said to me.

▲ A former soldier describing his return to the USA. He was in an airport bar, speaking to people of his own age (nineteen).

Source D

He called it the madman theory. He said: 'I want the North Vietnamese to believe I've reached the point where I might do anything to stop the war. We'll just slip them the word that I'm obsessed about communism. Tell them that I can't be restrained and that I've got my hand on the nuclear button. If we do that Ho Chi Minh himself will be in Paris in two days begging for peace.

▲ From *The Ends of Power* by H. R. (Bob) Haldeman, 1978, one of President Nixon's closest advisers during the Vietnam War. Haldeman is explaining Nixon's decision to extend the bombing campaign.

Source F

The USA was certainly weakened by the Vietnam War. At home, it prevented President Johnson building his Great Society. But more importantly, the USA became unwilling to involve itself in any international conflict until the Gulf War in 1991. When the Gulf War was over, Bush said: 'By God, we've kicked the Vietnam syndrome once and for all.'

▲ From a British history textbook written in 1998.

Source E

However we got into Vietnam, whatever the judgement of our actions, ending the war honourably was essential for the peace of the world. We could not simply walk away from an enterprise as if we were switching a TV channel. As the leader of democratic alliances we had to remember that scores of countries and millions of people relied for their security on the US' willingness to stand by allies.

▲ Henry Kissinger, National Security Adviser, speaking after the end of the Vietnam War.

Study Source A

a What can you learn from Source A about the impact of the war on US soldiers? (4)

Study Sources A, B and C

b Do Sources B and C support the evidence of Source A? Explain your answer. (4)

Study Sources A, B and C

c Use the sources and your own knowledge to explain why soldiers faced opposition when they returned home. (6)

Study Sources D and E

d How useful are these sources in helping us to understand US policies in Vietnam? (6)

Study all of the sources

e Source F suggests that the most important effect of the war on the USA was its unwillingness to become involved in world conflicts. Use the sources and your own knowledge to say whether you agree that this was the most important effect of the war on the USA. (10)

CHAPTER 7

The end of apartheid in South Africa: 1982~94

The National Party and the nature of its rule

The National Party was set up in South Africa in 1914 to protect the rights and interests of the Afrikaners. When Afrikaner Jan Hertzog became prime minister in 1924, he made Afrikaans, the language spoken by Afrikaners, an official language. Hertzog also prevented non-whites from doing skilled jobs in mines.

In 1918, a secret society called the Broederbond was set up to protect Afrikaners. By 1930 the Broederbond, which was totally committed to maintaining white supremacy in South Africa, became the most powerful organisation in the country.

In 1948 the National Party, led by Daniel Malan, won the general election. The National Party won by using the slogan 'Swart Gewaar', which means Black Peril, to play on white fears. Malan became prime minister and appointed a cabinet that was made up entirely of Afrikaners. All cabinet meetings were now conducted in Afrikaans. The new government immediately began to develop the system of '**apartheid**'.

> **Who are the Afrikaners?**
> - Descendants of Dutch, German and Huguenot 17th century settlers.
> - Previously known as 'Boers' from the Dutch for 'farmer'.
> - Moved north on the 'Great Trek' to form Transvaal and Orange Free State.
> - Fought the Boer War against the British from 1899–1902.

The system of apartheid, and its economic and social consequences

Apartheid means 'apartness' – the belief of the National Party that the different races in South Africa should be kept apart. The system was already partly in existence when the National Party took power in 1948. But in the years after 1948, apartheid was extended and in some cases also applied to Asians and **coloureds**. Malan and his successors, Hendrik Verwoerd in 1958, and John Vorster in 1966, ruthlessly enforced the new system.

The National Party argued that apartheid meant 'separate development' – the idea that blacks, whites and coloureds should live their lives apart, and that each race should develop in its own way. But 'apart' came to mean control by the whites.

Acts relating to apartheid

The central feature of apartheid was the Population Registration Act of 1950. All people had to be classified into one of three categories: whites, natives and coloureds. Natives were Africans and coloureds were people of mixed race.

The next major change was the Group Areas Act, which divided South Africa into areas for whites and non-whites. People who lived in the 'wrong' area were forced to move, even if they had been living there for many years. This act was extended by the Promotion of Bantu Self-government Act in 1959. This set up Bantustans, or self-governing homelands for blacks. However, the white South African government could overrule any decision taken by a Bantustan government. The South African government tried to maintain that the homelands were independent countries for blacks within South Africa. However, they were not recognised by any foreign governments.

In 1953, the Bantu Education Act stated that black children were to be educated differently from whites. They received only a low level of education and were not taught either English or Afrikaans. They were also taught that whites were superior in every way. This was designed to prevent black children acquiring skilled jobs or developing careers. It was intended to keep the blacks 'in their place'.

In 1952, the **Pass Laws** were extended. All black men aged sixteen or over (and later, women) had to carry a pass book. The pass book had 96 pages and contained the owner's photograph, address, job, fingerprint impressions and other details. Blacks needed permission to be out after 9 p.m. and to be in white areas. These would be shown by stamps in the pass book. The police continually stopped blacks and demanded to see their pass books.

From 1956, only whites were allowed to vote in elections. Indians had lost the vote in 1948, but 48,000 coloureds retained it. Until 1956 they could vote for four MPs who were always white. South Africa now became a completely white **monopoly**.

Further measures extended apartheid even more. Mixed marriages were banned, as was sexual intercourse between whites and non-whites. Previously sex had only been banned between whites and blacks. The Motor Transport Act allowed apartheid on public transport, on beaches and in restaurants. Shops and all public places were segregated.

Increasingly, blacks were forced to live in townships on the edge of South African cities. The most famous was the South West Township of Johannesburg, known as Soweto. Here a million blacks were crammed together, travelling to work in Johannesburg every day. Concentrating such large numbers of blacks into such small areas made the townships difficult to control. They also became rich recruiting grounds for anti-apartheid groups like the African National Congress (ANC) and the Pan African Congress (PAC).

The power of the police

It was one thing to pass apartheid laws, but quite another to enforce them, so the National Party increased police powers.

From 1965 the police could detain those suspected of breaking the apartheid laws for up to 180 days without charge. Opponents of apartheid could be imprisoned without trial. Stories of the use of torture during imprisonment became widespread.

There were some other changes, too.

- To back up the uniformed police, a secret police force, the Bureau of State Security (BOSS), was set up.

- In 1972, the State Security Council was set up, which led to much greater influence for the military forces and the secret police.

- In the 1980s the Civil Co-operation Bureau (CCB) was set up. This carried out acts of sabotage and murder, including the assassination of ANC Paris representative, Dulcie September, in 1988.

- Blacks were not allowed to stay in a white area for more than three days. All blacks were stopped regularly by the police to check their passes and then move them away.

- Banning orders could be used to stop a person writing, broadcasting, attending a meeting or just leaving home. Journalists were constantly harassed and the Publications Board enforced rigid censorship.

The number of civil servants, policemen and soldiers needed to enforce apartheid grew rapidly. In the late 1970s, the manpower of the police and South African Defence Force rose from 328,000 to 592,000. At the same time, expenditure on military spending alone rose by 400 per cent. To back up the police, white citizens were asked to volunteer for the Active Citizen Force.

The National Party held power in South Africa from 1948 to 1994. In many ways this was a remarkable achievement for a party that represented only 12 per cent of the population. The National Party's hold on power increasingly came to rely on two factors. One was the limitations on the right to vote. The other was the National Party's increasing use of violence, which led to the declaration of States of Emergency.

By the late 1970s, the economic consequences of apartheid were becoming increasingly obvious. The cost of maintaining a police state was rising out of control. This, combined with the effects of **boycotts** and isolation, was hitting the South African economy very hard.

The education policy followed by the National Party was producing large numbers of poorly educated workers, who spoke little or no English or Afrikaans. This was based on the traditional view of blacks as agricultural labourers and miners. Increasingly, however, South African businesses wanted well-educated workers who could cope with the changing demands of modern industry. Between 1951 and 1976 the number of jobs in industry almost doubled, while the number of jobs in farming and agriculture fell. As a result, in the 1980s, politicians found themselves facing more and more demands for change.

Support for, and opposition to, apartheid in South Africa

Support for apartheid came almost exclusively from white Afrikaners. Apartheid was not just a way of preventing the Afrikaners being swamped by blacks, it was also a way of asserting their independence and rejecting British influence. In the 1980s many people still referred to the 'laager mentality' of some Afrikaners. This is because during the Great Trek the Afrikaners had protected themselves by drawing their wagons into a circle, or laager. When they were attacked or criticised, they barricaded themselves in and refused to have anything to do with anybody else.

The Afrikaners had originally been farmers, who had used blacks for labourers. This explained their contemptuous attitude to black Africans, who they often referred to, insultingly, as 'Kaffirs'.

Some white English speakers accepted apartheid, or at least went along with it. But the Liberal Party opposed apartheid in parliament; one of

the most outspoken opponents was the MP Helen Suzman. However, as the National Party won every election from 1948 to 1994, the opposition within parliament could do very little.

The most important opposition to apartheid came from Africans themselves. The African National Congress (ANC), was set up in 1912 to campaign for the rights of black South Africans. It was intended to be peaceful and to cut across all tribal divisions. Separate organisations were set up to represent Indians and coloureds (people of mixed race).

Organisations opposing apartheid

In 1949 Walter Sisulu became the ANC Secretary-General and it adopted a new Programme of Action including strikes, demonstrations and other forms of civil disobedience.

A second and more violent organisation was the Pan African Congress, which was set up in 1959. When President F. W. de Klerk announced the scrapping of all apartheid laws in 1991, the PAC refused to attend the convention that was set up to find a new constitution for South Africa. Its slogan was 'One settler, one bullet'.

A third organisation was Inkatha ya KwaZulu, set up by Chief Mangosuthu Buthelezi in 1975. Chief Buthelezi was prime minister of KwaZulu, one of the homelands set up by the South African government. His aim was to gain independence for the Zulu nation, which brought Inkatha into conflict with the ANC, which wanted a united South Africa. In the last years of apartheid the South African secret services tried to exploit this difference by inciting, and probably carrying out, massacres of ANC and Inkatha supporters. The government hoped that this would lead to conflict between the two organisations.

In the 1980s the ANC began a programme of violent attacks in South Africa. In 1980 it carried out a rocket attack on an oil refinery and in 1982 blew up a nuclear reactor. The ANC was supported by the newly independent countries of Angola, Mozambique and Zimbabwe. The South African government struck back by invading Angola and forcing Mozambique to sign a non-aggression pact. This convinced the ANC that it could not win by force alone, so in 1985 the ANC decided to make the townships ungovernable. Inhabitants built barricades, and organised strikes and boycotts. For two years there were continuing disturbances, which resulted in more than 2,000 deaths. By 1987 the country was in chaos.

In 1983 the United Democratic Front (UDF) was set up. This brought together more than 500 different anti-apartheid organisations and attempted to unite the ANC and the community groups that were developing in the townships. This was a sign that the opposition to apartheid was beginning to develop a truly national organisation. However, Inkatha remained outside the UDF and violence between its members and the ANC continued.

Commonwealth and world reactions to apartheid

There was great worldwide opposition to apartheid. It was condemned by the United Nations in 1952, which then recommended **economic sanctions** in 1962. By that time South Africa had resigned from the Commonwealth to avoid being expelled. South Africa was expelled from the Olympic Games in 1964. The Organisation of Petroleum Exporting Countries (OPEC) banned oil sales to South Africa in 1973 and in 1974 the country was expelled from the UN. By 1980, all South Africa's neighbours had black governments. The USA and the European Community began to impose economic sanctions in 1985, but these appeared to have little effect. On the surface, the South African economy showed little sign of strain.

Why action wasn't taken against apartheid
Persuading foreign governments to take positive action proved very difficult. One reason for this was the reluctance of African governments to make sacrifices. For example, Kenya broke off all trade with South Africa, only to see other black African countries take its place as a trading partner. Zambia and Zimbabwe, both landlocked developing countries, sent most of their exports and imports through South Africa. Two million migrant workers in Malawi and Mozambique depended on jobs in South Africa.

Other leaders, including Margaret Thatcher of Britain, saw South Africa as an ally against the spread of communism. Mrs Thatcher also claimed that sanctions would hurt black Africans more than they would hurt the government. In this she was probably right; unemployment among blacks rose after sanctions were imposed, but ANC leaders urged Britain and the Commonwealth to act nevertheless.

One form of sanctions that was applied was an arms embargo, but even here the South African government was able to get round it by developing its own arms industry with the support of the Israeli government. It was also able to buy arms from the Soviet Union. By the late 1970s the Soviet Union was desperate for foreign currency so it agreed to sell arms.

The most powerful bargaining counter in the South African government's possession was the country's vast mineral resources. It produced, for example, half of the world's gold and diamonds. With riches such as these, few countries could afford to ignore South Africa completely.

Sanctions
Nevertheless, there were significant changes in the 1980s. Some 277 companies withdrew their investments in South Africa and a number of famous names closed all of their plants. These included Peugeot, IBM and Pepsi Cola.

Perhaps the most significant form of sanction was the boycott imposed by foreign sporting associations. This began in 1969 when the South Africans opposed the inclusion of Basil D'Oliviera, a Cape coloured, in the English cricket touring team. The Afrikaners were devoted to rugby and cricket, and were desperate for foreign competition. In an effort to persuade the world that South African sport was multi-racial, rugby teams included coloured players, like Errol Tobias, but at home all clubs were segregated and it has remained almost exclusively a white sport. In the townships, black South Africans prefer to play soccer.

To break the boycott, rebel tours of Australian, English and even West Indian cricketers were organised, often at enormous expense. But the situation did not really improve until apartheid came to an end and sporting links were re-established.

Since the end of apartheid cricket has been much more successful in attracting blacks and the South African squad is now multi-racial. However, two members of the squad were accused of making racial remarks In 1998 and one announced his retirement from international cricket soon afterwards. Both men were Afrikaners.

Changes to apartheid in the 1980s

By the late 1970s there were clear signs that apartheid was not working. The central problem was that apartheid was based on the idea that a large majority of the population could be kept at a low level of education and could be given menial, unskilled jobs to do. This just did not work in a modern economy.

Solutions for integration

It was the prime minister, John Vorster, a determined supporter of apartheid, who first realised the extent of the problem; he set up two commissions to consider possible solutions. They recommended that jobs should no longer be reserved for whites and that black trades unions should be allowed.

In 1979 John Vorster was replaced as leader of the National party by P. W. Botha. He was also a determined supporter of apartheid, but realised that it was impossible to keep 20,000,000 black Africans in complete subservience forever. He explained to the National Party: 'We have to be prepared to adapt our policy to those things that make adjustment necessary, otherwise we die.'

Botha introduced a series of measures that ended many forms of segregation – what people often referred to as 'Petty Apartheid', meaning the use of separate public buildings, seats and beaches, or the reservation of certain jobs for whites. Employers were allowed to employ blacks in skilled jobs, black trades unions were legalised, and **desegregation** of hotels, restaurants and theatres was permitted, although not made compulsory.

There were also two more far-reaching measures. In 1984 a new constitution came into force, which created a parliament with three chambers. Whites, Indians and coloureds all elected MPs who sat in separate houses. However, since laws passed by the Indian and coloured houses had to be approved by the whites this made little difference. The new constitution also created the post of State President, a position that Botha himself filled. Then in 1986 the Pass Laws were abolished. These had been unpopular not only with blacks, but also with employers as they prevented the creation of a permanent workforce. In the townships community councils were set up, with councillors elected by the inhabitants.

P. W. Botha hoped that his concessions would save apartheid. He was wrong, because they made the situation worse. Non-whites who co-operated under the new constitution were attacked and some white extremists, who were appalled by his concessions, left the National Party to join the Conservative Party. This was an extreme right–wing racist party that adopted many of the slogans and emblems of the Nazi Party.

Botha found himself attacked by both the blacks and the whites. From 1985 there was increasing opposition in the townships and he had to make use of the new powers of the State President to order a State of Emergency across the whole country. From 1984 to 1988 more than 3,350 people died in disturbances across South Africa.

In January 1989, P. W. Botha suffered a stroke and resigned as leader of the National Party. He remained in office as State President for another seven months and in August 1989 arranged a meeting with Nelson Mandela, then the vice-president of the ANC, who had been in prison since 1964.

The end of apartheid: the roles of Nelson Mandela, the ANC and De Klerk

The meeting between Nelson Mandela and P. W. Botha in August 1989 produced no immediate results. When Mandela asked Botha to release all political prisoners, he was told that it was impossible and the meeting came to an end.

Botha resigned as president immediately after this meeting and was replaced by F. W. de Klerk. De Klerk realised that changes to the apartheid system were essential, but nobody expected the changes to be so sudden and so significant. In February 1990 de Klerk legalised the ANC, the PAC and the South African Communist Party. All political prisoners were freed and the death sentence was abolished. Nine days later Nelson Mandela was released from prison. By January 1993 all apartheid legislation had been repealed.

A change of course

De Klerk's actions took almost everyone by surprise, not least his own party. Many people left the National Party in protest. The Conservative Party grew in strength, but when de Klerk held a referendum in February 1992, 68.6 per cent of voters, all whites, backed reform. More dangerous was the increased support for the Afrikaner Weerstands Beweging (AWB), which translates as the Afrikaner Resistance Movement. The AWB was led by Eugene Terre Blanche, whose name means 'white land', and by 1993 there were 20,000 members.

In fact, de Klerk had no intention of allowing black majority rule; he was simply facing the facts that apartheid could not survive and hoped, that he could save the Afrikaners by making concessions. He had come to this conclusion after the worst general election result in the history of the National Party in 1989, and political and economic chaos throughout the country.

De Klerk, therefore, gambled that he would be able to play off the ANC and Inkatha, and that Nelson Mandela would lose his 'hero' status when he had to take real political decisions. This would enable de Klerk to create a new South Africa in which power was shared by blacks and whites. But he underestimated Nelson Mandela. Once free, Mandela proved to be a very skilful negotiator. His behaviour and moderation impressed many South Africans, who had previously regarded him as a communist and a terrorist. De Klerk also found out that it was impossible to halt the process of freedom half way. Once black Africans tasted equality, they were not to be put off with anything less than the real thing.

A new constitution

Negotiations to draw up a new constitution began in 1991, but collapsed the following year when the government refused to accept majority rule. The ANC responded with strikes, boycotts and mass protests. The government gave way when the ANC suggested a five-year period of power-sharing. De Klerk still hoped that Inkatha might refuse to take part in the general election that was planned for April 1994, but at the last moment Chief Buthelezi agreed to participate.

A month before the election the members of the AWB invaded Bophuthatswana, one of the tribal homelands. The black ruler had worked with the National Party and was refusing to take part in the election. The AWB hoped to take advantage of the situation and sabotage the whole process. It was a disaster. Soldiers and the police cornered the terrorists and shot them. Many South Africans watched the events on television, horrified at the attempts of the AWB to ruin the election.

The election gave a massive majority to the ANC and Nelson Mandela took office as president of South Africa on 10 May 1994. In a spirit of forgiveness and reconciliation, he appointed F. W. de Klerk as one of the two vice-presidents and Chief Buthelezi as a cabinet minister.

Nelson Mandela

Nelson Mandela became involved in politics in 1947. As organiser of the ANC, Nelson Mandela was acquited of treason in 1961. He then led the Umkhonto we Sizwu (Spear of the Nation), which organised attacks on power stations and public buildings. He was arrested again in 1962 on charges of sabotage and violence. He was sentenced to life imprisonment in solitary confinement on Robben Island. Mandela was released from prison in 1990.

The National Party and the nature of its rule

Source A

In 1976, all outdoor meetings were banned except for sports events and funerals. The Internal Security Act allowed the government to ban any organisation, individual or newspaper. In effect the Minister of Justice now decided what was a crime and what was not. Suspects were held without trial. But South Africa was a police state long before this happened.

▲ From an American textbook published in 1991.

Source B

The revolutionaries and radicals in our country never abolished their aim for South Africa to become a communist state. This is, of course, totally unacceptable to the majority of South Africans and the South African government is equally not prepared to accept that at any stage. Therefore it was necessary to curb the actions of certain persons and organisations.

▲ From the announcement of the State of Emergency in 1988 by the Minister for Law and Order.

Source C

Before the morning I was taken from the cell to the place where I was tortured the day before. I was handcuffed below the knees and my arms, and an iron bar was forced between my arms and my legs. I was left hanging between two tables. I was told to tell the truth. They put a rubber tube on my face and I was left bleeding from the nose. Somebody was stabbing me with a sharp instrument in my private parts. This went on for about four to five hours.

▲ From a description of the treatment received in prison by a detainee.

Source D

Botha needed the support of those Blacks who had achieved a degree of success under apartheid by acquiring skilled jobs and obtaining a higher standard of living. He therefore decided to water down apartheid. As he said, White South Africa had to 'adapt or die'.

Botha's reforms allowed some Blacks to buy property in white areas. These were the Blacks who had previously been allowed into those areas to work. The government also relaxed restrictions on trade unions, so that many black Africans were now able to join unions and improve their wages and working conditions. There was a massive increase in spending on education for black Africans, so that they would be better able to provide a skilled workforce suited to modern industry.

▲ A comment on the South African government's policies in the 1980s, from a modern school textbook.

Source E

▲ Armoured personnel carriers moving into Soweto in the 1980s.

Source F

On Tuesday 6 September 1977, a friend of mine named Stephen Biko was taken by South African political police to Room 619 of the Sanlam Building in Strand Street, Port Elizabeth, Cape Province. He was handcuffed, put into leg irons, chained to a grille and subjected to 22 hours of interrogation, in the course of which he was tortured and beaten. He sustained several blows to the head that damaged his brain causing him to fall into a coma and die six days later.

▲ From the book *Biko*, by Donald Woods.

Study Source A

a What can you learn from Source A about the methods used by the government in South Africa? (4)

Study Source A, B and C

b Do Source B and C support the evidence of Source A about the methods used by the government of South Africa? Explain your answer. (4)

Study Sources A, B and C

c Use the sources and your own knowledge to explain why the South African government acted in this way. (6)

Study Sources D and E

d How useful are these sources as evidence about the policies of the South African government? (6)

Study all of the sources

e 'During the 1980s, the South African government relied more and more on force to keep blacks under control.' Use the sources and your own knowledge to explain whether you agree with this view. (10)

The system of apartheid, and its economic and social consequences

Source A

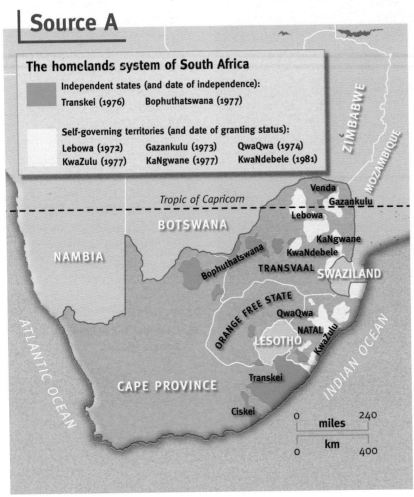

The homelands system of South Africa

Independent states (and date of independence):
Transkei (1976)   Bophuthatswana (1977)

Self-governing territories (and date of granting status):
Lebowa (1972)   Gazankulu (1973)   QwaQwa (1974)
KwaZulu (1977)   KaNgwane (1977)   KwaNdebele (1981)

▲ A map showing the Bantustans, or tribal homelands, set up by the South African government.

Source B

Between 1951 and 1986 at least 4,000,000 people were forced to move from white areas to Bantustans and black townships on the edge of white towns. Black people who had lived in Kenton-on-Sea for 25 years were given just 11 days' notice of their removal to the Ciskei Bantustan.

In these Bantustans black people would have their own government, but they would not be completely independent. The white South African government would still control defence and foreign policy.

It followed from this policy that blacks in white areas were now just visitors with no rights.

▲ From a modern school textbook.

Source C

It came so suddenly. They came with guns and police and all sorts of things. We had no choice. The guns were behind us. They did not say anything, they just threw our belongings in and off they went. There is nothing you can say or they will shoot you in the head. Soldiers and everything were there. We did not know, we still do not know, this place. When we came here they just dumped our things. What can we do now? We can do nothing.

▲ A description of a forced removal to a Bantustan.

Source D

White	68
Indian	61
Black	55
Coloured	51

▲ The life expectancy of people in South Africa in the 1980s.

Source E

A policeman checking the pass books of black South Africans.

Source F

We should get away from the idea that these homelands could be regarded as dumping grounds for people whom we do not want in white South Africa. However, at the same time, it must be realised that the white areas should not be regarded as the dumping grounds for the surplus labour, which comes from the Bantu homelands.

▲ From a statement by a representative of the National Party.

Study Source A

a What can you learn from Source A about the treatment of blacks in South Africa? (4)

Study Source A, B and C

b Do Source B and C support the evidence of Source A about the treatment of black South Africans? Explain your answer. (4)

Study Source A, B and C

c Use the sources and your own knowledge to explain why blacks were forced to go to Bantustans. (6)

Study Source D and E

d How useful are these sources as evidence about the effects of apartheid on black South Africans? (6)

Study all of the sources

e The writer of Source F suggested that the black and white areas of South Africa received similar treatment. Use the sources and you own knowledge to explain whether you agree with this view of apartheid. (10)

Support for, and opposition to, apartheid in South Africa

Source A

I don't know any blacks of my age and have never spoken to any. I don't think it is a good idea that black and white should know each other. I would just hate to live with them. I don't like anything about them. I don't know if our black maid has any children. I never speak to her. I have never been into a Bantu location and don't want to.

▲ From a statement by a seventeen year old Afrikaner.

Source B

White South Africans had one of the highest standards of living in the world. Many white homes were huge by British standards, with big gardens and a swimming pool. There would often be living quarters for a maid or a nanny. Well-off white families employed between one and four black servants.

White areas had properly made roads, not dust tracks; there was good street lighting, too. White areas had libraries, museums, public gardens and so on. The whites who ran them could decide when, and if, other races could use them.

▲ From a modern school textbook.

Source C

It was never intended that if you give something to one group that equal provision should be made in every respect for other groups. In our country we have civilised people, we have semi-civilised people and we have uncivilised people. The government of the country gives each section facilities according to the needs of each.

▲ From a statement by the South African Minister for Justice in the early 1970s.

Source D

Let me reminded you of three little words. The first is 'all'. We want all our rights. The second word is 'here'. We want our rights here in a united, undivided South Africa. We do not want them in impoverished homelands. The third word is the word 'now'. We want all our rights, we want them here and we want them now. We have been jailed, exiled, killed for too long. Now is the time.

▲ From a speech by the Reverend Allan Boesak in 1983.

Source E

We want a country that is united, democratic and non-racial. It must belong to all who live in it, in which all enjoy equal rights and in which the right to rule will rest with the people as a whole. Power must not rest with a collection of Bantustans and tribal groups, which are organised to maintain power for the minority.

▲ From a speech made by Oliver Tambo, the president of the ANC.

Source F

▲ Members of the Black Sash, an anti–apartheid movement, protesting in Johannesburg.

Study Source A

a What can you learn from Source A about relations between whites and blacks in South Africa? (4)

Study Source A, B and C

b Use Sources B and C and your own knowledge to explain the comments made in Source A. (6)

Study Source C and D

c These sources give very different opinions about the future of South Africa. In what ways are they different? (4)

Study Source D and E

d How useful are these sources as evidence about the aims of black South Africans? (6)

Study all of the sources

e 'Apartheid was so deep-rooted that it would be almost impossible to overturn it by peaceful means.' Use the sources and your own knowledge to explain whether you agree with this view. (10)

Commonwealth and world reactions to apartheid

Source A

There is no case in history that I know where punitive general economic sanctions have been effective in bringing about internal changes.

▲ From a speech by Margaret Thatcher in 1986.

Source B

Sanctions will help to convince white South Africans that it is in their own interests to dismantle apartheid and enter negotiations to establish a non-racial and representative government. The white minority must see that apartheid is no longer a real option because the economic and political cost is too high. Sanctions will undermine the power of the apartheid regime and weaken its determination to resist change.

▲ From a study on sanctions by the Commonwealth, published in 1989.

Source C

Sustained international pressure and economic sanctions played a very important role in ensuring that it became impossible to continue with apartheid.

▲ From a speech by Nelson Mandela in 1994.

Source D

	South Africa	The rest of Africa
Industrial production	38%	62%
Minerals	45%	55%
Motor Vehicles	49%	51%
Railways	50%	50%

▲ Percentage figures showing the production of goods and raw materials in the South African economy and for the rest of Africa combined in the late 1970s.

Source E

The foreign action that did South Africa the most damage occurred in 1985 when western banks refused to make any new loans and called in existing ones. South Africa was forced to repay US$13,000,000,000 by December 1985. As a result, the rand, the South African currency, lost 35 per cent of its value in thirteen days.

From 1989 to 1992 South Africa went through a serious recession, which saw its national income fall by 3 per cent every year.

▲ ▲ **From a modern school textbook.**

Source F

Breaking the Afrikaners' will by rising economic pressure abroad will not work. The government sees black rule as a mortal threat to language, to property, to identity and to physical security. It is pointless to think that fears such as these can be overcome by threats to the economy.

▲ **From an article in the newspaper *Johannesburg Business Day* in 1986.**

Study Source A

a What can you learn from Source A about the impact of sanctions upon South Africa? (4)

Study Sources A and B

b Sources A and B give very different accounts of the impact of sanctions upon South Africa. Use the sources and your own knowledge to explain why they are so different. (6)

Study Sources A, B and C

c Does Source C support the view of sanctions given in Source A or Source B? Explain your answer. (4)

Study Sources D and E

d How useful are these sources as evidence about the impact of sanctions on the South African economy? (6)

Study all of the sources

e The writer of Source F believed that sanctions would have no effect on the South African government. Use the sources and your own knowledge to explain whether you agree with this view. (10)

Changes to apartheid in the 1980s

Source A

The world does not remain the same, and if we as a government want to act in the best interest of the country in a changing world, then we have to be prepared to adapt our policy to those things that make adjustment necessary, otherwise we die.

▲ From a speech made by P. W. Botha to a conference of the National Party in 1979.

Source B

While the National Party respects the multicultural nature of South Africa's population, it rejects any system that amounts to one nation or group in our country dominating the others. If Mr Mandela gives a commitment that he will not instigate or commit acts of violence, I will, in principle, be prepared to consider his release. My government and I are determined to press ahead with our reform programme. I believe that from today there can be no turning back.

▲ From a speech made by President Botha to a conference of the National Party in August 1985.

Source C

One of Botha's first moves was to recognise blacks as permanent residents of white cities, and grant them the right to own houses and property in the townships. He got rid of some of the more unpleasant apartheid laws and offered a vote of sorts to the coloureds and Indians. He started pouring money into black education and easing restrictions on black enterprise, hoping to create a black middle class as protection against revolution. To pay for this he taxed white South Africans. To whites who complained, P. W. had this to say: 'Adapt or die.'

▲ From a book written by an Afrikaner.

Source D

	Whites	Blacks
1970	33.3	15.9
1985	40.0	32.1
2000	44.2	53.6

▲ Population statistics shown in an advertisement published by the South African government in the 1980s.

Source E

▲ Protas and Susan Madlala, who were married in 1985.

Source F

I have no hope of real change from this government unless they are forced. We face a catastrophe in this land and only the action of the international community by applying pressure can save us. I call upon the international community to apply punitive sanctions against this government to help us establish a new South Africa – non-racial, democratic and just.

▲ From a news conference given by Archbishop Desmond Tutu in 1986.

Study Source A

a What can you learn from Source A about the policies of P. W. Botha? (4)

Study Sources A, B and C

b Use the sources and your own knowledge to explain how P. W. Botha tried to change South Africa. (6)

Study all of the sources

c How useful are these sources in helping you to understand the success of Botha's policies? (6)

Study Source F

d Source F gives a different view of South Africa in the 1980s from all of the other Sources. In what ways is it different? (4)

Study all of the sources

e 'P. W. Botha tried to change South Africa because he believed that blacks should be treated as the equals of whites.' Use the sources and your own knowledge to explain whether you agree with this view of Botha's policies. (10)

The end of apartheid: the roles of Nelson Mandela, the ANC and de Klerk

Source A

It is time for us to break out of the cycle of violence and break through to peace and reconciliation. We will offer a new democratic constitution, universal franchise, equality before the law, better education, health services, housing and social conditions for all. The time for talking has arrived.

▲ From a speech made by President de Klerk in the South African parliament on 2 February 1990.

Source B

We reject black majority rule. We stand for power-sharing and group rights. We are not selling out to anyone. We are going to make it safer for our descendants to live in South Africa.

▲ From a speech made by President de Klerk in the Transvaal on 18 October 1990.

Source C

▲ A photograph of de Klerk, Mandela and Buthelezi in April 1994.

Source D

I told de Klerk that the ANC had not struggled against apartheid for 75 years only to yield to a disguised form of it. If it was his intention to preserve apartheid through group rights, then he did not truly believe in ending apartheid.

I saw my mission as one of preaching reconciliation, of binding the wounds of the country. I knew that many people, particularly the minorities, whites, coloureds and Indians, would be feeling anxious about the future, and I wanted them to feel secure.

▲ From Nelson Mandela's book *Long Walk to Freedom*, published in 1994.

Source E

Overseas investment is growing all the time. Tourism has more than trebled. The government has three priorities right now, Health, Education and Housing. Starter homes are being provided, funded by the government and building societies. An important factor in the whole process is lack of bitterness and desire for revenge. Mandela provides an excellent role model of forgiveness in his efforts to 'nation-build'.

▲ **From comments by a South African businessman in January 1996.**

Source F

▲ **A cartoon published in a British daily newspaper in 1993. The figures are de Klerk and Mandela.**

Study Source A

a What can you learn from Source A about the aims of President de Klerk? (4)

Study Sources A and B

b i Source B suggests that de Klerk had different aims from those given in Source A. In what ways were they different? (4)

b ii Use the sources and your own knowledge to explain why the sources differ. (6)

Study Sources C, D and E

c How useful are these sources as evidence about the role of Nelson Mandela in bringing about a peaceful solution to the problems facing South Africa? (6)

Study all of the sources

d The cartoonist in Source F suggested that de Klerk and Mandela played equal parts in ending apartheid in South Africa. Use the sources and your own knowledge to explain whether you agree with this view. (10)

Outline Studies

Introduction

Although Edexcel Syllabus A offers ten alternatives for Outline Studies, the vast majority of centres make their selection from the following four topics:

The impact of war on Britain c.1900~50

The rise of the communist state: The Soviet Union, 1928~91

A divided union? The USA 1941~80

Superpower relations 1945~50

These four topics are covered in detail in Chapters 8~11. Together they form a coherent study of the main events of the twentieth century and allow for links to be made with a number of Depth Studies (such as The Russian Revolution, The war to end wars, Depression and the New Deal, the world at war). Each chapter exemplifies the level of knowledge and understanding that students will need in the GCSE examinations. This takes away the uncertainty that many teachers and students feel when they study history at GCSE. Questions in this section of the book are designed to aid comprehension and learning of the issues covered in each chapter. Practice exam-type questions, together with mark schemes, sample answers and comments can be found in the Teachers' Guide.

CHAPTER 8

The impact of war on Britain: c.1900~1950

Introduction

This chapter looks at the ways in which two world wars affected Britain. The wars have become part of the British public's consciousness even though they ended such a long time ago. Films, books and plays about the wars are very popular and the Imperial War Museum in London is one of the most visited museums in the country.

The first part of the chapter spends some time on the outbreak of the First World War and examines in detail the impact of the war. There are sections about the ways in which different groups in society (particularly women) were affected by the war. There is also an analysis of the changing role of the government.

The second part of the chapter examines the impact of the Second World War. Themes similar to the First World War are identified, but the effects of new technology are also analysed. Moreover, the consequences of Dunkirk, the Battle of Britain and the crucial issue of evacuation are also discussed. Finally, the chapter examines some of the reforms introduced by the Labour government after 1945 when the welfare state was created. It is interesting to note that there were few social reforms after 1918, yet there was a tremendous commitment to change at the end of the Second World War.

More than one million British soldiers were killed in the two world wars. Technology had changed the way wars were fought by 1939 and, in the Second World War, British civilians found themselves on the front line just as much as the soldiers. The bombing of towns and cities in the years 1940–45 left more than 60,000 dead and approximately one million homes destroyed or uninhabitable.

Britain was certainly a changed country by 1950. Women had secured the vote on equal terms with men, and their contribution to victory in 1918 and 1945 was immeasurable. In the years after 1945, the new Labour government set up a welfare state which promised to look after its citizens from 'the womb to the tomb'. Some of the changes that Britain experienced were clearly the results of war, but other changes were actually slowed down by the wars.

The First World War

When Britain declared war on Germany in August 1914, it happened to be a Bank Holiday weekend and so there was already a festive mood in the nation. Moreover, there had been a feeling for some time that there might be a war against Germany. The Bank Holiday was extended and the festive mood continued. When mixed with the war-like atmosphere the result was an intense feeling of patriotism in the country.

All sections of society were keen to support the war, though some Labour Party members, who were opposed to warfare of any kind, opposed it vehemently. Businessmen promoted the phrase 'business as usual'.

Parliament was quick to see the need for a large army and authorised an increase to 500,000 men on 6 August and by the middle of September asked for 600,000 more. By December 1914, parliament had sanctioned the recruiting of up to four million men for the army.

Source A

▲ New recruits queuing at a recruiting office in London in 1915.

Source B

Recruitment in the early weeks and months of the war

August 1914	300,000
September 1914	450,000
December 1914	117,000
February 1915	88,000

Recruitment

Young British men hurried to enlist in the army. Recruiting offices all over the country reported that there were huge queues containing men from all ages and sections of society. For many men the war was an opportunity to secure paid employment.

It is interesting to note that in places where employment was high – for example, Leicester and Northampton – the recruiting figures were lower than the national average. There was a general idea that the war would 'be over by Christmas' and therefore it would all be a 'lark' or 'a bit of fun'.

For other recruits the war was a chance to see something of the world. At this time the average working-class man could never really hope to see a foreign country. Of course, many joined the Forces because they were patriotic and wished to fight for Britain and protect 'little Belgium'.

The numbers enlisting were quite astonishing – the chart above indicates the extent of recruitment in the early months. Women encouraged men to enlist, and those men who were seen out of uniform were offered a white feather to symbolise cowardice. Eventually the mass recruitment was to have sad consequences when local battalions (Pals Battalions) were slaughtered as at the Battle of the Somme in 1916, when there were nearly 60,000 casualties on the first day of the campaign.

Thus by the end of August 1914, there was widespread acceptance of the war. The Secretary of War, Lord Kitchener, was one of the few who believed that the war would not be over by Christmas – perhaps by Christmas 1917, but not 1914.

Source C

▲ A recruiting poster which appeared on 7 August 1914.

Source D

Women knitted socks, waistcoats, helmets, mittens, body belts. They knitted in theatres, trains, trams, parks and parlours, in the intervals of eating in restaurants, of serving in canteens ...

▲ Mrs C. S. Peel, from *How we lived then*, 1929.

Propaganda

When the war first began, there was little need for the government to rely on propaganda to foster a hatred of the Germans. There were soon stories in Britain that the Germans had killed Belgian children, mutilated their bodies and raped nuns. Such rumours served only to magnify the anti-German feelings in Britain. The depth of feeling can be seen early in the war, when Prince Louis of Battenberg, the British First Sea Lord, was forced out of office because of his German origins.

The government set up a secret War Propaganda Bureau but initially, newspapers were able to maintain attitudes and enthusiasm for the war. In September, the Kaiser called the British Expeditionary Force (BEF), which had been sent to France to fight the Germans, 'a contemptible little army'. This was seized on by the government and was used to encourage recruiting.

Much was made of a German naval attack on Scarborough, Whitby and Hartlepool in December 1914. Posters and newspaper accounts of the attack are said to have created a surge in recruitment. When the liner *Lusitania* was sunk on 8 May 1915 by a German U-boat, the British propaganda machine went to work, despite the fact that there were grounds for the Germans to think that the ship was carrying war materials.

The Propaganda Bureau found its task of managing opinions and attitudes relatively easy until 1916. By the end of 1916, almost everyone had been touched by the war and there was some disillusionment and even discontent about the war beginning to set in.

Prime Minister Lloyd George set up a Department of Information to control the cinema and material for news consumption. The men in charge of the Department were newspaper owners and senior journalists. One of the most famous propaganda stories emerged soon after the Department was created – that the Germans were converting the bodies of dead soldiers into oils, pig-food and manure.

In June 1917, a National War Aims Committee was established. The Committee held rallies and distributed thousands of leaflets. The emphasis was placed on those areas which seemed to show that morale was diminishing. The Committee tried to create a feeling of national unity but also a climate which would disapprove of any anti-war sentiment. It realised that films, such as *The Battle of the Somme* could be used to great effect. Many short films were made to publicise the contribution of a number of types of workers such as munitions, nurses, Land Army girls and housewives.

Source A

REMEMBER SCARBOROUGH!

The Germans who brag of their "CULTURE" have shown what it is made of by murdering defenceless women and children at SCARBOROUGH.

But this only strengthens

GREAT BRITAIN'S resolve to crush the

GERMAN BARBARIANS

ENLIST NOW!

▲ A recruiting poster published after the German naval bombing of Scarborough.

Though many devices were used to try to maintain the public's pro-war position, it seemed as if the Germans were their own worst enemy. The shelling of Scarborough, the sinking of the *Lusitania,* the use of poison gas, the execution of Edith Cavell, Zeppelin and Gotha raids and unrestricted submarine warfare were seen as atrocities and welded the nation together. Little was needed to convince the British people that they had right on their side.

Edith Cavell

Edith Cavell was a nurse who worked for the Red Cross in occupied Belgium. She was arrested for helping British soldiers to escape. She was court-martialled and shot on 12 October 1915.

Source B

▲ **The evil Hun. A cartoon by Edmund J. Sullivan published in Britain portraying the Kaiser Wilhelm II (the German Emperor) as evil.**

Questions

1   Why was there little need for propaganda at the beginning of the war?

2   How did the British use propaganda during the war? Use Sources A and B to explain your answer.

3   Why do you think the government used Edith Cavell as part of its propaganda?

The role of women

The war had a major impact on the position of women in society. By the end of 1918, the number of women in the workforce had increased by 25 per cent, women over 30 had been given the vote and large numbers had served in the armed forces or as nurses near to the front. However, some of the changes that women experienced in the war were to be short-lived and when war broke out again in 1939, people spoke of women winning their rights – again!

Working-class women had been badly hit in 1914 when wealthy women stopped buying expensive new dresses. So thousands of seamstresses and dressmakers lost their jobs. It has been estimated that more than 40 per cent of all female workers were unemployed by September 1914. It was not until April 1915 that the pre-war level of employment of women was reached.

Suffragettes and the WSPU

An interesting feature of the impact of the war is the way in which the suffragettes reacted to the crisis. The Women's Social and Political Union (WSPU), led by Mrs Pankhurst, had been campaigning for women to have the vote. It announced the end of **militant** activities and began a campaign to become more involved in the war effort.

By the middle of 1915, the overall picture of female employment was somewhat dispiriting. Women wanted to work but there were few opportunities to do so. The feelings of frustration grew, and Mrs Pankhurst and the WSPU organised a march in the centre of London in July 1915 to demand a greater involvement in the war effort. Some 30,000 women participated.

Increased involvement did begin in the summer of 1915, but this arose because of necessity not pressure from women. The Munitions of War Act allowed the introduction of semi-skilled, unskilled or female labour into jobs reserved for skilled craftsmen. There was further expansion of female labour in 1916 when conscription was brought in for all males between the ages of 18 and 41. However, there was much antagonism between the sexes. The men's fear was understandable; their role was being challenged for the first time and the idea that a woman could do the same job as a man was unheard of, although women were rarely granted equal pay with men. There remained the notion that women were unskilled and only temporary. In some factories there were no toilets for the women, and there had to be distinct rotas for 'natural breaks'.

In August 1915, the government introduced a National Register which included all persons,

▲ Women campaigning in 1915 to be part of the war effort.

Source B

The men led us a devil of a life ... they cut a petrol pipe half through, they would unscrew a valve, they would change the leads on the spark plugs ... They would give us the wrong directions.

▲ An interview with a woman driver during the war.

Industry/Occupation	July 1914	July 1918	Gain (%)
Building	7,000	+22,000	320.2
Metal industries	170,000	+424,000	249.2
Chemicals	40,000	+64,000	158.9
Government industries	2,000	+223,000	10,150.0
Gas, water, electricity	600	+4,000	704.3
Transport	18,200	+99,000	545.4
Other 'white-collar'	50,500	+69,000	136.5
Civil service	66,000	+168,000	254.4
All industrial occupations	2,176,000	+565,000	25.9
Total for all occupations	**3,276,000**	**+1,659,000**	**50.6**

▲ Increases in women's employment 1914–18.

male or female, between the ages of 15 and 65. The purpose of this was to determine who was available for work. Each person had to carry a National Registration certificate at all times. Women became more 'visible' during the war – that is they were seen doing men's jobs.

Jobs for women

At the beginning of the war, there were about 210,000 women employed in the munitions industries. By 1918, this had risen to about 900,000 women employed in munitions. The jobs were often dangerous and there were some 300 women killed in explosions or other related industrial accidents – some died from poisoning but there are no accurate figures available.

In the munitions factories, women came into contact with trinitrotoluene (TNT), a poisonous substance. Despite protective clothing, hair and skin would often turn yellow (leading to the nickname 'canary') and in extreme cases the inhalation of TNT led to death. Pay in the munitions industry was considered good – for women – sometimes they could earn two pounds per week. Such an amount gave some women a greater degree of independence and the opportunity to go to the cinema, music hall and public house.

Source C

... never throughout the whole of that fight (for the vote) did we for one single moment forget the love we had for our country or did we relax our patriotism ... one of the mistakes the Kaiser made ... was that he thought under all circumstances the British people would continue their internal quarrels.

▲ A speech by Mrs Pankhurst, November 1914.

Questions

1 Suggest reasons why there was an unwillingness to employ women at the beginning of the war.

2 Look at Sources A and C. What can you learn about the attitudes of the Suffragettes to the war?

3 Why was it important to have a National Registration of people?

4 Why do you think that even trade unionists objected to the employment of women?

Over the whole war, the largest increase in female employment came in transport where women were employed as porters, conductors and ticket collectors and were often paid the same rate as men. Men had always done many of these jobs. All society could appreciate the part that women were playing.

Women found that there were opportunities in commerce, banking, the civil service, teaching and working for government establishments. Though many of these jobs were lost at the end of the war, the idea that women had a role to play in employment was established.

The Land Army, nursing and the WAAC
One area that did not enjoy great success was the Land Army. Working conditions were often quite harsh and there were restrictions placed on social life.

The need to grow as much food as possible within Britain led to the creation of the Land Army in 1917. There were about 100,000 women working on the land in 1914 and it was hoped to recruit many thousands more.

Women recruited to the Land Army were told to behave like 'good English girls who expect chivalry and respect from everyone she meets'. Wages were poor and if possible farmers preferred to employ schoolchildren, who could be paid even lower wages. There was an increase of only 13,000 women working on the land during the war years.

Working in the armed forces and nursing are the two areas that are highly regarded when considering the role of women in the war. The women who worked in **munitions** and other key industries tended to be working class. Those who became nurses were mainly of middle class origin.

By 1918 there were about 45,000 nurses. There were various nursing groups in the war – Voluntary Aid Detachment, First Aid Nursing Yeomanry, Scottish Women's Hospitals. The work did enable many women to be close to the front line and in some cases the shortage of male doctors provided new opportunities for women.

In January 1917, the Women's Army Auxiliary Corps (WAAC) was formed in order to supply clerks, cooks and domestic workers for the army and had 18,000 recruits by 1918. The Women's Royal Naval Service (WRNS) was formed in 1917 and the Women's Royal Air Force (WRAF) in April 1918. Most of the WRAFs were clerical workers but some were employed as welders, carpenters or drivers.

Source D

▲ Inside a munitions factory.

Source E

I think it was the happiest time I ever spent, for it was all so worthwhile ... and no matter how tired I was, what horrible things I had to do , I was helping to make things a little better.

▲ A VAD nurse speaking in 1919.

Votes for women

In 1916 the government called a conference to discuss the issue of women and the vote. A law granting women the vote was passed by the Lords in February 1918. The role of women in the war and changing views of the role of women in society helped some MPs to press for them to have the vote. However, there were restrictions placed on those women who could vote – a woman had to be over 30 years old, own a house or be married to a householder, whereas men could vote at the age of 21. This act gave over eight million women the vote – most of the women who had joined the workforce between 1914 and 1918 were under 30. What upset many women in 1918 was the fact that the right to vote came only at the age of 30 and, for many, depended on their husbands being a householder. In 1928, women were given the vote on the same terms as men.

Source F

These women are quite serious and although uniform is compulsory, we are told that they are by no means to be a merely ornamental corps ...

▲ The *Blackpool Herald* in 1915 writing about the Women's Volunteer Reserve.

If women had secured the vote, they did not secure the right to hold on to their jobs. The Pre-war Practices Act (1919) could force them to surrender them to a man.

The Act allowed men to reclaim jobs which had not been covered by the trades union agreements made during the war. Yet again, women were treated as second-class citizens.

Source G

▲ **Members of WAAC on parade during the First World War.**

Questions

1 Why do you think some historians say that women became 'visible' in the war? Use the text and the sources to help you explain.

2 Why do you think that the nurses are often remembered more readily in the war than other workers?

3 Why did women receive the vote in 1918?

DORA

The British government acted quickly after war was declared on Germany. On 8 August 1914, the Defence of the Realm Act (DORA) was passed. The act allowed the government to 'issue regulations as to the powers and duties of the Admiralty and Army Council ... for securing public safety and defence of the kingdom.' There was a second DORA later that month increasing government power.

War-time regulations

DORA meant that the government could censor newspapers and place people in prison without trial (though trial by jury was restored in 1915). The government was soon using its powers under DORA and altered licensing laws by means of the Intoxicating Liquor Act. The opening hours of public houses were restricted and eventually most opened for about five hours a day (opening hours had been between eighteen and nineteen hours before 1914). The level of alcohol in beer and spirits was gradually reduced and consumption was further hit when excise duties on alcohol were increased. The price of a pint of beer more than tripled during the war years (it is worth noting that the average man spent about one–sixth of his wages on alcohol before 1914). Civilians also found that DORA could alter time. The government introduced 'British Summertime' – clocks were put forward one hour so that farmers and other workers could have an extra hour of daylight.

Source A

... productivity is less now than it was before the war ... this is principally due to drink ... 80 per cent of absenteeism is caused by drink ... The takings of public houses that have had their hours of opening reduced have actually increased ...

▲ A letter to Lloyd George from the Shipbuilding Employers Federation in March 1915.

Source B

▲ A government poster from 1917 encouraging people to save food.

Rationing

By the end of the war, prices of most food and household items had increased by more than 200 per cent. Prices of some foodstuffs, such as bread, were eventually fixed. It was the shortages of food, not price rises, which sapped the morale of civilians. Queues for foodstuffs became commonplace in the poorer, working-class areas. When the German U-boat campaign was at its height in April 1917, and merchant ships bringing food to Britain were sunk, it was estimated that there were only four days' supply of sugar and nine weeks' supply of wheat. Prime Minister Lloyd George appointed Lord Devonport as Food Controller and also demanded an increase in output of domestic food production. By early 1918, wheat and potato production had increased by one million and one and a half million tons respectively. There was a half-hearted attempt to bring in voluntary rationing in early 1917. The scheme failed because the government did not understand that most working-class people relied on bread as the major part of their diet.

Food	Percentage imported
Sugar, cocoa, chocolate	100%
Cheese	80%
Fruit	73%
Butter	65%
Meat	40%

▲ Britain's reliance on imported food.

▲ A food queue outside a London soup kitchen in 1917.

The voluntary scheme tried to move people from eating bread to meat, but the poor could not afford meat. Lord Rhondda, the Minister of Food, eventually introduced rationing in early 1918 on items such as meat, tea, bacon, sugar and butter. Rationing continued into the immediate post-war years – indeed milk rationing was actually introduced after the war ended. It was not until 1921 that rationing finally ended.

The role of the government

DORA indicated how far the government was prepared to go to secure victory in the war. The role of the government did alter drastically during the war. The control of munitions production was finalised when a specific ministry was created and in other areas of production, the government was not slow to act. Transport, railways, shipping shipbuilding and mines were among the key industries taken over for the duration of the hostilities.

The people of Britain found that government was involving itself in every aspect of their lives. The men were conscripted after 1916, and huge numbers of workers were now literally employees of the government. In order to pay for the war, the government increased not only taxes on alcohol but also income tax. Income tax rose from 4 per cent to 30 per cent during the war and, more importantly, the number paying it rose from just over one million people to over seven million. For many, Britain would never be the same.

Source D

The following foodstuffs have been listed as in short supply.

Sugar, tea, butter, lard, dripping, milk, bacon, pork, condensed milk, rice, currants, raisins, spirits, Australian wine.

▲ *The Times* newspaper, December 1917.

Questions

1 Why was DORA important to the government?

2 In what ways were the daily lives of British civilians changed by government actions?

3 Why was rationing introduced?

4 In what ways did the role of the British government change during the war?

Civilians and the front line

The First World War was the first war that brought the front line to civilians. Improvements in technology before 1914 and progress in aircraft construction meant that the war could be taken to Britain's capital city and other urban areas. The first instance of civilians coming under attack came in November 1914 when Yarmouth was shelled.

On 15 and 16 December 1914, German ships bombarded the east-coast towns of Scarborough, Whitby and Hartlepool. At Scarborough, 19 people were killed and 80 injured. The nation was horrified – the idea that civilians were liable to be killed made people realise that this war was different to previous ones. It was a total war which involved soldiers and civilians alike.

The war in the air

Although the German fleet did not make any similar raids for the remainder of the war, there were new forms of warfare that brought the war to the civilians from 1915 onwards. In January 1915, the Zeppelin attacks began. Zeppelins were huge airships that contained hydrogen gas, making them lighter than air. They were powered by engines and could travel at about 50 mph. The first attacks were on King's Lynn and Yarmouth. Zeppelins continued to bomb towns throughout the war. By 1918, some were as long as eleven cricket pitches, were powered by six engines and contained more than two

Source A

We had a pretty terrifying time with the Zepps last night ... There was a tremendous glare in the sky to the west of us which came from a big fire in Wood Street ... I believe most of the damage was done along Oxford Street, Holborn, Euston Road ... a lot of people were killed in a motorbus ... it must have been terrifying to be out, as I believe there was a fearful panic in the street.

▲ **A British nurse writing in September 1915.**

Source B

▲ **A British recruiting poster from 1915.**

million cubic feet of hydrogen gas. However, once aircraft technology improved the Zeppelins were no match for the British fighter planes. Nevertheless, they had created panic and fear in the early years of the war.

Improved technology during the war meant that London was an easy target for the German Gotha bombers and there were several instances of widespread death from bombing. For example, there was one raid on London on 13 June 1917 when 162 civilians were killed and 432 were injured. One bomb fell on a school, and 16 children were killed and 30 injured.

When one considers the damage and destruction caused by bombing in the Second World War, the raids of 1915–18 were quite minor. However, they caused terrific fear and panic and it has been estimated that about 300,000 Londoners sheltered in the underground railway stations to avoid the effects of the bombs. Some Londoners actually left their homes and moved to places such as Bath and Bournemouth, which were much safer.

January 1915 – April 1918	
51 Zeppelin raids	1,913 casualties
December 1914 – June 1918	
57 aeroplane raids	2,907 casualties

Total civilian casualties, 5,611 – including 1,570 fatalities, of whom 1,413 were killed in air attacks.

▲ **The number of civilians killed in Britain 1914–18.**

Though London was an easy target, Dover suffered most aerial attacks. The local caves were used as shelters and by the end of 1917, there was space for 25,000 people to shelter in the event of prolonged attacks.

The German aerial attacks meant that special air defences had to be set up. By the end of 1916, more than 17,000 men and 110 aircraft were involved in the air defence of Britain. There was no permanent '**blackout**' system like the one adopted after 1939. However, DORA allowed local military authorities to impose some form of blackout. The scheme eventually adopted was to dowse all lights within twelve minutes of receiving warning of the approach of an enemy attack.

To help those people whose property was damaged in the raids, the government set up the National Relief Fund. This gave payments to the boarding-house keepers of the East Coast, and those people whose houses were damaged were also given funds.

The bombing raids never really sapped the morale of the British people. If anything they led the people to demand more energetic measures from the government in the fight against the Germans.

Source C

▲ **A Zeppelin.**

Questions

1 Why did the naval attacks on Scarborough and Whitby create such indignation in Britain?

2 Few people were killed in air raids during the war. Nevertheless, why were the raids important to both sides?

3 Why do you think that the government did not operate a full blackout during the war?

4 How effective do you think the German air raids were?

Changing attitudes to the war

Although there was tremendous enthusiasm for the war in 1914, opponents of the war formed the Union of Democratic Control (UDC) in September 1914. The UDC argued that there should be an early negotiated peace and that in future Britain's foreign policy should be based on the wishes of its people. The Labour leader Ramsay MacDonald supported this group but he was out of touch with the feelings of the majority of the Labour Party and he gave up the leadership post.

Enthusiasm for the war, however, dwindled from 1916. The Battle of the Somme did not bring the much hoped for breakthrough and the huge loss of life for so little gain could not be explained away as a victory. For many people, both at home and at the front, the Somme was a major turning point in the war. The optimism of 1914 was gone, and so was the blind faith in the government and the generals' ability to win the war. Many soldiers wondered how the generals could have ordered an attack that brought nearly 60,000 casualties on the first day. As news of the losses at the front reached home there was widespread horror. From 1916 onwards many soldiers saw the war as a job to be done and prayed they would survive. Few talked about winning glory and the fear of 'missing the fun' as they had in 1914.

Fate	Total
Non-combatant corps	3,000
Ambulance drivers/stretcher bearers	2,400
Worked under government guidance in the UK	3,964
Went to prison (1,500 of whom were absolutists)	6,260

▲ A table showing the fate of conscientious objectors.

Source A

I was bullied horribly when I was tried, and sentenced to 28 days' detention in solitary confinement – to be given raw rations and to cook food for myself. This does not sound bad, but I found that the confinement was in a pit which started at the top as three feet by two and tapered off to two feet six inches by fifteen inches. The bottom was full of water and I had to stand on two strips of wood all day long to keep above the water line.

▲ An extract from a letter written by a conscientious objector, 24 June 1917. The letter was smuggled out of prison by a sympathetic soldier.

Conscription

By late 1915, recruitment to the armed forces was slowing and Kitchener was keen to maintain the flow at a level at about 35,000 new recruits per week. The government eventually introduced conscription in January 1916 for all single men between the ages of 18 and 41. The Military Services Act was extended in April that year to include married men. There was active opposition to conscription from the No Conscription Fellowship which had been formed in 1914. This body ensured that there were clear rights for those individuals who did not wish to serve in the armed forces. Those men who refused to fight because of religious or political reasons were called conscientious objectors or conchies. If a conscript wished to challenge conscription, he had to prove himself before a tribunal.

A **conscientious objector** was often criticised by the general public as a coward, shirker or worse still, a traitor. Those who passed the tribunals were still recruited, but to do non-combatant work. There were numerous examples of conscientious objectors acting with great bravery at the front as stretcher-bearers or ambulance drivers. Those who wanted nothing to do with the war were known as 'absolutists'. These men were committed pacifists who refused to have

▲ Conscientious objectors in Dyce, near Aberdeen.

Source C

'Good morning; good morning!' the General said

When we met him last week on our way to the line.

Now the soldiers he smiled at are most of 'em dead,

And we're cursing his staff for incompetent swine.

'He's a cheery old card,' grunted Harry to Jack

As they slogged up to Arras with rifle and pack.

But he did for them both by his plan of attack.

▲ 'The General', by Siegfried Sassoon.

anything to do with the war – even in a non-fighting capacity. Figures show that there were only about 16,000 conscientious objectors and perhaps 1,500 absolutists.

The table opposite indicates the kind of work that conscientious objectors were given following a tribunal. A prison sentence usually meant hard labour. Some 71 conchies died in prison and more than 30 suffered mental breakdowns. At the end of the war, conscientious objectors were forbidden to vote for five years.

Conscientious objectors came to be hated and reviled by large sections of the population. This was understandable. Most families had members who were serving in the armed forces and by 1916, many had relatives who had been killed in the war. Those who sought to avoid call-up could only, in the public's mind, be cowards, and were therefore treated accordingly. The conchies were treated horribly by their Army guards, but it must be remembered that many won medals for bravery as ambulancemen in the front line.

Questions

1 Why was the Battle of the Somme a turning point in the public's wholehearted support for the war?

2 Why was conscription such an issue in the First World War?

3 Why did attitudes to war change by 1918?

The Second World War

War broke out again in Europe in September 1939, but this time it was to be far different from the Great War of 1914–18. There had been a threat of war in September 1938, but when Prime Minister Neville Chamberlain and Hitler reached agreement at Munich, it was hoped that there would be a lasting peace. Following the German occupation of Czechoslovakia in March 1939, Britain made a treaty with Poland, agreeing to give support in the event of a German invasion. In April 1939, Britain announced military conscription in peacetime for the first time in its history.

The call to arms

Before war was actually declared (3 September 1939) many preparations had been made for the protection of British civilians. Many children and their mothers were evacuated during the summer months. The government had a clearer idea of the way recruiting should take place and had even drawn up a Schedule of Reserved Occupations. The Military Training Act of 1939, which called up men of 20–21 years, was extended to include all 18–41 year olds. However, the 'call-up' was rather slow and there were some criticisms made of the government's inefficiency. Nevertheless, there were those who remembered the problems of recruiting a generation before and some men in specific jobs were allowed to be '**deferred**'. By this, employers were able to stop the call-up of key workers in specialist occupations.

By the end of 1940, more than 200,000 had been deferred. Despite conscription, there were over one million men who volunteered for military service or who asked for their 'call-up' to be speeded up. There was not the enthusiasm and fervour as there had been in 1914, but some did join up out of patriotism and others did so to fight Nazism.

Some of the volunteers could see the horror of war, but felt that dictators such as Hitler had to be opposed in order to have a free world. Basic human rights had to be preserved even if this resulted in going to war.

Source A

▲ A painting by Charles Cundall showing troops being rescued from the beaches at Dunkirk.

The 'phoney war'

In 1936, during Spanish Civil War, German planes had carried out tests on bombing cities from the air. The town of Guernica became famous because of the damage caused by the Luftwaffe. In 1939 it was presumed that British cities would be bombed within days of the outbreak of war, but the dreaded bombing attacks did not take place. Local Gas Identification Squads had been set up, and adults and children were issued with gas masks that had to be carried at all times. Local authorities had been issued with thousands of tents which would act as temporary homes for air raid casualties. But for months nothing happened. The period has since become known as the '**phoney war**' but was originally called the 'bore war'.

Date	Figures given by RAF in 1940	Figures given by RAF after war	Figures in German High Command Diary
15 August	185	76	55
18 August	155	71	49
15 September	185	56	50
27 September	153	55	42
Totals	**678**	**258**	**196**

▲ German air losses on four days during the Battle of Britain.

Dunkirk

The 'bore war' ended abruptly on 10 May 1940, when German forces invaded Holland, Belgium, Luxembourg and France. By coincidence, this was the day that Winston Churchill replaced Chamberlain as prime minister. The British had sent troops to France to help fight the Germans, but by 21 May they had been pushed back onto the beaches at Dunkirk. To rescue the troops an armada of small boats set off from Britain. These ships helped the Royal Navy to rescue men from the beaches. The British lost 68,000 men in the evacuation and left behind 120,000 vehicles, 90,000 rifles and 2,300 guns. What followed was to be an indication of how even the worst defeat could be turned into a victory by the clever use of propaganda.

The 'Dunkirk spirit'

Newspapers and broadcasts from the BBC assured the British people that the withdrawal from Dunkirk had been magnificent. The writer and broadcaster J. B. Priestley spoke eloquently of the little boats that rescued the British army. (These boats were probably responsible for bringing back about 20,000 out of 340,000 men.) The idea grew of 'the Dunkirk spirit', of a nation pulling together, and it is something that British people speak of nearly three generations later. The propaganda machine stepped into action again during the summer of 1940, when the Battle of Britain took place. This was Hitler's attempt to destroy the RAF so that he could launch an invasion of Britain. Although he came close to victory, Hitler was eventually forced to call off the attack as the RAF had not been defeated. The press and the BBC published inflated figures of German aircraft losses and the nation spoke readily of 'the few' (from Churchill's speech about the battle). The fame of the Spitfire fighter plane stems from the accounts of 1940, even though there were more Hurricanes involved.

Source B

Never in the field of human conflict have so many owed so much to so few.

▲ A speech made by Churchill congratulating the RAF pilots on their victory in the Battle of Britain.

Questions

1 Why was it important to give a positive interpretation to the events at Dunkirk?

2 Why do you think that so many people today have a romantic view of Dunkirk and the Battle of Britain?

Propaganda

Propaganda became a vital weapon for both sides in the war – each was able to broadcast to enemy civilians in order to undermine morale. The Ministry of Information was responsible for ensuring that the British public was given details of the war in order to ensure continued support.

Radio

The BBC was not taken over by the Ministry, but was careful to run its own censorship. Morale was maintained by means of keeping the nation as informed as much as was possible and also by means of comedy programmes. The programme *It's That Man Again* (ITMA) was hugely popular and poked fun not only at Hitler and the Germans but also at the British. There were programmes that were broadcast from factory canteens (*Workers' Playtime*) and others which played requests for soldiers (*Sincerely Yours,* starring Vera Lynn). By the end of the war, there were more than ten million wireless (radio) licences, indicating that it would be easy to reach more than 25 million people.

Cinema

The cinema played a very important role in propaganda during the war. Before 1939, about three-quarters of the adult population were keen cinemagoers. During the war, the number of British made films declined but the quality did improve. Many documentary films were made, such as *Fires were Started* and fictionalised ones such as *The Way Ahead* about the average British soldier. Feature films such as *The Gentle Sex* and *Went the Day Well* were able to show ordinary people of all classes working together to defeat the enemy. However, perhaps the film most obviously used for propaganda purposes was *Henry V,* which was released at the time of the D-Day invasion in early summer 1944. It has been estimated that there were about 1.5 billion cinema tickets sold in Britain in 1945.

Newspapers and posters

Newspapers were not allowed to 'record or communicate to any other person which might be useful to an enemy'. The circulation of papers did not get smaller even though they were reduced in size and volume (there was a shortage of newsprint). In fact, in 1943, people were buying papers in greater numbers than ever before.

Wherever civilians went during the war, they could not avoid posters and notices encouraging them to 'win the war'. Food production was especially crucial and the German U-boat campaign of the First World War was still fresh in people's minds. There was the 'Dig for Victory' campaign, which encouraged people to grow their own food. Even the moat around the Tower of London was dug up so that vegetables could be grown there. The Ministry of Food issued factsheets about how best to use and cook different and unusual types of food.

The use of posters was very widespread and the best ones were those that expressed a feeling of the nation working together. The cartoon of the nation behind Churchill (see Source B) is very powerful and the image of Britain is captured in the spirit of the struggle.

Source A

▲ **A government poster from the 'Dig for victory' campaign.**

Source B

ALL BEHIND YOU, WINSTON

▲ A British cartoon from 1940: 'All behind you Winston'.

Questions

1 What is the purpose of propaganda?

2 Why were radio and the cinema important during the war?

3 What does Source C tell you about newspapers in the Second World War?

4 Do you think it is right for the government to control what is published or broadcast during a war?

It should be noted that the government was careful to plan what the public saw. One should always ask in a war what was not seen – there were no photographs published of the looting that took place in Coventry after the bombing raids and the deaths of children at Catford School, nor was there any reporting of the 173 people killed when a panic-stricken crowd pushed into the Bethnal Green tube station.

Of course, the Germans also used propoganda. For example, the broadcasts of Radio Hamburg could be picked up in Britain. A regular contributor to Radio Hamburg was William Joyce. He was born in the USA and moved to Ireland at the age of 16. In 1922 he came to live in England. He was so much in agreement with Nazi views that he went to live in Germany before the Second World War. From 1939–45 he made radio broadcasts mocking the British war effort. His tone was so mocking that the British people nicknamed him 'Lord Haw Haw'. At the end of the war he was brought back to Britain, found guilty of treason and hanged.

The Blitz

British civilians did not really experience the horror of war and realise that they were on the front line until 7 September 1940. This date signalled the beginning of the bombing campaign against London and other major cities which was known as the 'Blitz'. In the 1930s there had been government analyses of the number of casualties Britain could expect to suffer when aerial attacks began. Figures as high as 600,000 were quoted and it was thought that law and order would break down. The evacuation of millions of civilians is evidence of government fears.

Source C

There must be some sign of guts in the BBC announcers. They can show the hate of the Germans and contempt for the Italians in their voices ... Have we no patriotic tunes to play? ... politicians should not refer to Herr Hitler unless the word 'Herr' is spat out or sneered.

▲ A report from the *Daily Express*, 16 September 1940.

On the first night of bombing 430 people were killed. London then experienced 76 consecutive nights of bombing and, after November, other major cities were attacked. The most famous raid was on Coventry in November, when the raid lasted several hours. Some 400 people were killed and the cathedral was destroyed. By the time the first Blitz stopped on 10 May 1941 more than 40,000 civilians had been killed. Around 800,000 houses were destroyed or damaged, which created problems for local authorities as people needed re-housing.

Some of the heaviest raids were on Hull and Belfast. Belfast suffered only a couple of raids but these devastated the city because there were no anti-aircraft guns in Belfast, as it had been thought that the Germans would never fly so far. The intensity of the raids was never the same after 1941, but in 1942, there were attacks on some historic towns such as York, Norwich, Canterbury and Exeter. These were called the Baedeker raids. They were called this because the German Baedeker tourist guide books indicated the places of historical and architectural interest in Britain. The towns chosen from these guides were those that were weakly defended. Many people had their views confirmed that the Germans were barbarians.

V1 and V2

The second phase of bombing began on 16 June 1944 when rocket powered pilotless aircraft attacked London. These were called V1s – from the German word *Vergeltungswaffe* – literally retaliation weapon. The V1s were nicknamed **'doodlebugs'** or 'buzz bombs'. The V1 attacks lasted for 80 days and by the end the home anti-aircraft defences had been massed on the south coast and were becoming skilled in shooting them down. About 10,500 V1s were launched against Britain and of these 4,000 were destroyed. They killed and wounded 20,000 civilians. The V1 did not affect morale, but it worsened the housing problem. At the height of the V1 campaign, more than 20,000 houses per day were being damaged. By the

Source A

▲ Catford School after a bombing raid.

Source B

... It will take ten years at the present rate for half the houses of London to be demolished.

▲ Churchill speaking in Parliament in October 1940, expressing his relief that casualties were lower than anticipated.

end of January 1945, 145,000 men were employed in repair work on London's houses.

The second devastating secret weapon of the Germans first fell on London on 8 September 1944. This was the V2 – a rocket that could travel at speeds of up to 5,000 kilometres per hour at a height of 95 kilometres. Because of their speed, there was no possible warning of their impending arrival. Fortunately they were not particularly accurate. About 500 landed on London, almost 3,000 people were killed by them and more than 6,000 were injured. The V1 and V2 attacks stopped in March 1945.

More than 60,000 civilians died as a result of the bombing campaigns. A major aim of the Blitz was to destroy the morale of the British people and encourage them to put pressure on their government to make peace. Of course, government propoganda ensured that few people realised how severe the damage being caused by German bombers was. Only those living in the areas where bombing was concentrated knew the real situation. In general the British morale was not broken, but for thousands of British civilians the Blitz was a terrifying ordeal which they would never forget.

Source C

▲ **Bomb damage to Coventry Cathedral after an air raid.**

Questions

1   What was the Blitz?

2   Why do you think Churchill was keen to point out how long it would take to destroy London's houses by bombing? Use Source B to help you with your answer.

3   What were the effects of the Blitz on Britain?

Living through the Blitz

Taking shelter

There were many methods used to overcome the threat of bombing raids. First, trenches that had been dug in the crisis of 1938 were added to, and by the outbreak of war there were enough to shelter half a million people. More important were the two million Anderson Shelters provided by the government by the start of the Blitz. The Anderson Shelter was two curved sheets of corrugated steel bolted together at the top. They were sunk about a metre into the ground and then covered with about 40 cm of soil. The entrance was protected by a steel shield and a blast wall. Later, in 1941, the Morrison Shelter was introduced. This could be erected indoors and 500,000 had been distributed by the end of the year. Civilians had a wide choice of shelters and only a tiny percentage of Londoners sheltered in the tube. Despite this, it is the pictures of people sleeping in the tube which have come to be the lasting image of the Blitz.

As protection against the effects of bombing, windows were taped up to avoid flying splinters and sandbags used to protect buildings. For example, school children in Plymouth helped fill 16,000 sandbags in January 1940 to protect a local hospital.

One form of avoiding the bombing raids was 'trekking'. People would often leave their home town or city in the late afternoon and move into the countryside. They would return early next morning after the air raid.

The 'blackout'

The 'blackout' had perhaps the most immediate effect on the British people. So that German bombers could not see cities from the air (and therefore bomb them more easily), people had to ensure that no light was visible from their homes as soon as lights were put on. Failure to do so meant a visit from the Air Raid Warden. Streetlights were not lit and cars had to drive without lights. One small town in Northumberland was bombed when a German bomber caught sight of lights and dropped his last few bombs before returning to base. What he had seen was the local bus turning around at the end of its run – with its headlights on. In December 1939 over 1,500 people were killed on Britain's roads. This was nearly three times the pre-war average of 600 deaths per month. Many people fell into canals, fell downstairs or from railway platforms. Eventually, civilians could use dimmed torches in the streets and car drivers could use dimmed headlights. To assist pedestrians and drivers, kerbs and roadsides were painted black and white. Some pavements were even painted to ensure pedestrians did not collide with each other.

The Air Raid Wardens' Service had been set up in 1937 and had almost half a million recruits at the beginning of the war. The wardens were key figures in the event of a bombing raid, ensuring there

Source A

▲ **The delivery of Anderson Shelters.**

Source B

▲ The Home Guard.

Source C

People would rush to get to the tubes, almost knock you down to get at the escalator ... We lived like rats underground ... People spread newspapers on the floor to show it was their territory ... sometimes you'd get people squaring up and fights.

▲ An extract from an interview with a Londoner remembering the early days of the Blitz.

was calm, that people knew how the raid was progressing and that people were helped after the raid. About one in six wardens was a woman. There were barrage balloons above several cities, but these could not prevent aerial bombardment. The use of anti-aircraft guns was more of a morale booster for people living in cities – bombers were rarely shot down by them.

The fear of invasion

There was a constant fear that the Germans would invade Britain and on 14 May 1939 Anthony Eden, Secretary of State for War, broadcast to the nation (see Source D).

Within 24 hours 250,000 men had put down their names to join and by the end of June 1940, about 1.5 million had volunteered. The new force was renamed the Home Guard in July. Those who joined were often too old to be in the regular army or worked in an industry essential to the war effort. This led to it having the nickname 'Dad's Army'. The Home Guard took on duties that relieved the pressure on the regular army. It was able to guard the coastline, man roadblocks, secure telephone exchanges – above all it permitted involvement in the defence of the nation. It was a clear sign of the spirit of Britain's resistance.

Source D

We want large numbers of men between the ages of 17 and 65 to come forward now and offer their services in order to make assurances that an invasion will be repelled. The name of the new force will be the Local Defence Volunteers.

▲ Anthony Eden speaking in May 1939.

Questions

1 In what ways were civilians prepared for air attacks at the beginning of the war?

2 Why do you think that there is still an image of all Londoners sheltering in the tube?

3 Why were the Air Raid Wardens' Service and the Home Guard important?

Evacuation

The Second World War was a total war that involved the whole home-front population from young children to the very old. The development of heavy bomber aircraft meant that civilians were at risk at home just as much as soldiers on the front line. The bombing of cities during the Spanish Civil War in the 1930s had shown how much devastation could be caused.

Because of this, the British government made plans that in the event of war, children of school age would be evacuated away from London and other areas of high population.

The government was convinced that bombing would be inevitable and thought there would be at least half a million civilian casualties in the first few weeks of fighting. Orders had even been made to have one million shrouds and coffins made.

Moving to the countryside

By the time war was declared on 3 September 1939, the government had already completed a survey which showed there was surplus accommodation outside the urban areas considered to be at risk for over four and a half million people. During the period 1–3 September 1939, about 1.5 million people were moved to 'reception areas' in country towns and villages.

When the evacuees arrived at their destination they were placed in accommodation by a Billeting Officer. In some cases, children were just lined up for the local people to choose who they wanted. This process was frequently cruel and resulted in families and friends being split up.

Source A

▲ Three very young children, with their belongings, being evacuated in September 1939.

Types of evacuees	Number evacuated
Schoolchildren	827,000
Mothers and under 5s	524,000
Teachers and helpers	103,000
Pregnant women	13,000
Handicapped people	7,000

▲ Types of people evacuated in September 1939.

Resistance to evacuation

Despite this huge movement, about half of the children in urban areas were not evacuated in this first phase. Parents often preferred to take a chance and keep their children with them, but in some cases the success of the evacuation depended on how vigorous the local authority was in implementing the programme. For example, in Sheffield many parents refused to allow their children to be sent into rural Lincolnshire because they would be closer to Germany than they were at home.

For many people living in the countryside it was a shock to see the state of some of the evacuees. Reports soon emerged of dirty, disease-ridden, ignorant and unruly children. Lord Chandos, who took in some 31 evacuees, complained that the children in his house regarded 'the floors and carpets as suitable places on which to relieve themselves' and Prime Minister Chamberlain wrote to a friend 'I never knew such conditions existed.'

The poor health of the evacuated children led to the government introducing measures to provide cheap milk for children and expectant mothers. Vitamins and cod liver oil were also provided as part of their rations.

Private evacuation

As well as those sent as part of the government schemes, it is estimated that a further two million people were privately evacuated to the countryside and more remote areas of Britain. The government also arranged for some children to go overseas and almost 3,000 were sent to British colonies and dominions, mainly Canada. This stopped when a ship carrying evacuees was sunk by the Germans.

Many of this first phase of evacuees soon returned home. The 'phoney war' meant that no German bombers came until September 1940. The evacuated children were homesick and their parents could not afford to send them money or come and visit them. Further evacuation occurred in the summers of 1940 and of 1944.

Source B

We were told to sit quietly on the floor while villagers and farmers' wives came to choose which children they wanted. Eventually only my friend Nancy and myself were left – two plain, straight-haired little girls wearing glasses, now rather tearful. A large, happy-looking middle-aged lady rushed in asking, 'Is that all you have left?' A sad, slow nod of the head from our teacher. 'I'll take the poor bairns.' We were led out of the hall with this stranger and taken to a farm where we spent two years.

▲ Beryl Hewitson describes what happened to her when she was evacuated.

Source C

The local ladies would walk through the mob and make a selection. If you were similar to Shirley Temple [a popular child film star of the 1930s] you were grabbed right away. The little angelic girls always went first ... most girls went into the best homes. If you were like me who always looked filthier than others, your chances were pretty bleak.

▲ John Wills, an evacuee, describes his experiences on arrival at a reception centre.

Questions

1 Why do you think the government evacuated so many people in the period 1–3 September 1939?

2 Read the text and look at Sources A, B and C. Can you suggest reasons why evacuation was such a negative experience for some children?

Rationing

As in the First World War, German submarines sank merchant shipping bringing food and supplies to Britain. This resulted in shortages and rationing.

The system adopted was quite simple. Everyone was issued with a ration book and registered with a local grocer and butcher. They then bought their food from those shops and would hand in coupons in the ration book when they paid for their purchases.

Rationing of many foodstuffs, like butter, bacon and sugar, began in January 1940. Gradually more and more items were rationed, and luxury items such as silk stockings and cosmetics were included in this list by 1941. There was little opposition to rationing, which most people considered to be a fair way of sharing goods in short supply. Rationing was regarded as most fair in those sections of the population and regions where food had been plentiful before the war. It was least popular with workers in heavy industries, and those who lived in pre-war depressed areas. Workers felt they needed more than the daily allowance of 3,000 calories – heavy work requires a substantial diet.

By 1941, Britain was having to import large quantities of food on the Lend-Lease Scheme. Items such as dried eggs, evaporated milk, cheese, beans, lard and tinned meat were among the goods that were becoming scarce. At the end of 1941, the government introduced the points system. By this, each rationed item had a points score. The scarcest items were given the highest value – so, for example, 1lb (0.5kg) of

Source A

A woman from Middlesbrough was fined 10s (50p) after being found guilty of wasting food. The court heard that she threw buttered slices of bread into the garden. It was the first charge of its kind in the town under the Waste of Food Order, 1940.

▲ *Middlesbrough Evening Gazette, 2 February 1942.*

Source B

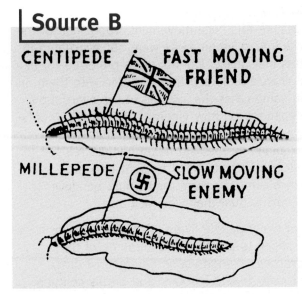

▲ A cartoon for gardeners. This reminded gardeners that centipedes prey on garden pests but millipedes eat vegetables.

dried peas was 1 point, but 1lb of salmon was 32 points. Some foods on the points system were often not available and so when they came into the shops there was a made rush to buy them. Often foods, such as horsemeat, were not rationed, but could only be bought by queuing for hours outside the butchers.

By the end of 1942, Britain's food imports were less than half those of 1939 – the points system made people think carefully about spending. Nevertheless, there was plenty of food, but little variety. Bread and potatoes were not rationed and so people could fill up on these bulk items. After four years of war, potato consumption had increased by 40 per cent, milk by 30 per cent and vegetables by 30 per cent on the 1939 figures. As could be expected, because they had a high points score, meat consumption fell by 29 per cent and poultry/fish by 40 per cent during that same period.

A clear indication that diet was more balanced came when infant mortality figures showed higher survival rates.

Grow your own

The 'Dig for Victory' campaign began at the start of the war. Ten million leaflets were issued

Source C

▲ Londoners queuing for horsemeat in the 1940s.

Source D

I used to go shopping for my mother. This could sometimes take a whole morning even though the shops were just round the corner. Most of the time was spent queuing – especially for bread and meat. One day word went round that a certain shop had some 'viyella' material. My mother and her friends queued for hours. For years afterwards you would know whose mother was in that queue because the children had dresses and skirts, blouses, shirts and shorts all made from either pale blue or pale pink spotted viyella!

▲ A woman remembering how rationing affected her as a child during the war.

about it in 1942 alone and a survey showed that by 1943, more than half of the working classes kept either an allotment or garden. The number of allotments grew from 815,000 in 1939 to 1,400,000 in 1943. More than a quarter of hens' eggs were produced by domestic keepers and pig keeping became something of a craze. There were eventually 6,900 'Pig Clubs' with hundreds of thousands of members.

There were ways of avoiding rationing. The '**black market**' existed – sometimes goods might find themselves mysteriously moved from the docks and shopkeepers could acquire these extra goods. The extra goods were kept 'under the counter', or out of sight. The Ministry of

Food had 900 inspectors to ensure that all regulations were kept to. Many people, however, found clever ways to make their rations go round – for example, using flour and baking powder to produce six omelettes from one egg. The new carrot toffees, said to improve vision in the blackout, also proved very popular.

However, rationing of food and other goods did not stop with the war. Some items were still being rationed up to fourteen years after the fighting stopped.

Questions

1 Why was rationing introduced so soon in this war?

2 What methods did the government use to make people aware of diet and availability of food?

3 Can you suggest reasons why the British people put up with rationing?

Women in the Second World War

As with the First World War, women also played a crucial part in the Second World War. Like British men, British women were conscripts, but of a different kind. Not only were they called up to join the armed forces (but not to fight) they also did the jobs left empty by their husbands, fathers and brothers. Moreover, they had to look after families and much of the propaganda about saving for the war effort was targeted at them. But they had to cope not only with new jobs, caring for their families, rationing and air raids, but also with the arrival, from 1942, of American GIs.

Working women

The decision to conscript women was taken in 1941, when the shortage of manpower was more widespread. This was the first time that any democratic nation had done this. A wartime survey showed that 97 per cent of women agreed that they should undertake some kind of war work. By 1943, over seven million women were involved in the armed forces, industry and defence. Just as in the First World War, there was some opposition to female employment. Nevertheless, almost half of all females between the ages of 14 and 59 undertook some kind of national service.

Many of the same issues cropped up again during this war. There was no government commitment to equal pay because it was felt that if concessions were given, there would be industrial unrest among the men. An Equal Pay Commission was set up in 1943 and it was to report in 1946. It had no powers to make any recommendations. The Ministry of Health was unwilling to set up nurseries because there was still the idea that female employment was only temporary and that as soon as hostilities the status quo would resume.

By 1944, there were approaching half a million women working in the armed forces. They did not fight on the front line but their involvement did permit the release of men for such activities. In some cases women took on skilled jobs in the forces, as pilots (but, of course, not at the front line) and radio operators, but there were many who believed that the traditional jobs were the

Auxiliary Territorial Service	198,000
Land Army	30,000
Civil Defence	375,000
Armed Forces	470,000

▲ **The number of women involved in uniformed services.**

only ones women were capable of doing. The commonly held attitudes that women could only perform simple tasks and that certain jobs were unglamorous or not feminine were difficult to change. Indeed, many women when interviewed during the war were happy to say they were looking forward to giving up their jobs, marrying and having children. Nevertheless, by 1951, the proportion of married women at work was 21 per cent (in 1931, it had been 10 per cent).

Source A

▲ **A Land Army girl.**

Source B

▲ An advertisement in a woman's magazine in 1942.

Evacuation

Women had to cope with the problems of evacuation – more than three million endured this trauma at the beginning of the war. The surveys carried out in the war by Mass Observation show that women were often more dispirited and resigned than their male counterparts. This can be readily explained because they were the ones who had to deal with food shortages, bombings, damages to houses and the absence of their partner. More than 63,000 British women were killed during the war.

The arrival of the GIs

From January 1942 American troops started arriving in Britain. There were nearly two million American troops (more commonly called GIs

Source C

Americans were 'cheeky' compared to our usual 'Mr Frigidaire Englishman', but what a boost to her ego when one is greeted with 'Hello Duchess!' (and you were treated like one!) ... As we got to know these boys, how generous they were; we never lacked for chocolates or cigarettes or even precious luxuries like nylons that they could get for us.

▲ Comments from a woman who was a teenager during the Second World War.

because their uniforms were supposed to be stamped with 'General Issue') stationed in Britain ready to take part in the Allied invasion of Hitler's Europe. These troops had a huge impact on the British people with whom they came into contact.

Most of the GIs who came to Britain were part of the United States Army Air Forces (USAAF). However, many were non-combat troops, that is they were responsible for supplying everything from vehicles, planes, ammunition to food and uniforms. Many of these men became involved with local people in the towns and villages near their bases. Two US supply bases were at Burtonwood and Warton in Lancashire. The men stationed there stayed on the same base all the time and spent their time off in local towns such as Manchester and Liverpool. Some of these men married local girls. In fact during the Second World War there were 75,000 British GI brides in Britain – most of whom went to join their husbands in the USA after the war.

Questions

1 Why were women conscripted in 1941?

2 In what ways did job opportunities for women change during the Second World War?

3 Why did the arrival of the US soldiers have such an effect on women?

Post-war developments

Just as in the First World War, the government had taken control of all those industries that were vital to the war effort. This greater government involvement continued after the war. William Beveridge, a minister, was asked to look into social security. He said that there were 'five giants' which had to be removed if Britain were to end poverty. The 'giants' were 'Want, Disease, Ignorance, Squalor and Idleness'. The Report was published in December 1942 and sold 100,000 copies within one month.

The Report proposed an insurance scheme for all, which would cover:

- people against sickness, unemployment and old age
- a national health service with free medical treatment for all
- that the unemployed would receive benefits during a period out of work
- family allowances
- an improvement in the quality of housing.

Source A

BEVERIDGE REPORT PLANS TO ABOLISH WANT

CIVIL DEFENCE & POLICE PAY RAISED

£2 Pension for Married Couple: Medical Aid Free to All: Housewives' New Status

INCREASES UP TO 4s 6d A WEEK

TRAINING UNEMPLOYED: NO MEANS TEST

BY OUR POLITICAL CORRESPONDENT

▲ The front page of a newspaper in December 1942 announcing the plans outlined in the Beveridge Report.

There is no wonder that the Report was well received – it promised to attack poverty and would bring security and peace of mind to the vast majority of Britain's citizens.

Some reforms were introduced before the end of hostilities – the 1944 Education Act at last made education for 11–14 year olds free. Family allowances were introduced in 1945 and 25p was paid to the mother for each child after the first born. The Labour Party was committed to the Beveridge Report and after its landslide victory in the 1945 General Election it began to act on its proposals.

The National Insurance Act 1946
The Labour government made this compulsory, thus extending the system of insurance cover. Workers were covered for sickness and unemployment – moreover, it provided old age and widows' pensions, maternity and death grants. Everyone paid the same flat rate weekly contributions and would receive the same in benefits. There was no need for the Means Test.

National Health Service Act
This Act ensured that all people were able to have free medical treatment in hospital and from a general practitioner. Dental and optical treatments were also now available free of charge. Most of Britain's hospitals were taken over by the state and run by regional hospital boards. The act also enabled local authorities to provide facilities such as welfare services, maternity clinics and ambulances.

National Assistance Act
This set up the National Assistance Board which could give weekly payments or lump sums to those who had fallen below the poverty line and were in urgent need of help. Essentially, the Act tried to ensure that every individual would be guaranteed a minimum basic income.

The Housing Acts of 1946 and 1948
There was a shortage of over one million houses in 1945 and as a result of these two Acts, the construction of council houses was encouraged. More than 800,000 council houses were built by

Source B

▲ Prefabs in York.

Source C

On Monday morning you will wake up to a new Britain in a state which 'takes over' its citizens six months before they are born, providing care and free services for their birth, early years, their schooling, sickness, workless days, widowhood and retirement. All this with free doctoring, dentistry and medicine for 5 shillings (25p) out of your weekly pay packet.

▲ From the *Daily Mail*, 3 July 1948.

1951. There were also about 150,000 'prefabs' built in the early post-war years.

With the establishment of the Welfare State, it could be said that the British people were looked after from 'the womb to the tomb'.

In 1918, people were, of course, happy that hostilities were over, but many wanted to go back to life as it had been before 1914. At the end of the Second World War, most people wanted to look to the future, to build a better country. The bombing, blackout, rationing – all of these hardships had to have been for something.

It was said in 1945 that Labour government offered 'Bread and butter and a DREAM!'

Source D

One morning Dad went to see our doctor to ask about the new National Health Service. The doctor said: 'Mr Dawson, I didn't think you wanted that kind of service'. But we joined all the same.

▲ A woman who was a teenager at the end of the war commenting on the new National Health Service.

Questions

1   What were the 'five giants'?

2   Why could the 'five giants' not be tackled separately?

3   Which do you think was the most important act introduced by the Labour government after 1945?

4   If Labour offered 'Bread and butter and a DREAM!', what do you think was meant by the idea 'DREAM'?

Overview

How far did a) attitudes to women and b) the role of the government change in the period 1900~50?

A divided union?
The USA: 1941~80

Introduction

The history of the USA since 1776 has been stormy and tempestuous. The middle years of the twentieth century have perhaps been the most eventful since independence was declared. This chapter examines events within the USA during a time when it became one of the two strongest nations in the world.

The chapter begins by analysing the impact of the Second World War and it explains how the USA emerged as the leading economy of the world. It also shows that there were many tensions within US society during the war which would later lead to great unrest and upheaval. The quest for civil rights led to the emergence of such powerful figures as Martin Luther King and Malcolm X, and forced the Americans to re-think their views on race.

There is also an analysis of the great fear that the Americans had of communism and looks at McCarthyism and US politics. Moreover, the darker side of politics is also examined with the Watergate Affair, and the upheavals within US society during the 1960s and early 1970s are examined through the developing student and women's movements.

If the USA in the period 1941–80 gave an image of a united country ready to fight Nazism and communism, then this chapter shows that the reality was that at home it was very much 'A divided union'.

The USA and the Second World War

After the First World War the USA pursued a policy of isolationism. It did not want to be involved in European disputes that could drag it into another war. An opinion poll in 1937 found that almost two-thirds of Americans felt that US participation in the First World War had been a mistake. During the 1930s isolationism was strengthened when a series of laws was passed which prohibited the sale of US weapons to nations at war and stopped its citizens from travelling on ships belonging to nations at war.

Nevertheless, President Roosevelt realised that the problems caused by Japan and Germany's aggressive foreign policies could affect the USA and in 1939, he asked Congress for US$1.3 billion to strengthen America's armed forces.

When war started in Europe in 1939, there were many Americans who believed that the USA should not become involved. Others, however, wanted to help the 'old country' and support Britain – though there were also, of course, many Germans, Italians and Japanese in the USA. In 1940, President Roosevelt arranged the transfer of 50 US destroyers to Britain and introduced conscription to build up US armed forces.

Then, on 7 December 1941, the Japanese launched an attack on the American fleet at Pearl Harbor, Hawaii. The attack resulted in 2,400 American deaths and the sinking of eight battleships. On the following day, the USA officially declared war on Japan and on 11 December, Germany and Italy declared war on the USA. The war that followed lasted almost four years and brought significant changes within the USA. Some of those changes were to be short-lived, but others had an influence way beyond 1945 and into the next generation.

Source A

▲ Pearl Harbor after the attack.

Chapter 9 *A divided union? The USA: 1941–80*

167

The impact of the war on American society

The war severely disrupted the lives of the average American citizen. By 1945 almost 16 million of them had served in the armed forces. Some of these men had never previously been outside their home towns and many had never even left home. For those men who had not been recruited there were opportunities, too. Many moved to other areas in search of high-paid jobs in the defence industry. Some 700,000 black Americans travelled north or west from their homes in the southern states hoping to secure decent jobs that would help them escape the poverty and racial discrimination they experienced in the south. In total almost 1.5 million Americans moved to California looking for a better life. Many of these **migrants** were farm labourers hoping for work in the Californian arms industry.

To help promote support for the war the government set up schemes such as the Office of Civilian Defence, which asked the American people to give 'an hour a day for the USA'. People were encouraged to start 'victory gardens' and eventually these were producing 40 per cent of all the vegetables grown in the USA. Recycling of scrap materials was encouraged, and these efforts produced half the tin and paper that the USA needed during the war.

For most Americans the war was the first experience of food rationing, which the government introduced to keep prices down by controlling the amount that could be bought.

For young people the war provided employment opportunities, and many students dropped out of school to start jobs. The number of workers between sixteen and nineteen years of age tripled to almost three million by 1944. Because married women were employed in greater numbers, a generation of children grew up who had to look after themselves. They were often known as 'latch key kids' or 'eight hour orphans'. One distressing feature of this change in family life was the recorded increase of juvenile delinquency.

The impact of war on women

The war had an immediate impact on the role and position of women. In 1941 women made up only 27 per cent of the workforce, but by 1945 the figure had risen to 37 per cent. More than 350,000 served in the armed forces and of these about 25 per cent served overseas. Like most of the men who served abroad, this was the first time that many of them had left the USA. The largest increase in female employment came in the defence industries, where there were four times as many women working as there had been in peace time.

However, women often had a hard time gaining acceptance by their male co-workers, many of whom had not been used to seeing women in their workplace. Others did not believe that women should be working, but felt that they should be at home looking after their families. The government, however, appreciated the need for women to work and there were campaigns to encourage them into the factories. 'Rosie the Riveter' became the symbol of the overall-wearing, blue collar female worker and posters of her could be seen everywhere.

The greatest change came for many black women. Their opportunities for employment increased and thousands of them found employment in the war industries. Some black women joined the armed forces as nurses, but in keeping with attitudes towards race in the USA in the 1940s, they were only allowed to tend to black soldiers.

Source B

We must begin the great task of what is before us by abandoning once and for all the illusion that we can ever again isolate ourselves. There is no such thing as security for any nation in a world ruled by the principles of gangsterism. There is no such thing as impregnable defence against powerful aggressors who sneak up in the dark and strike without warning.

▲ Comment made by Roosevelt on 9 December 1941 on why the USA had to join the war.

At the end of the war the men returned home from the fighting. They wanted their jobs back. So the US government and many industries urged women to 'go back home' and 'give your job to a veteran'. Many women did leave their jobs and, of course, the end of the war brought a reduction in the number of workers needed in factories as demand for war goods ended.

Some women were only too happy to return to the familiar roles of full-time mothers and 'home-makers'. But others were resentful at losing the independence that their work pay packet gave them. Nevertheless, there were more women in work in 1950 than there had been in 1940 and the breaking of the stereotype of the 'wife at home' had begun.

Source C

▲ A poster showing Rosie the Riveter.

Source D

The men really resented the women very much and in the beginning it was a little bit rough. After a while the men that you worked with realised that it was essential that women worked there and the women were doing a pretty good job. However, I always felt that they thought it wasn't your place to be there.

▲ Written in 1987 by Helen Studer, a riveter recalling her work during the war at Douglas Aircraft.

Questions

1 Describe the effects of the war on American family life.

2 Look at Sources C and D. Do you think that attitudes towards women changed in the war?

Chapter 9 *A divided union? The USA: 1941~80*

169

The impact of the war on black Americans

One million black Americans served in the US armed forces during the Second World War. As in American society at the time, there was segregation in the armed forces too. There were only twelve black officers at the beginning of the war and black Americans were usually assigned to all-black units commanded by white officers. Black soldiers would often be given menial jobs such as labourers and cooks instead of being sent into combat. As the war developed, racially integrated units became more common as General Eisenhower was a strong supporter of them. Such units performed with distinction at the Battle of the Bulge in late 1944. By the end of the war the number of black officers and integrated units had increased significantly. There were also several units of black pilots, whereas in 1941 there had been no black pilots.

Black Americans found themselves fighting for 'democracy and freedom' against the tyranny of Nazi Germany and the oppressive rule of the Japanese. In Europe, Hitler was condemned for his racial policies and promoting the Aryan (Germanic) race as superior to all others. Yet these soldiers lived in a country where most blacks were treated as second-class citizens. Many were not permitted to vote and were discriminated against in education and job opportunities.

So the war gave black Americans the opportunity to press for equality of **civil rights**. The black press set up the 'Double V' campaign. This would involve victory at home in terms of civil rights as well as abroad on the battlefield. Philip Randolph led blacks in their struggle for equality using the slogan 'We loyal American citizens demand the right to work and fight for our country'. He set up the 'March on Washington Movement' and hoped to mobilise between 50,000 and 100,000 people.

Source E

▲ Black American soldiers in action in the Second World War.

- Women's Auxiliary Army Corps
- Women Appointed for Voluntary Emergency Services (WAVES)
- Woman Ordnance Worker (WOW)
- American Red Cross

▲ Women in the armed forces.

▲ **A victim of the race riots 1943.**

1 What was meant by isolationism?

2 How did the USA help Britain yet at the same time remain neutral in the years 1939–41?

3 Why did large numbers of American citizens move location during the war?

4 In what ways did the war affect:
   i women, and
   ii black Americans?

Government reaction

The campaign by black Americans for better treatment pushed President Roosevelt into action. In 1941 he issued Executive Order 8802, which stated the following:

> 'Government agencies, job training programmes and defence contractors must put an end to discrimination.'

The Fair Employment Practices Committee was set up to investigate violations of that Order. Encouraged by this progress, black civil rights leaders set up the Congress of Racial Equality (CORE) in 1942. As Black people's expectations rose, they became more active. Membership of the National Association for the Advancement of Coloured People grew rapidly during the war years. By 1946 it had 460,000 members, ten times the membership in 1940.

However, progress towards equality was not always smooth. The arrival of large numbers of black Americans created racial tensions in some cities. Race riots broke out in Detroit on 21 June 1943 in which 25 blacks and nine whites were killed. More than 700 people were injured and there was US$2 million worth of damage to property. There were also riots at nine black army training camps where the soldiers resented the unequal treatment they received. Further riots occurred in the summer of 1943. The worst took place in Harlem, New York, when six blacks were killed and 300 people injured.

However, despite the pressure from the black community, President Roosevelt felt that he could not make any further reforms. Despite the changes during the war the basic inequalities still existed and it was more than a generation before some of the worst features of discrimination in the USA were removed.

Japanese-Americans

If there was mixed treatment for black Americans during the war, then the treatment of the Japanese-Americans was appalling. When war with Japan started in December 1941, the government decided that immigrant Japanese families were a threat to the USA. So in the spring of 1942, more than 100,000 Japanese-Americans were moved from their homes to relocation camps in bleak parts of the USA. One-third of the number were **Issei** (foreign-born Japanese) but about two-thirds were their children, **Nisei** (that is, children of Issei, born in the USA).

Chapter 9 *A divided union? The USA: 1941–80*

171

Source G

▲ **The vandalised home of a Nisei family in May 1945.**

On 19 February 1942, President Roosevelt authorised the removal of Japanese-Americans to internment camps. It was felt that these people would commit acts of sabotage to aid Japan in an attack on the West Coast and perhaps set up spy networks to undermine the American war effort. The Nisei were forced to sell almost all of their belongings, and their property was often vandalised or illegally seized. It was estimated that Nisei losses totalled about US$500 million. Yet, at the same time, more than 8,000 Nisei were conscripted and 9,000 volunteered to fight for the USA. The 442nd Regimental Combat Team, almost entirely made up of Nisei, was the most decorated combat force in the US army.

The impact of the war on the economy
The war finally brought the USA out of the Depression of the 1930s. President Roosevelt had spent billions of dollars on job creation schemes in his New Deal, but it was only when production was stepped up to prepare for the war that unemployment in the USA fell to the level that it had been in 1929 before the Wall Street Crash.

Source H

What'd you get, black boy,

When they knocked you down in the gutter.

And they kicked your teeth out,

And they broke your skull with clubs,

And they bashed your stomach in?

What'd you get when the police shot you in the back,

And they chained you to the beds

While they wiped the blood off?

What'd you get when you cried out to the Top Man?

When you called to the man next to God, as you thought,

And you asked him to speak out to save you?

What'd the Top Man say, black boy?

Mr Roosevelt regrets ...

▲ **An extract from a poem written in 1943 by a black student disappointed by Roosevelt's failure to make further reforms.**

Questions

1   Look at Source G. Why was there such hatred of the Japanese-Americans inside the USA?

2   Look at Source H.
    How useful is this source in helping you to understand attitudes to black Americans during the war?

Modern World History

The war had an even greater impact than reducing unemployment. It resulted in the USA becoming the richest country in the world. Unlike other nations, in particular the Soviet Union, Germany and Britain, the USA did not suffer destruction to its cities and industries. Therefore it was not faced with an enormous task of repair when the war ended in 1945.

Also, the smooth transition from war production to peace-time working helped the USA to experience high degrees of prosperity until the late 1950s.

The war created 17 million new jobs in the USA and there was frequently overtime for those workers who wanted it. With extra wages in their pockets, Americans were able to buy more goods and so help boost demand which, in turn, created more jobs. Farmers, too, were able to enjoy prosperity for the first time in almost a generation. European agriculture was disrupted by the war and so it was easy to export American foodstuffs.

The America government spent billions of dollars on equipping its armed forces in the war and this was paid for by raising taxes and borrowing money by selling '**bonds**' to the public. Those buying the bonds were guaranteed their money back after a set period plus a guaranteed rate of interest. By the end of the war, Americans had bought war bonds totalling US$129 billion. Even children were encouraged to buy bonds, and comic-book heroes like Batman were used to advertise them.

The War Production Board was set up in January 1942 to maximise production of war materials. Within weeks it had cut the production of 300 'non-essential' products such as refrigerators, bicycles, beer cans and toothpaste tubes. It was much more important to produce tanks and aircraft.

By the end of 1942, one-third of the economy was devoted to the production of war goods, doubling the 1941 figure. By this time, US production equalled the combined total of Germany, Italy and Japan.

The war changed the role of the US government. During the New Deal, Roosevelt gained increasing power as he used government agencies to create jobs. Some Americans complained that this went against the American ideal of '**rugged individualism**' and called him a dictator. But during the war the government became even more involved in the lives of its citizens. Apart from the War Production Board and conscription, the government employed almost 4 million civilian workers in 1945 – double the number in 1941.

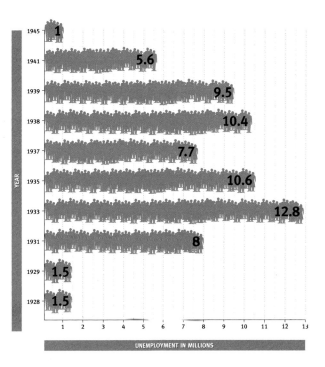

▲ **Unemployment in the United States 1928–45.**

Source I

The USA was the only great power to emerge from the war stronger economically than it went into it. Its cities and farmlands, its oil wells and mines were all undamaged. It had many new factories, built during the war to turn out weapons and equipment and these were available afterwards to make peacetime goods. Between 1939 and 1947, US industrial output trebled and the number of jobs in industry increased by 52 per cent.

▲ **A modern historian writing in 1995.**

Chapter 9 *A divided union? The USA: 1941–80*

173

Questions

1 In what ways did President Roosevelt help the development of civil rights during the Second World War?

2 Why were there race riots in the USA in 1943? (Use the sources and your own knowledge to explain your answer.)

3 Why were the Japanese-Americans treated so badly by the US government?

4 What was the impact of the war on the US economy?

Source A

▲ An American cartoon showing US fears of a communist takeover of the world.

McCarthyism and the 'Red Scare'

During the Second World War, the USA fought on the same side as the Soviet Union. Relations deteriorated towards the end of the war and after 1945 there was a 'Cold War' between the democratic USA and the communists of the Soviet Union. The Americans were convinced that the Soviets were trying to spread communism throughout the world.

After 1945, this distrust grew rapidly following the Soviet occupation of Eastern Europe, the Berlin Blockade and the development of the Soviet atomic bomb (See chapter 11). The victory of the Chinese Communist Party in 1949 and the outbreak of the Korean War in 1950 seemed to confirm to many Americans that unless it was checked, communism would take over the world. Steps had to be taken both abroad and at home.

In the 1930s the American government had set up the House Un-American Activities Committee (HUAC) to deal with groups whose views were considered unacceptable, but little had been done before war broke out in 1941. With the coming of the Cold War after 1945, however, the committee became much more active. In 1947, ten prominent Hollywood writers and directors were asked by the Committee to confirm whether they had ever been members of the Communist Party. The Committee already had documents which proved their membership, but belonging to a political party – even to the Communist Party – was not a criminal offence in the USA. So the 'Hollywood Ten' refused to answer the Committee's question. They used the American Constitution's First Amendment to avoid incriminating themselves. Despite this they were imprisoned. The **'Red Scare'** in America had begun.

The Alger Hiss case

In 1947 President Truman approved a scheme called the Federal Employee Loyalty Programme. This was designed to ensure that there were no security risks among government staff. There was a growing feeling that some government employees were not loyal to the USA and were, in fact, working for the Soviet Union. From 1947–50, FBI Loyalty Boards investigated more than three million government workers. They did not find a single case of government employees carrying out acts of espionage, but they did identify 212 people who were regarded as security risks and they were forced to resign from their jobs.

It was in this growing climate of suspicion, that the Alger Hiss case occurred. Hiss had worked for President Roosevelt and there had been allegations of espionage made against him, which proved to be unfounded. Further charges were made against him in 1948 when he was accused of being a high-ranking member of the Communist Party. During the investigation, some microfilm was found containing State Department secrets. The documents shown on the microfilm had been copied on a typewriter that was eventually traced to Hiss. Hiss was convicted of perjury in January 1950 and sentenced to five years in prison. To this day Hiss has denied any wrong doing. Later that year, the McCarran Act was passed. It stated the following things.

- It was illegal for Americans to engage in activities that might create a communist government in the USA.

- Communist organisations had to be registered with the federal government.

- Communists were not allowed to work in defence factories or to obtain US passports.

President Truman thought it was wrong to punish people because of their views:

'In a free country, we punish men for crimes they commit, but never for the opinions they hold.'

Despite his opposition, Congress passed the act. Anti-communist feeling in the USA was reaching hysterical levels.

Congress shall make no law respecting an establishment of religion, or prohibiting the free excercise thereof; or abridging the freedom of speech, or of the press; or the right of the people peaceably to assemble, and to petition the Government for a redress of grievances.

▲ The First Amendment.

Source B

▲ Alger Hiss.

Chapter 9 A divided union? The USA: 1941–80

175

McCarthyism unleashed

Directly after the Hiss case, an engineer, Julius Rosenberg and his wife, Ethel, were arrested and charged with conspiring to transmit top secret bomb specifications to the Soviet Union. They were sentenced to death and executed in 1953. Both protested their innocence and refused to make any deal that was offered to them – even though such a deal would have saved their lives.

Anti-communism in the USA found a leader in Senator Joseph McCarthy of Wisconsin who began to whip up anti-communist fears to fever pitch. On 9 February 1950, he claimed that he

Source D

▲ Senator McCarthy showing 'evidence' to the House Un-American Activities Commission.

had a list of 205 communists who were working in the State Department. However, when his claims were investigated he wavered on the exact number from 205 to 81 to 57 to 'a lot'.

McCarthy's claims were investigated by a Senate committee which found no substance in them and said they were 'a fraud and a hoax'. McCarthy then turned on the committee chairman Senator Tydings and accused him of being a communist. In the autumn elections in 1950, Tydings was defeated by a supporter of McCarthy. This made other politicians very reluctant to criticise him publicly.

Although Senator McCarthy never produced a shred of evidence, he made attacks on public figures that ruined many government officials. Nobody was safe from his accusations. McCarthy had so much public support that in the face of public opinion those people who were accused either resigned or were sacked as a security risk. Millions of Americans believed that McCarthy was a crusader, fighting the unseen enemy, making America safe for democracy.

The list of the accused grew until it included scientists, diplomats, members of the Democratic Party (McCarthy was a Republican), writers and actors. Some actors were **blacklisted** and could not secure work for many years. McCarthy claimed to have evidence in his briefcase, but never allowed anyone to see into it. His accusations, however, made terrific stories for the press and so received extensive publicity. His main weapon has been described as the 'multiple untruth'. President Truman disliked him and did not believe what he was saying, but would not stand up to him, fearing that he might appear to be unpatriotic and that he would lose votes at the next election.

In 1952 President Eisenhower of the Republicans was elected. He ordered a fresh investigation into the Civil Service. He wanted any person who was a security risk to be removed from office. Between May 1953 and October 1954, 6,924 government workers lost their jobs, although none was ever put on trial. In 1953, McCarthy became Chairman of the Senate Committee on Government Operations, but the following year he went too far. He accused 45 army officers of being communist agents. The Army-McCarthy hearings that resulted were televised and the nation saw a side of McCarthy they did not like. While being questioned, he was rude, abusive and had a bullying manner. In contrast the army's attorney, Joseph Welch, was constrained and polite in the face of McCarthy's aggressiveness. McCarthy's popularity now began to decline dramatically. In December 1954, the Senate condemned McCarthy's behaviour and **censured** him for 'improper conduct'. McCarthy died in 1957.

The McCarthy era shows how easy it was to whip up public opinion into a frenzy – simply on the basis of unsubstantiated evidence. The affair showed how fearful the USA was of communism.

Fear of communism did not die with McCarthy. The hysteria that had been created by the 'Red Scare' had led to the formation of a number of vigilante-style watchdog groups run by private citizens who were still convinced that there were 'reds under the beds'. Indeed, the government itself produced films and brochures that encouraged people to expose anyone they suspected of having communist leanings – the Communist Party was officially banned in the USA in 1954 – and as late as 1960, some American states demanded a pledge of loyalty from their employees.

Source E

I do solemnly swear that I will oppose the overthrow of the government of the USA ... I am not a member of the Communist Party.

▲ **State of Massachusetts Oath of Loyalty, 1960.**

Questions

1 Why was there a fear of communism in the USA after 1945?

2 Why did President Truman set up the Federal Employee Loyalty Programme?

3 What were the effects of the Hiss case?

4 What were the key features of McCarthyism?

5 Why did McCarthyism die out?

Chapter 9 *A divided union? The USA: 1941~80*

177

The civil rights movements and their impact on American society

Though there had been some progress for black Americans in the Second World War, their position in society after the war was clearly that of second-class citizens. In 1948, President Truman introduced a civil rights plan which included an anti-lynching bill and a ban on measures designed to stop poor people from voting. However, Truman faced opposition from his own party and many of his plans had to be dropped. So there was little progress, though the armed forces were at last desegregated and the government was told to employ a higher percentage of black Americans.

Source A

▲ An example of discrimination in the USA. Often coloured people were not allowed to use the same facilities as white Americans.

Education

The issue that aroused great passion was that of education. In the early 1950s, only sixteen states required their schools to be integrated (to teach black and white children together) and even these requirements were often ignored by individual school districts. But in 1950, the Supreme Court made two decisions (listed below) about education that gave fresh hope to black Americans in their struggle for equality.

- Black American students could not be segregated within a school attended by whites.

- When comparing the education provided for black Americans and whites it was not enough just to look at buildings or books. 'Intangible factors' such as the quality of teaching had to be considered.

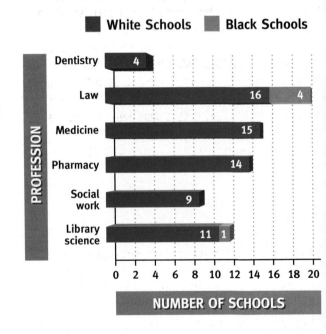

▲ Statistics showing the small number of schools where blacks could learn a profession before 1950.

▲ Elizabeth Eckford, one of the nine black students arriving at Little Rock Central High School on 5 September 1957.

These decisions encouraged the National Association for the Advancement of Coloured People (NAACP) to challenge a 1896 Supreme Court decision that segregation in education was legal as long as there was 'equal provision'. In other words, it was acceptable to have separate schools for blacks and whites so long as they had equal facilities. NAACP took the Topeka school board in Kansas to court as a test case. In 'Brown vs Topeka, Kansas', NAACP argued that it was simple logic that it was sensible to send seven-year-old Linda Brown to her nearest school (a few blocks away) rather than the all-black one several miles away. Chief Justice Earl Warren of the Supreme Court delivered the verdict of the court. On 17 May 1954 it was ruled that 'in the field of public education the doctrine of "separate but equal" has no place.' The verdict also stated that separate educational facilities really meant unequal ones and that states should set up education systems where black and white children attended the same schools. This was to be done 'with all deliberate speed'.

There was, however, enormous resistance to integration. Some states were able to introduce

Source C

The mob was jeering and spitting. It had to be the most frightening thing, because she had a large crowd of white people threatening to kill her. And she had nobody. There wasn't a black face anywhere. Then this white woman came out of the crowd and guided her on to the bus and got her home safely. Elizabeth was in tears.

▲ One of the 'Little Rock Nine' explaining how Elizabeth Eckford was refused entry to the Little Rock Central High School.

it with little difficulty, but in others students refused to attend integrated schools. In some places 'White Citizens' Councils' were formed to resist integration. The Ku Klux Klan also campaigned to prevent integration.

One of the most famous incidents occurred in September 1957 at Little Rock Central High School, Arkansas. Nine black students were scheduled to begin their studies at what had previously been an all-white school. The Governor of Arkansas, Orval Faubus, said he had heard that there would be trouble and surrounded the school with state National Guard soldiers to prevent the black students entering.

Questions

1 Why was President Truman unable to introduce a number of laws to improve civil rights for black Americans?

2 Why was education a key issue in the struggle for civil rights?

3 What were the key features of the Brown vs Topeka case?

4 What were the key features of the Little Rock case?

5 Why was Little Rock important to the development of civil rights?

Chapter 9 A divided union? The USA: 1941~80

179

After a court ruling, Faubus was forced to remove the troops and the nine black students turned up for school on 5 September. They were met by a hostile crowd of 1,000 people and the nine returned home at lunch time under police protection.

Eisenhower then sent federal troops to Little Rock to protect the nine students. They remained until the end of the month, then the state National Guard, this time under the orders of President Eisenhower, protected the black students until the end of the school year. In September 1958, Faubus closed all the schools in Little Rock to prevent **integration**. But the Supreme Court ruled this action was against the constitution, and the schools were re-opened to both black and white students. In December 1958, a nation-wide opinion poll in the USA put Faubus in the top ten of most admired men in the world.

The Montgomery bus boycott
Both the Brown case and the dispute at Little Rock had shown that progress could be made by using the law. But there were other methods, too. A bus boycott in Montgomery, Alabama showed the power that the black Americans had if they took action together. In Alabama, as in most states in the south of the USA, blacks were only allowed seats at the rear of buses and had to give up their seats if white people had nowhere to sit. In 1955, Rosa Parks took a place in the middle of the bus and refused to give it up when asked to do so by a white person. She was ejected from the bus and arrested.

Source D

There comes a time when people get tired. We are tired of being segregated and humiliated, tired of being kicked about by the brutal feet of oppression ... If you protest courageously and with dignity historians will have to pause and say there lived a great people – a black people who injected a new meaning and dignity into the veins of civilisation.

▲ **Martin Luther King explaining the purpose of non-violent opposition.**

Her arrest was just the spark that some blacks had been waiting for, and many historians see the true beginning of the civil rights movement stemming from Rosa Parks' decision not to give up her seat. The incident caused tremendous outrage in the black community. Immediately, black leaders met and planned a boycott of the bus company. Martin Luther King, a local Baptist minister, lead the protest. He was strongly influenced by the ideas of Mahatma Gandhi, who had campaigned for Indian independence from British rule.

King called on blacks to avoid violence and to show their opposition to racial discrimination by peacefully practising civil disobedience against the laws that they thought were wrong. King believed that such an approach would show people the dignity of black people and expose the brutality of the white authorities in enforcing discriminatory laws.

Questions

1 What were the key features of the Montgomery Bus Boycott?

2 What was the role of Martin Luther King in the civil rights movement?

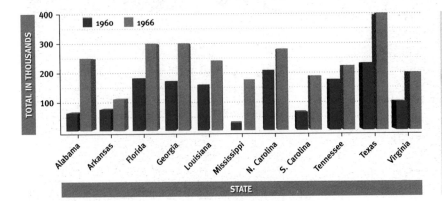

▲ **Percentage of Blacks registered to vote in the southern states of the USA.**

The black community felt so strongly about the 'bus' issue that they supported King's call to stop riding on city buses. King knew that without black people's fares the buses would lose money. For over a year the bus boycott continued and the bus company lost 65 per cent of its income. Finally, in December 1956, the Supreme Court ruled that the Montgomery bus segregation law was unconstitutional (and so, therefore, were similar laws in other cities and states). A few days later the boycott ended and Montgomery integrated its buses. Black people had won a significant victory in the battle for civil rights.

The campaign continues

In the winter of 1959–60 civil rights groups stepped up their campaigns. They organised marches, demonstrations and boycotts to end segregation in public places. They especially challenged the practice of not serving blacks at lunch counters. Where this was the case large numbers of black people would arrive and stage sit-ins. No matter how much abuse they received at the hands of white people, they tried to maintain a non-violent approach.

By 1960, the crusade for civil rights had become a national movement. Although major changes in the law were slow in coming and defenders of segregation often used violence against civil rights supporters, many Americans were becoming aware of the unfair way in which blacks were treated, particularly in the southern states.

Source E

▲ **White Americans pick on civil rights demonstrators holding a sit-in at a sandwich bar.**

Chapter 9 *A divided union? The USA: 1941–80*

181

The Kennedy years

Martin Luther King won increased support for the civil rights movement by appealing to students, and from this emerged, in April 1960, the Student Non-violent Co-ordinating Committee (SNCC). Many SNCC workers dropped out of their studies to work full time in those areas that were most resistant to integration. This was a very brave thing to do as there were very deep-rooted feelings in some communities against equal rights for blacks. There were many examples of civil rights workers being beaten up and several of them were murdered.

Though President John Kennedy endorsed sit-ins and promised to introduce a civil rights bill, there was no mention of these issues in his inaugural address as president. Obviously more pressure would have to be applied.

A group of civil rights activists working for an organisation called the Congress of Racial Equality (CORE) was determined to ensure that the Supreme Court's decision to integrate bus stations and buses was enforced. Throughout the summer of 1961, members of this group, calling themselves 'Freedom Riders', were arrested, but achieved their aim of gaining a huge amount of publicity. By the end of September 1961, the Interstate Commerce Commission (a body set up to regulate trade and business between states) announced that there would be no segregation in bus stations and terminals.

President Kennedy was keen to bring about improvements for black Americans and his brother, Robert Kennedy, the Attorney General, had meetings with the main civil rights groups – SNCC, CORE and NAACP – in the summer of 1961. Together they devised the Voter Education Project, which aimed to get more blacks to register to vote and to use that vote. As a result there was a large increase in the number of black voters, but at a cost. Some whites carried out a policy of intimidation in which black communities sometimes found their homes and churches attacked, and individual blacks were subjected to beatings, shootings and evictions.

In 1962, the city authorities at Birmingham, Alabama closed parks, playing fields, swimming pools and other public places to avoid integrating them. So in 1963, Martin Luther King organised a campaign of marches and demonstrations that would ensure maximum media coverage. He was fortunate in some ways because the local police commissioner, Eugene 'Bull' Connor, was determined to take strong action against the black campaigners. He set dogs on the demonstrators and when they refused to disperse, he also turned fire hoses on them.

Source F

The boys dared Emmett to speak to a white woman in the store. Emmett walked in confidently, bought some candy from Carolyn Bryant, the owner's wife, and as he left said, 'Bye, baby.' The store owner was so outraged that he and his half-brother took Emmett away. His body was found three days later with a bullet in his skull and his head crushed. The store owner and his half-brother were tried for murder. Local people raised money to pay for their defence and at the end of the trial the all-white jury took just one hour to find them not guilty.

▲ The story of Emmett Till, a black boy from Chicago visiting relatives in Mississippi in 1955.

Source G

I have a dream that one day this nation will rise up, live out the true meaning of its creed: 'We hold these truths to be self-evident that all men are created equal.' I have a dream that one day on the red hills of Georgia sons of former slaves and sons of former slave-owners will be able to sit down together at the table of brotherhood. I have a dream that one day the state of Mississippi, a state sweltering with the heat of injustice, will be transformed into an oasis of freedom and justice.

▲ Martin Luther King's famous 'I have a dream' speech.

▲ Marchers caught by a fire hose in Birmingham, Alabama in 1963.

These demonstrations were broadcast across the USA, and the world and many Americans were horrified at the brutality. During the campaign Martin Luther King was jailed, but the most important thing was that television viewers were able to see the outrageous treatment meted out to young demonstrators. The campaign was successful, meaning that there was an end to segregation in Birmingham. The publicity had a much wider effect, too. At the end of the campaign, President Kennedy announced that he would submit a civil rights bill to Congress.

King continued his campaign for civil rights in the summer of 1963. He organised a huge march on Washington DC. The original aim was to call for more jobs for blacks, but he decided to demand the passage of Kennedy's civil rights bill. More than 250,000 people attended the march, including over 50,000 white supporters. The gathering is best known for King's emotional speech, which begins 'I have a dream ...' (see Source G).

King was awarded the Nobel Prize for Peace in December 1964, because he had worked so hard for 'the furtherance of brotherhood among men'. Yet the fame he achieved did not prevent him from going out on the streets to campaign. A few days after the announcement of his award he found himself in jail in Selma, Alabama. He was involved in the campaign to ensure that blacks registered for the vote – and, as usual, his presence secured national coverage. His campaigning was rewarded when the new Voting Rights Act was passed in 1968 and a further a million blacks were able to vote.

Questions

1 What problems faced President John Kennedy when he tried to improve civil rights?

2 In what way had civil rights improved by 1963?

Black Power

The demands of the civil rights campaigners slowly but surely brought results, but for many black Americans the new laws were not being introduced fast enough, nor did they approve of the methods being used. They argued that non-violent civil disobedience was just trying to convince white people that black people were 'nice'. They did not want to be 'nice'; they wanted to take what they thought was theirs by right – and by force if necessary. They also did not want white and black integration. They wanted blacks to be separate because they were better than whites.

So there began to emerge a call for black separatism. This was a view promoted by such people as the Black Muslims, the best known of whom was Malcolm X. He strongly criticised Martin Luther King's methods. Instead, he advocated the use of weapons for self-defence because he felt that non-violence simply encouraged white racism. Shortly before his death in 1965, Malcolm X said:

> 'The white people should thank Dr King for holding black people in check.'

Malcolm X made an impression on the young militant blacks. In 1966, Stokely Carmichael was elected Chairman of the SNCC. Carmichael believed in **'Black Power'**. He said that blacks should take control of all aspects of their lives – social, political and economic. It meant separation from white society by violent means if necessary. One of the most militant black-power groups was the Black Panthers. Founded in 1966, the Panthers urged blacks to arm themselves and confront white society in order to force whites to grant them equal rights.

Influenced by the growing militancy and frustrated by their lack of success, blacks began to riot in many US cities. The riots in the Watts district of Los Angeles in August 1965 were particularly serious. During the six days of rioting, 34 people died, 1,072 were injured and 4,000 were arrested. Almost 1,000 buildings were destroyed and property loss totalled nearly US$40 million. There were riots across the USA throughout the summers of 1965, 1966 and 1967. During the first nine months of 1967, more than 150 US cities reported incidents of racial disorders.

Source I

Our enemy is the white man! And when you know who your enemy is he can no longer keep you divided and fighting, one brother against another.

I am for violence if non-violence means we continue postponing a solution to the American black man's problem. If we must take violence to get the black man his human rights in this country, then I am for violence.

We are the only black organisation that black people support. These so-called 'Negro progress organisations' – they insult your intelligence, claiming they are fighting on your behalf, to get you the equal rights you are asking for, claiming they are fighting the white man who refuses to give you rights.

▲ Some of the sayings of Malcolm X.

Source J

▲ The aftermath of rioting in the Watts district of Los Angeles in 1965.

President Lyndon Johnson appointed a Commission of Enquiry headed by Governor Kerner of Illinois to find out what was causing the riots. The resulting report found that the riots were brought on by a sense of frustration among black people at the way they were being treated and concluded:

'The nation is rapidly moving towards two increasingly separate Americas.'

To stop this break-up, the report recommended the elimination of all racial barriers in jobs, education, housing, greater public response to problems of racial minorities and increased communication across racial lines. But race riots did not end with the Kerner Report. In April 1968, Martin Luther King was assassinated and an outburst of rage swept through nearly 130 American cities. The black movement had already lost another leader when Malcolm X was assassinated in 1965.

The civil rights movement found it difficult to be effective without strong leadership in the years after the death of King. For many Americans the war in Vietnam, crime on the streets and drugs became the new issues on which to campaign. Nevertheless, the 1950s and 60s had been years of progress – though as Source L shows the issue of race had not gone away.

Source K

▲ A Black Panther poster from the 1960s.

Source L

Mississippi whites were responsible for at least twelve separate lynchings of blacks in 1980. On 12 October 1981, the body of Douglas McDonald was pulled from a lake in Eastover, Mississippi. The black man's ears had been hacked off.

▲ From a recent book on race relations in the USA.

Questions

1 Why do you think that Martin Luther King was awarded the Nobel Peace Prize?

2 Why did the Black Power movement emerge in the 1960s?

3 Why were there riots in many US cities after 1965?

4 What were the key features of the Kerner Report?

The New Frontier and the Great Society

In 1960, Kennedy was nominated for the presidency of the USA by his party, the Democrats. In his acceptance speech he talked of how the USA stood on the edge of a 'new frontier of unknown opportunities and paths and of unfulfilled hopes and threats'.

The 'New Frontier', as it became known, was the rather personal vision of Kennedy and it was difficult to pin down specific policies from the general things he spoke about. He said he wanted to 'get the country moving again'. He sought to create economic growth and strengthen public programmes such as housing and education. Moreover, he wanted to restore US prestige abroad.

The economy
Measures were taken to encourage investment in industry by reducing taxes for those firms that bought new equipment. Kennedy also tried to limit prices and wages to ensure that inflation did not spiral out of control. Jobs were created as a result of increased defence spending and the space programme. He tried to help the less well off by increasing the minimum wage from US$1.00 an hour to US$1.25 an hour. He also proposed a general tax cut in 1963, which he hoped would put more money in people's pockets and encourage a boom in spending – resulting, therefore, in a demand for manufactured goods. However, the tax cut was not introduced until after his death.

Social welfare
Kennedy tried to reduce poverty in both urban and rural areas by the Area Redevelopment Act of 1961. The federal government could give loans, grants and technical assistance to those states – for example, Pennsylvania, Kentucky and Tennessee – that had serious problems with long-term poverty. The Housing Act could provide money for urban renewal and also made available loans over long-term periods at low interest rates.

Kennedy wanted to tackle the social and economic problems caused by unemployment and in 1961 the Manpower Development and Training Act was passed. It concentrated on retraining jobless workers. A US$900 million public works programme was authorised to provide jobs for the retrained workers.

Source A

▲ **Kennedy speaking in the 1960s.**

Source B

This is a great country but I think it could be greater; and this is a powerful country, but I think it could be more powerful ... Economic growth means strength and vitality; it means we are able to sustain our defences and meet our commitments abroad.

▲ **An extract from a speech made by Kennedy in 1963.**

Source C

It ought to be possible for American citizens of any colour to register and to vote in a free election without interference or fear of reprisal ... in short, every American ought to have the right to be treated as he would wish to be treated. But this is not the case.

▲ President Kennedy, June 1963, speaking on television.

Source D

EXTRA

PRESIDENT SLAIN

Texas Assassin Hits Kennedy in Automobile

News Call Bulletin

SAN FRANCISCO'S EVENING NEWSPAPER

Volume 5, No. 90 — FRIDAY, NOVEMBER 22, 1963 — Phone EX 7-5700 — Price 10c

Mystery San Carlos Gun Battle

PRESIDENT JOHN F. KENNEDY

DALLAS---President John F. Kennedy is dead. He died after an assassin fired on his car leading a motorcade into Dallas, third stop on his Texas tour.

DALLAS (UPI)—President John F. Kennedy and Gov. John B. Connally of Texas were cut down by an assassin's bullets as they toured downtown Dallas in an open automobile today.

▲ The front page of a newspaper reporting Kennedy's assassination on 22 November 1963.

Civil rights

As a Democrat, Kennedy relied on the support of senators and representatives from the southern states. Many of these people were not keen to see radical changes made to improve black civil rights, as it could cost them votes. But Kennedy was committed to correcting the inequalities he saw in American society (see Source C). So the President had to tread carefully. He filled several key government posts with black Americans – for example, Carl Rowan became Ambassador to Finland, Robert Weaver became Home Finance Administrator and Thurgood Marshall was appointed to the US Circuit Court. A Committee on Equal Employment was also set up in March 1961 to try to improve job opportunities for black Americans.

Robert Kennedy, as Attorney General, also worked to end inequality. He brought 50 cases in four states where black Americans were denied the right to vote. The most famous case in John Kennedy's presidency was that of James Meredith, a black student who was prevented from taking up his studies at the University of Mississippi. President Kennedy sent in US marshals to escort Meredith to classes. There were riots and two people were killed and 70 injured. Soldiers remained at the university until Meredith was awarded his degree. President Kennedy also threatened to use federal troops to allow black students into the University of Alabama, where the Governor of Alabama, George Wallace, was trying to prevent integration.

In June 1963, President Kennedy put forward a comprehensive civil rights package that would ban discrimination in employment, guarantee equal voting rights and provide all Americans with equal access to public housing. Before this measure could be passed, Kennedy was assassinated in Dallas, Texas. However, his proposals were taken up by his Vice-President, Lyndon Johnson who took over as president.

Chapter 9 *A divided union? The USA: 1941~80*

187

1964	**Civil Rights Act** Banned discrimination in public accommodations, in federally assisted programs, and in employment; gave federal government new power to enforce desegregation and prosecute voting rights violations
	Economic Opportunity Launched the 'war on poverty,' creating nationwide federal programs such as Head Start, the Job Corps, and VISTA, within the Office of Economic Opportunity
1965	**Elementary and Secondary Education Act** First major federal aid package for education in US history
	Medical Care Act Federally funded health care for the elderly (Medicare) and for welfare recipients (Medicaid)
	Voting Rights Act Ended literacy tests for voting; allowed federal agents to monitor registration
	Immigration Act Ended discriminatory ethnic quotas
1966	**Minimum wage law** Raised the rate from $1.25 to $1.40 an hour
	Model Cities Act Funded the clearing of slums and building of new housing projects, recreational facilities and mass transit

▲ Some of the Acts and laws passed as part of President Johnson's Great Society legislation.

Source E

In the past we have often been called on to wage war against foreign enemies which threaten our freedom. And now we are asked to declare war on a domestic enemy which threatens the strength of our nation and the welfare of our people.

▲ President Johnson addressing Congress in March 1964.

The Great Society

President Johnson wanted to continue the dream of Kennedy's New frontier and went beyond it to create his own vision of a 'Great Society'. He said that his society was one where 'freedom from the wants of the body can help fulfil the needs of the spirit'.

Johnson saw poverty as the greatest evil in society and set out to end it. He also wanted to bring an end to racial discrimination in employment and education. Speaking to students at the University of Michigan in 1964, he described his dream of 'The Great Society' where there was 'abundance and liberty for all'.

President Johnson was well aware that Americans had been greatly affected by the death of John Kennedy and that his easy victory in the presidential election of 1964 was a reflection of the respect felt for the assassinated president. While he had the support of the people, and of

Congress, he pushed ahead with new laws as quickly as he could. He was an experienced enough politician to know that the '**honeymoon period**' would soon come to an end.

The Great Society did achieve some success despite the fact that President Johnson lacked money because of the cost of the Vietnam War. But Johnson had critics on all sides. Many in his own party accused him of wasting money on the war, Republicans accused him of wasting money on welfare programmes and many black Americans could not see the logic of waging the Vietnam war when poverty was still rampant in the big cities.

Finally, Johnson was worn down by the problem created in trying to win the Vietnam War. He decided not to stand for re-election in 1968. His successor, Richard Nixon, was to have even greater problems in his presidency.

Source A

▲ A mother in a traditional 'stay at home' role.

Influences to change this picture came from a variety of directions. There were women in the civil rights movement who experienced discrimination and who wanted to do something about it.

The Feminine Mystique, written in 1963, was a **milestone** in the women's rights movement. The author, Betty Friedan, wrote that women should have political, economic and social rights equal to those of men. Moreover, she ridiculed the notion that women were only suited for low-paid jobs and that achievement could only be measured by their success as wives and mothers.

Women

Though many women in the USA had retained their war-time jobs, the majority returned to the traditional roles of housewife and home-maker. Television programmes and advertising re-inforced the commonly held view that a woman's place was in the home.

During the Second World War, many women had won a taste of independence when they took up full-time employment for the first time. But after the war many women gave their jobs up to returning soldiers. The prosperity of the 1950s did lead to an increase in females attending college and securing skilled/professional jobs, but the most significant changes in attitudes to women – and women's attitudes to themselves – came in the 1960s. A major reason for this was that in 1960 the birth control pill went on sale. Many women felt that 'the pill', as it was referred to, gave them the opportunity to be sexually active without the risk of becoming pregnant. This not only changed women's attitudes towards sexual relations, but also gave them much greater opportunities to succeed in employment.

Source B

Women experience discrimination as widespread and deep-rooted and every much as crippling as the assumptions of white supremacy are to the black Americans. We need to come to understand that this is no more a man's world than it is a white world.

▲ An extract from a SNCC paper, 1964.

Questions

1 Why was President Johnson able to pass many laws aimed to end discrimination and inequality in such a short time?

2 Describe the problems President Johnson faced in trying to establish his 'Great Society'.

3 Why in the 1950s and 60s did many women begin to challenge their accepted role in society?

Chapter 9 *A divided union? The USA: 1941–80*

189

Source C

▲ Members of the Women's Liberation Group demonstrating in August 1970.

The campaign for women's equality also received a boost from the government. In 1961 President John Kennedy appointed Eleanor Roosevelt as chair of the Presidential Commission on the Status of Women. The Commission reported in 1963 and showed just how much work there was to do to bring equality. In 1960, women made up 5 per cent of the nation's managers and administrators and 12 per cent of all professions and technical workers. In the 1960s, a woman doing the same job as a man on average earned only 59 per cent as much. At the beginning of Kennedy's presidency, women made up only 35 per cent of the nation's undergraduates.

Across the USA, 32 states set up their own commissions. During the 1960s, two very important laws were passed.

1 In 1963 the Equal Pay Act required employers to pay women the same as men for the same work. However, it did not address the discrimination that women faced in securing a job in the first place.

2 In 1964 Civil Rights Act made it illegal to discriminate on grounds of gender.

Women were in an increasingly stronger position to challenge their stereotyped position in society. In 1966, the National Organisation for Women (NOW) was set up. The members felt that progress towards equality had been slow and that even the Equal Employment Opportunities Commission had not taken female issues seriously.

By the early 1970s, NOW had 40,000 members and had inspired the formation of other groups such as the National Women's Caucus and the Women's Campaign Fund. Minority women also formed their own groups – for example, the North American Indian Women's Association and the National Black Feminist Organisation.

In July 1972, *Ms.* – a feminist magazine – published its first issue, selling 300,000 copies in eight days. Women's Studies courses appeared at universities and the US armed forces relaxed some restrictions against women in 1976, by allowing them to train at the academies at Anapolis and West Point.

Many radical feminists took extreme steps, which often brought public ridicule. The 1968 Miss World Contest was caricatured when a sheep was crowned as winner in a mock competition. In what feminists called an attack on 'feminine enslavement', girdles, bras, hair curlers and false eyelashes were publicly burned. These actions won as much support as they lost. Support was lost because it is often thought in a democracy that change will come through peaceful, not violent, methods.

In 1972, the Educational Amendment Act outlawed sex discrimination in education and courses had to be rewritten to ensure that gender stereotyping did not occur in the curriculum. This was extremely important since it ensured that women were treated equally in education and that a positive image of them was given in teaching.

Only by means of **legislation** have some women secured equality. What men have by right, women now have only by law. Yet despite the the new laws, women do not compose half of Congress, or half of the key positions in business or industry. They are still issues in which women seem not to have gained an equal say – for example, abortion.

▲ **A successful 1980s career woman.**

Occupational Group	1950	1960	1970	1980
All workers	28	33	38	44
White-collar	40	43	48	55
Professional	40	38	40	46
Managerial	14	14	17	28
Clerical	62	68	74	81
Sales	34	37	39	49
Blue-collar	24	26	30	34
Crafts	3	3	5	6
Operatives	27	28	32	34
Labourers	4	4	8	11
Private household	95	96	96	97
Other services	45	52	55	61
Farm Workers	9	10	10	17

▲ **The percentage of women working in various occupations 1950–80.**

Chapter 9 *A divided union? The USA: 1941–80*

191

Source E

Even those of us who have achieved precarious success in a given field still walk as freaks in a man's world since every profession is still structured as a man's world.

▲ **Betty Friedan speaking in 1970.**

Source F

It's obvious why there's so much delinquency now – working women. They should stay at home and look after the kids. Men should go out to work; women are the homemakers.

▲ **An interview from 1959 with a US male born in 1895.**

The student movement

The 1960s was a decade of social unrest, with many groups campaigning for improved civil rights or opposing government policies. Not surprisingly, this unrest spread to America's youth and there was widespread political activity in the colleges and universities. By the mid-1960s, many students across America were heavily involved in demonstrations. The death of John Kennedy in 1963 came as a great shock to the American people. Coupled with the stories of atrocities coming from the Vietnam War, Kennedy's assassination destroyed the optimism that had existed in the USA in the early part of the decade. Many students began to see their society as corrupt. To begin with, students demanded a greater say in running their own education, but as time passed they turned their attention to protesting at what they saw as the evils in society. The Vietnam War and racial discrimination were the two main targets.

It should also be remembered that the 1960s saw the pop music explosion, and the age of the protest singer had arrived. This was epitomised by singer/songwriter Bob Dylan whose lyrics covered the theme of changing times, nuclear war, racism and the hypocrisy of waging war.

The 1960s was also a time of student unrest across the world. In 1968, student demonstrations in Paris were so serious that they almost overthrew the government of France.

One of the first student protest groups to emerge in the USA was Students for a Democratic Society (SDS). The SDS formed groups in 50 universities and its anti-Vietnam stance won it increased support after President Johnson announced bombing raids on North Vietnam in 1965.

By the end of 1965, the SDS had 10,000 members at 150 colleges and universities. These members held anti-war marches and in April 1965 some 20,000 students converged on Washington DC.

Questions

1 Why did a women's movement develop in the 1960s?

2 What were the key features of the women's movement?

3 Why has legislation been important in the development of equal rights for women?

4 Do women have equality with men in the USA?

5 Why did a student movement develop in the 1960s?

6 What were the key features of the student movement?

Source A

▲ One of the students killed at Kent State University in 1970.

Source B

Come senators, congressmen
Please heed the call,
Don't stand in the doorway
Don't block up the Hall.
For he that gets hurt
Will be he who has stalled.
There's a battle
Outside and it's ragin'
It'll soon shake your
windows
and rattle your walls
For the times
they are a changin'

▲ Some lyrics from the song
'Times they are a-changin''
written by Bob Dylan.

Demonstrations against the war continued, and between January and June 1968 almost 40,000 students at more than 100 colleges staged protests.

Most of the demonstrations were peaceful, but in some places feelings ran so high that violence erupted. One such example occurred at Kent State University, Ohio in 1970. Students were holding a peaceful protest against President Nixon's decision to bomb Cambodia as part of the Vietnam War. National Guardsmen were called to disperse the 600 students, but some students refused to go so tear gas was used against them. Still many refused to disperse and in the confusion shots were fired. Four people were killed and eleven were injured.

The nation was shocked to hear that its troops were firing on students at university.

Although the SDS declined and student protest did not bring an end to the Vietnam War, there is no doubt that it helped force a shift in government policy and make the USA's withdrawal from Vietnam much more likely.

It should be remembered that the bulk of students were of middle-class origin. They would have been expected – in previous generations – to support the government in a war. For such people to oppose the government was virtually unheard of.

Chapter 9 *A divided union? The USA: 1941~80*

193

Source C

▲ Part of the Hippy movement from the 1960s.

Flower power

One part of the youth movement in the 1960s was clearly identified with protesting against the Vietnam War. The anti-war movement was also linked to the rapidly developing pop music culture. Other young people became involved in developing what is now called 'an alternative lifestyle'.

These people were known collectively as 'hippies'. They converged on San Francisco and were clearly recognisable by their long hair, weird clothes (by normal standards) and every-day acceptance of drugs such as marijuana and LSD. They followed such groups as the Grateful Dead, Jefferson Airplane, The Doors, and Big Brother and the Holding Company. The hippies often wore flowers in their hair – as depicted in the worldwide hit song of 1967 by Scott McKenzie called 'San Francisco (Be sure to wear flowers in your hair)'. Their slogan was 'Make love, not war', which fitted in with their anti-Vietnam War stance.

The youth hippy movement culminated in two massive pop concerts – Woodstock and Altamont – at the end of the 1960s. Four people were killed by Hell's Angels (who were security guards) at Altamont.

1950	1 million
1960	4 million
1970	8 million

▲ The growth in student numbers 1950–70.

The Watergate scandal and its impact

On the night of 17 June 1972, police arrested five burglars in the offices of the Democratic National Party Committee, which were based in the Watergate building, Washington DC. Among other things, the arrested men had lock picks, rolls of film, two cameras and US$1,754 in cash. An address book was also found, containing a name (Howard Hunt), a telephone number and a note, 'W. House'. The repercussions of this discovery were to be so dramatic that just under two years later President Nixon went on television to announce that he was resigning his presidency.

▲ **The Watergate Building in central Washington DC.**

CREEP

The five men arrested in the Democratic Party headquarters were not ordinary burglars. They had been sent to the Watergate building as part of a campaign to get President Nixon re-elected. Nixon was so concerned that he might not win the presidential election in 1972 that he set up a committee to ensure he would secure a second term of office. This 'Committee to Re-elect the President' (CREEP), was organised by John Mitchell, a close adviser of Nixon, and soon US$60 million had been illegally collected for the presidential campaign. Some of this money (US$350,000) was allocated for **dirty tricks** against Nixon's opponents. CREEP had a group of workers – the plumbers – who were used to prevent damaging security leaks. A leading plumber suggested 'bugging' (using microphones to listen in to private conversations) the Democrats' offices. The idea was accepted and Mitchell gave the go-ahead.

However, two newspaper reporters, Carl Bernstein and Bob Woodward, were intrigued by the Watergate burglary and carried out their own investigations. They uncovered some facts that were very embarrassing for the White House – for example, the fact that the burglars were employed by CREEP and that CREEP had a fund controlled by the White House.

More worryingly, the reporters discovered that the break-in was one of many planned illegal activities financed by CREEP. In August 1972, President Nixon said that no one at the White House was involved in this 'bizarre incident', but at the same time, secretly authorised US$460,000 of CREEP's funds to be paid to the Watergate burglars. This was just one of the many lies that Nixon was to tell – and which were to rebound on him when the public became aware of the truth.

Questions

1 What was CREEP?

2 Why was CREEP set up?

3 Who were the 'plumbers'?

4 How was the connection between the Watergate burglars and the White House made?

Chapter 9 *A divided union? The USA: 1941~80*

195

Nixon won the presidential election and Watergate seemed to have died. It was only resurrected when the five burglars were put on trial. One of the burglars, James McCord, was frightened of a lengthy prison sentence and admitted that White House officials had lied about their involvement and pressured the burglars to 'plead guilty and remain silent'. The burglars were convicted, then the Senate held its own investigation. The Senate Committee heard evidence from a large number of officials between May and November 1973. Nixon's closest advisers – John Dean, H.R. 'Bob' Haldeman and John Ehrlichman – resigned, but Nixon still maintained that he knew nothing about the break-in.

In April 1973, Nixon went on television and told the nation that 'there can be no whitewash at the White House'. He then appointed a special prosecutor to investigate the Watergate affair. The man chosen for this was Archibald Cox.

Through the summer of 1973, there were more twists and turns to the scandal. Dean claimed that there had been a cover-up and that Nixon had directed it. Nixon denied this. Then a White House aide told the Senate Committee that in

1971 Nixon had installed a tape-recording system in the White House. All the President's conversations were taped. So it would be easy to hear exactly what Nixon had said to whom about Watergate. But when the Senate asked for Nixon to surrender the tapes, he refused and claimed **'executive privilege'**. Moreover, he insisted that the release of the tapes would endanger national security.

There followed a series of bewildering events on 20 October 1973, which became known as the Saturday Night Massacre. Nixon ordered the Attorney General to sack Cox. But the Attorney General refused, as did his deputy. Both resigned their posts, and eventually Cox was sacked. However, his replacement, Leon Jaworski was not prepared to be Nixon's 'yes' man, and he demanded to have the tapes. Some transcripts of the tapes were released but the most **incriminating** comments had been omitted.

The tapes were a shock to the nation. Nixon was shown as a man who used foul language and ethnic insults, and who was petty and vindictive. **'Expletive deleted'** became a national catch phrase because it appeared so often in the transcripts!

Source B

Meeting between President Richard Nixon, Chief of Staff H.R. Haldeman and Counsel to President, John W. Dean at the Oval Office on 15 September 1972.

Nixon: Boy, you never know when those guys get after it – they can really find it.

Dean: The resources that have been put against this whole investigation to date are really incredible. It is truly a larger investigation than was conducted against the after inquiry of the JFK assassination.

Nixon: Oh.

Dean: Good statistics supporting the finding.

Haldeman: Isn't that ridiculous – this silly thing.

Nixon: Yes (expletive deleted). Goldwater put it in context when he said '(expletive deleted) everybody bugs everybody else. You know that.'

Dean: That was priceless.

Nixon: It happens to be true. We were bugged in '68 on the plane and in '62 even running for Governor – (expletive deleted) thing you ever saw.

▲ **An extract from the Watergate transcript published in the *Los Angeles Times*, Sunday, 5 May 1974.**

Nixon continued to refuse to release the unedited tapes. So Jaworski took the case to the Supreme Court, where judgement was made that the President must release the unedited tapes. To make matters worse for Nixon, the Senate decided that his behaviour had been so unacceptable that steps should be taken to **impeach** him. This would mean being tried by Congress. At the end of July 1974, the House Judiciary Committee voted to recommend the impeachment of President Nixon on three counts. (See Source D.)

Nixon now relented and handed over unedited tapes of his conversations. They showed that he had ordered the CIA to halt the FBI investigation of the Watergate burglary. Whether he had known about the original burglary was now irrelevant. The President had tried to stop the investigation and had told the Senate and the people of the USA that he had not. Nixon had ordered a cover-up and then lied. Impeachment was now a certainty. However, to avoid being impeached, Nixon opted to resign on 7 August 1974. On 8 August, Gerald Ford was sworn in as 38th president of the USA.

Source D

1 Obstructing justice by trying to cover up the role of the White House in the Watergate burglary.

2 Violating the rights of US citizens by using the FBI, CIA and IRS (Internal Revenue Service) to harass critics of the President.

3 Defying Congressional authority by refusing to hand over the tapes.

▲ The reasons given by the House Judiciary committee to impeach President Nixon.

Source C

▲ The television broadcast of President Nixon's resignation speech.

Chapter 9 *A divided union? The USA: 1941~80*

197

Aftermath

One month later Nixon was pardoned by Congress. After Watergate, Congress introduced measures to restrict the power of the president.

- The War Powers Act, 1973, required the President to consult with Congress before sending American troops into prolonged action.

- The Congressional Budget and Impoundment Control Act, 1974. This meant that the President could not use government money for his own purposes.

- The Election Campaign Act of 1972 was strengthened in 1974, setting limits on campaign contributions to prevent corruption.

- The Freedom of Information Act was extended by passing the Privacy Act, which allowed citizens to have access to any files that the government may have gathered on them.

Watergate had threatened the foundations of US democracy. Some 31 Nixon advisers went to prison for Watergate-related offences. Yet despite the attempts by Congress to restrict the powers of the President, many of the people of America felt they could no longer trust their most senior politician.

The Americans had experienced two traumatic decades of change. Watergate came at a time when defeat in Vietnam was still fresh in the nation's mind, and events in the Middle East were showing that the USA was not necessarily the superpower it was believed to be. Israel was for once not completely victorious in the 1973 Yom Kippur War despite a vast amount of aid from the USA. When the Arab states decided to stop the supply of oil to the USA, its economy soon went into depression.

The confidence of the US in 1945 had evaporated in just over one generation.

Source E

▲ Front cover of a newspaper reporting Nixon's resignation after the Watergate affair.

Questions

1 What did President Nixon mean when he said: 'There can be no whitewash at the White House'?

2 Why were the tapes so important to the Watergate affair?

3 What is meant by impeachment?

4 What were the results of Watergate?

Overview

'Although the USA had become an extremely rich country by 1980, it was still a divided society.' How far do you agree with this statement?

The rise and fall of the communist state. The Soviet Union: 1928~91

Introduction

By 1928 Joseph Stalin had out manoeuvred his rivals and had emerged as Lenin's successor. During the next ten years he gradually extended his influence over all aspects of the lives of the peoples of the Soviet Union; industry, agriculture, entertainment, the arts and even people's personal lives came under his control.

Stalin's position in the Soviet Union was only seriously threatened when Nazi Germany invaded in June 1941. In desperation he appealed to the patriotism of the Soviet peoples to stand firm and resist the invader. But when victory was won in 1945 it was Stalin who claimed the credit. Such was Stalin's power that when he died in 1953 his legacy of fear and suspicion lived on in the Soviet Union.

Nikita Khrushchev was unable to reform the Soviet economy and when he fell from power in 1964, his successor Leonid Brezhnev refused to make any further attempts at change. It was only in the 1980s that serious attempts to unpick Stalin's system of central control were made.

But it was too late. By then the Soviet Union was bankrupt and Mikhail Gorbachev's desperate attempts to save communism and the Soviet Union failed.

This chapter looks at the development of communism in the Soviet Union, the effect of communist rule on the Soviet people and the downfall of the communist state in 1991.

In May 1924, Lenin's 'Political testament', which named Leon Trotsky as his successor, was handed by his widow to the Bolshevik Central Committee. After it had been read, Joseph Stalin left the room and burst into tears. Lenin had suggested that Stalin should be dismissed from his post as General Secretary of the Communist Party, as Source A shows. It seemed that the enormous power base, which he had begun to build for himself inside the Party, was about to be wiped out in a single blow. He was saved, not because the other Bolshevik leaders had any great liking for him, but because they were afraid of Leon Trotsky taking Lenin's place. In that fateful moment, millions of lives, including those of the Bolshevik leaders themselves, were thrown into the balance.

Many of Stalin's actions in the Soviet Union over the next fifteen years were aimed at destroying the evidence that showed that Lenin had wanted him to be dismissed, and also destroying the people who knew the truth about the relationship between Lenin and Stalin.

In the years from 1924 to 1928, Joseph Stalin removed almost all of the Old Bolsheviks from positions of power inside the Soviet Union and the Communist Party. Lenin's former colleagues were isolated within the Party, then forced to resign. When they tried to resist, they found that Stalin, in his position of General Secretary, had filled the Party with his own loyal supporters. This pattern was repeated throughout Stalin's reign. Senior figures were dismissed, tried or executed without warning and replaced by younger men who owed their promotion to Stalin. He demanded complete loyalty to himself and complete acceptance of his decisions in every respect. This involved total control over all aspects of life in the Soviet Union. Stalin's main way of achieving this was through terror inflicted by the NKVD, his secret police force.

Stalin's basic policy was Socialism in One Country – the belief that if communism was to survive, it must be made absolutely secure inside the Soviet Union. By 1928 he was ready to put that policy into practice.

Changes in industry and agriculture

In 1928 Joseph Stalin launched a revolution, the beginning of the First Five-Year Plan. He wanted to reorganise and modernise Soviet industry and agriculture so that it could compete with the West.

The Five-Year Plans
From 1928 Stalin set about creating a command economy, where each factory and works was set targets by **Gosplan**, which was based in Moscow. Specially trained workers in Shock Brigades showed how new ideas could be put into practice. These included introducing the ideas of Frederick Taylor, who had been the basis of

Source A

Comrade Stalin, having become General Secretary, has too much power in his hands, and I am not sure that he always knows how to use it with sufficient caution. Therefore, I propose to the comrades to remove Stalin from the position and appoint another man who will in all respects differ from Stalin. He should be more patient, more polite and more attentive to his comrades.

▲ Part of Lenin's political testament, May 1924.

Source B

We are 50 or 100 years behind the advanced countries. We must catch up this distance in ten years. Either we do it or we go under.

▲ Stalin explaining the purpose of the Five-Year Plans.

Henry Ford's mass-production methods in the USA. The most famous of all workers was the coal miner Alexei Stakhanov, who dug 102 tonnes of coal in a single shift, instead of the normal seven tonnes. However, Stakhanov was given the most modern power tools, a perfect coal seam to work in, and a gang of workers to back him up and clear away all of the coal. Nevertheless, his record was soon broken by a rival who managed to dig 311 tonnes.

Stakhanovites were backed up by volunteers from Komsomol, the youth wing of the Communist Party. Around 250,000 volunteers went to work in industrial plants every summer. There were also massive propaganda campaigns using posters and paintings of Stalin meeting happy but determined workers.

Although the existing industries around Moscow and Leningrad were developed, the real effort went into vast new engineering plants in the Urals and Western Siberia. The most well known were the new industrial city of Magnitogorsk and the tractor plant at Chelyabinsk. The Dnieper Dam supplied electrical power for expansion in the Ukraine.

In Magnitogorsk there were more than 50,000 workers, about one-third of whom were kulaks who had been forced from their homes. They worked in teams around the clock living in appalling conditions in tents and sharing bunks. It was desperately cold in the winter. Ruts froze solid on every road and then became transformed into a quagmire in the summer when the temperature rose dramatically.

Source C

▲ **Stakhanovite miners in the 1930s.**

The whole emphasis during the first Five-Year Plan, which began in October 1928, was on heavy industry. Stalin ordered that production was to double in five years in the key industries of iron and steel, engineering and electrical power. It is true that production in engineering, electrical power, tractors, iron and steel, chemicals, coal and oil all developed dramatically, or so the official figures suggested. In practice, however, many of the figures were faked and the emphasis was on quantity not quality.

Chapter 10 *The rise and fall of the communist state. The Soviet Union: 1928~91*

201

The second Five-Year Plan began in 1933. At first it included more emphasis on consumer goods. But from 1934 Stalin ordered big increases in military expenditure as the threat from Nazi Germany grew. Despite that, the targets set for the second Five-Year Plan were much more realistic.

This table compares the Soviet figures for meeting targets in the first two Five-Year Plans with estimates compiled by Western economists.

A third Five-Year Plan was begun in 1938, but was cut short by the German invasion of the Soviet Union in June 1941.

Industrial production	First 5-Year Plan	Second 5-Year Plan
Official Soviet figures	100.7	103.0
Western estimates	65.3	75.7

Why did Stalin introduce the Five-Year Plans?

On the face of it Stalin believed that Soviet industry and agriculture was 100 years behind the West and it needed to catch up as quickly as possible. This was because Stalin distrusted the West. He knew that Britain, France and the USA had all intervened in the Russian Civil War, and from 1934 he began to suspect that they were supporting Hitler against him.

Stalin also wanted to destroy the New Economic Policy (NEP), which Lenin had introduced as a temporary measure in 1921 after the devastation of the First World War and the Russian Civil War. This had allowed small businesses with up to 25 workers to develop and had also made it possible both to pay taxes and to make profits, rather than hand over produce to the state. The main result of NEP had been the creation of the

Source A

НЕ ПОСТУПИМОСЬ У ЛЕНІНОВІЙ СПРАВІ

▲ A soviet poster urging support for the first Five-Year Plan

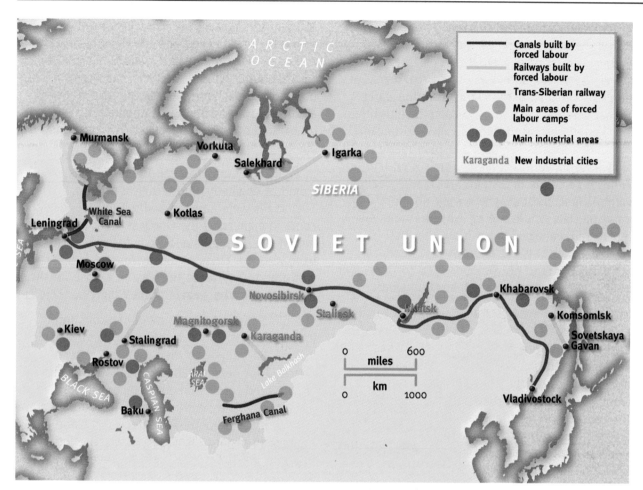

▲ The growth of the Soviet Union as an economic power.

kulaks, richer peasants who owned their own farms and employed labourers. The term kulak, meant 'tight-fisted', and this was how they were viewed by some people in the Soviet Union. Stalin hated the kulaks and wanted to destroy them. He thought that they were parasites. He also realised that they were a class that owed him no allegiance; they were, therefore, beyond his control.

The Five-Year Plans were also an attempt by Stalin to increase his control over the Soviet peoples. By exaggerating the threats to the Soviet Union from the West, they gave him the opportunity to enforce regulations, which would have been unacceptable in other circumstances. By 1934 the Soviet people had lost many basic rights, including the freedom to change jobs and move around the country.

Questions

1 Explain the meanings of the following terms: Five-Year Plan, Targets, Gosplan, Stakhanovite.

2 Why did Stalin decide to begin the Five-Year Plans in 1928? Look for some economic reasons, some political reasons and explain why he chose the date 1928.

Chapter 10 *The rise and fall of the communist state. The Soviet Union: 1928–91*

203

What went wrong with the Five-Year Plans?

At first Stalin's plans were greeted with enthusiasm by most Soviet citizens. The targets set were realistic and there was a real sense of purpose, but this mood changed in the early 1930s, when many people became disillusioned. The targets increased dramatically and became completely unattainable, as Gosplan made no allowance for local conditions and often had no knowledge of the industries that it was dealing with. At first, most planners were no more than party officials who came up with the numbers that Stalin wanted. To cap it all, the first Five-Year Plan was cut short by one year – it actually only ran from October 1928 to December 1932 – yet the targets remained the same.

No criticism of the Plans was accepted. Failure to meet targets usually led to accusations of sabotage, disgrace and prison or even death. Engineers and technical experts were often arrested because the machinery that they were responsible for had broken down. More often, the real reason for the arrests was that these workers knew that the demands of the Five-Year Plans were impossible. Gosplan wanted people who were prepared to attempt the impossible, so less experienced and more poorly trained engineers were preferable.

Pig iron	3.2
Steel	4.0
Coal	35.0

▲ Production figures for Soviet Union in 1928, in millions of tonnes.

	Pig iron	Steel	Coal
Soviet Union	14.8	18.4	164.6
USA	31.9	47.2	359.0
UK	6.7	10.3	227.0
Germany	18.3	22.7	186.0

▲ Comparative production figures for the Soviet Union in 1940, in millions of tonnes.

Many of the new industrial workers were peasants, who flocked into the cities to find work and earn the higher wages available in industry. They were poorly educated and had no experience of handling machinery, which often broke down, as they did not know how to operate it. This led to a disastrous fall in agricultural production.

The large number of breakdowns in machinery led to accusations of wrecking. These were usually aimed at engineers and technical experts. Thousands were arrested and put in trial, including some foreigners. In the Donbass area, more than half of the engineers and skilled workers had been arrested by 1931, mostly for wrecking. Stalin was able to use these trials as an excuse for the failure to met the targets of the Plan.

The difficulties of transforming peasants into industrial workers led to strict regulations being introduced from 1931. Prison sentences were imposed for defying labour discipline. Workbooks were issued to all workers to record their productivity. The death penalty was introduced for theft of state property. Absenteeism for one day resulted in instant dismissal. Finally, the internal passport was introduced, which prevented free movement about the Soviet Union.

As mentioned earlier, the emphasis was on quantity not quality. Stalin saw tractors as the key to increased agricultural production. But of the 170,000 tractors planned in the first Five-Year Plan, only 50,000 were built and 50 per cent of these broke down.

Despite all this, the Plans did increase industrial production by about 400 per cent during the 1930s.

Questions

1 Draw up two columns headed 'Successes of the Five-Year Plans' and 'Failures of the Five-Year Plans'. List as many examples of successes and failures as you can.

2 Why is it difficult to decide whether the Five-Year Plans did actually succeed or fail?

Collectivisation

Collectivisation was part of the first Five-Year Plan. It was an attempt to get rid of the ownership of land by ordinary people and move peasants to large collective farms where machinery and skilled labour could be used more effectively.

There were two types of collective farms.

- **Sovkhozy**, or state farms, where all the land was owned by the state, all the produce went to the state and workers were paid wages. The wages were paid whether the workers worked well or badly. These farms proved very expensive and few were set up.

- **Kolkhozy**, or collective farms, where workers kept plots of land for themselves and had to supply fixed amounts of food to the state at fixed prices. The workers kept what was left for themselves. If there was nothing left, then they starved.

Additionally, machine tractor stations were to be set up to provide the mechanisation in which Stalin placed so much faith.

At first Stalin tried to persuade peasants to join collective farms, but food shortages in 1928, when rationing was introduced, and again in 1929, led him to order the seizure of food to feed industrial workers. Seizures were resisted by peasants – especially by the kulaks who had taken advantage of NEP. In December 1929, Stalin went even further – see Source C.

Communist Party officials began to use the term **'dekulakisation'** to describe the attacks throughout the Soviet Union that began in early 1930. The populations of whole villages were rounded up and sent by train to the labour camps of the north. The secret police who carried out the operations called them 'white coal'. Resistance resulted in death. Villagers who tried to defend their property were shot on the spot.

How many kulaks died is uncertain; for one thing no one actually knew exactly what the term meant, although it was loosely defined as a peasant who made a profit. Stalin estimated that there must be 5,000,000–6,000,000 kulaks

▲ **A Soviet poster encouraging women to work.**

in the Soviet Union, but he later claimed that as many as 10,000,000 suffered at the hands of the NKVD. The kulaks reacted by destroying their livestock and property, rather than hand them over to the collective farms. By the summer of 1930, 14,000,000 cows and one-third of the pigs in the Soviet Union had been destroyed. The result was the worst famine in Russian history.

Russia had always suffered from large-scale famines. The last major one before the Revolution, in 1891–92, had killed 430,000 people. The famine of 1919–20, brought on by Lenin's War Communism, had cost the lives of 5,000,000 people, but Stalin was to beat those figures comfortably. Some 5,000,000 died in the Ukraine alone, and as much as a quarter of the population of Kazakhstan. Altogether, 20,000,000 people may have died during the famine of 1932–33.

Did collectivisation work?

It seems strange that a policy that killed perhaps 20,000,000 might have worked, but in Stalin's eyes it certainly did. He achieved what he set out to do, which was to destroy the kulaks. This gave him complete control over the peasants who made up more than half of the population of the Soviet Union. Stalin believed that dekulakisation would also give him the opportunity to rebuild and modernise agriculture in the Soviet Union and to end the repeated shortages of food that Russia had faced for centuries.

Despite the opposition of the kulaks and the appalling suffering of the Soviet people, collectivisation went ahead remorselessly. By 1932, 62 per cent of farms were collectivised and by 1940, a total of 400,000 farms had been set up. By 1937, when collectivisation was almost complete, wheat production was up by a third on the 1928 figure. But these figures do not tell the

	Cattle	Pigs	Sheep
1928	70.5	26.0	146.7
1933	38.4	12.1	50.2

▲ **Numbers of animals in Soviet union (in millions).**

whole story. The Soviet Union never solved its problems of food shortages. Forcing peasants to join collective farms did not work in the long run; there was no incentive to increase productivity when produce had to be given to the state at a fixed price. No matter how hard Stalin exalted the peasants, they worked far harder on the plots of land that they were allowed to keep for themselves, than they did for the collective. In 1937, 52 per cent of the Soviet Union's vegetables were produced on these plots of land and 71 per cent of its meat and milk. The problems of feeding the ever-growing Soviet population were to continue until the 1990s.

On 7 November 1932, at the height of the famine and the terrible persecution of the kulaks, Stalin's wife left an official banquet celebrating the fifteenth anniversary of the Revolution and killed herself with a gun, which had been smuggled into the Soviet Union by her brother. Some historians believe that Stalin never recovered from the shock and that this was a factor in his decision to begin the purges in 1934.

Questions

1 Explain the meanings of the following terms: collectivisation, kolkhozy, kulak.

2 In 1928 Stalin tried to persuade peasants to join collective farms. Use the text to design a leaflet encouraging peasants to move.

3 Why did many peasants refuse to move to collective farms in 1929 and 1930?

Source C

We must smash the kulaks, eliminate them as a class. We must strike at the kulaks so hard that they will never rise to their feet again.

▲ **Part of a speech by Stalin attacking the Kulaks.**

Source A

▲ A socialist realist painting called 'Higher and Higher', urging the Soviet people to achieve more.

How did life change for the peoples of the Soviet Union in the 1930s?

On the face of it, the results were impressive. Industrial production rose by about 400 per cent in the 1930s. Education and housing improved, the numbers of doctors increased and medical treatment improved. Industrial workers were given higher pay and rewarded with medals. Some social security benefits were provided.

For the first time in the Soviet Union, women achieved some form of equality. The Bolsheviks had declared equality for women in 1917, but it was only in theory. The modernisation programme needed all the workers it could get; it was like a war. Factories were provided with nurseries so that women could go to work after giving birth. Facilities were provided for mothers to express their breast milk, so that their babies could be bottle-fed in a crèche while they worked. Women began to attend university and many of the new doctors trained in the Soviet Union were women. Some 80 per cent of new workers in the second Five-Year Plan were women; in 1927, 28 per cent of industrial workers were women; and by 1937 it was 40 per cent.

However, the encouragement of women to work was not merely a means of achieving equality; there was a much more sinister reason behind it. Most of the Soviet citizens who disappeared during the purges were men; women were vital if the Five-Year Plans were to succeed. The situation became even worse after the outbreak of war with Germany, with the vast number of Soviet dead and prisoners. By the 1950s, women outnumbered men three to two in European Russia.

But there was another side to Stalin's regime. As more people crowded into the cities to work in industry, living standards fell. Flats, which had been intended for one family, housed two families, then one family to a room, and sanitation was very basic. This led to violence, crime and increasing alcoholism. Pay did not keep up with rises in prices. The NKVD were more and more in evidence as a means of keeping order. At the same time the higher ranks of the Communist Party began to enjoy special privileges, such as foreign foods, luxury goods, private estates and holidays at exclusive resorts on the Black Sea.

Chapter 10 *The rise and fall of the communist state. The Soviet Union: 1928–91*

207

▲ A workers' canteen in Moscow showing the poor, overcrowded conditions in which some people live.

After 1932 Stalin claimed that unemployment no longer existed in the Soviet Union, but many of the jobs were of little value and there was no incentive, except fear, to work harder. The command economy created a way of life in which the Soviet people came to expect to be told what to do. Stalin's regime destroyed individuality and initiative. When later leaders, like Nikita Khrushchev, tried to recreate these qualities, they found that Stalin had done his work only too well.

Questions

1 Look through this section in the textbook for the ways in which life changed for the people of the Soviet Union during the 1930s. On a poster on a double page, list the changes and say whether life improved or got worse.

2 Use the evidence you have collected for Question 1 to write a report on Stalin rule in the 1930s. Did he change the Soviet Union for the better or the worse?

▲ Stalin with his closest associates in 1934. Back row left to right: Abel Yenukidze (executed in 1938), Klementi Voroshilov (survived Stalin), Lazar Kaganovich (survived Stalin), Valorian Kuibishev (murdered in 1935). Front row: Sergei Ordzhonikidze (died 1936), Stalin, Vyacheslav Molotov (survived Stalin), Sergei Kirov (murdered 1934).

The nature of Stalin's dictatorship

In 1932 and 1933 opposition to Stalin's economic policies grew. Stalin's second wife committed suicide in November 1932 in protest at the appalling costs to people's lives. The following year, 800,000 party members were expelled and in 1934 at the XVIIth Party Congress Stalin almost lost his position as General Secretary of the Party. These were signs of real opposition to Stalin.

The purges

In 1934 the XVIIth Party Congress was known as the Congress of Victors, but this proved to be very inaccurate. It marked the beginning of the purges, which lasted until 1938 and led to the deaths of many millions of Soviet citizens. The most important event at the Congress was the election of Sergei Kirov as secretary. Kirov was the party leader in Leningrad and a popular figure in the country.

In December 1934, Kirov was murdered and his apparent murderer died soon afterwards. Suspicion fell on Stalin, who used the event as an excuse to eliminate anyone whom he suspected of disloyalty. Of the 1,966 delegates to the Congress,

Source B

My defective Bolshevism became transformed into anti-Bolshevism, and through Trotskyism I arrived at Fascism. Trotskyism is a variety of Fascism and Zinovievism is a variety of Trotskyism.

▲ Grigory Zinoviev's confession at his trial. He was accused of taking part in Kirov's murder.

Chapter 10 *The rise and fall of the communist state. The Soviet Union: 1928–91*

209

1,108 were executed. Of the 139 members of the Central Committee who were elected at the congress, 98 were shot in the following years. In Leningrad, more than 30,000 citizens were arrested and sent to labour camps. The death penalty was extended so that it could be used on boys as young as twelve years of age.

From 1934 anyone who was suspect in Stalin's eyes was purged. At best this would mean ten or more years in a labour camp; at worst it meant being arrested, tortured and shot by the NKVD.

Who were the victims of the purges?

Stalin distrusted anyone who he regarded as an 'expert' – all those, therefore, who appeared to know more than he did and who put forward ideas different to those of his own. Among his main victims were the following groups of people.

- Poets, writers, artists and musicians – in fact, anyone creative who might have ideas that Stalin did not approve of. The composer Sergei Prokofiev and the poet Osip Mandelstam were both attacked. Mandelstam was imprisoned and Prokofiev fled to the West, although he did return to the Soviet Union to write the sort of music that Stalin liked.

- Managers of industry or collective farms, who did not meet their targets for production. This policy had begun during the first Five-Year Plan.

- Scientists, engineers, experts of any kind who Stalin did not trust or understand. Only loyal party officials who accepted Stalin's decisions without question, were safe.

- Army and Navy officers; all eight Admirals of the Soviet fleet, three of the five Marshals of the Red Army, 90 per cent of the Generals and more than half of the officers of the Red Army – 35,000 in all – were executed in 1937–38.

Source C

▲ A Soviet sketch of Lenin and Stalin at work in the offices of *Pravda* (Truth), the Bolshevik newspaper.

What effects did the purges have?

The Red Army lost almost all its experienced officers. In 1941 it stood no chance against the German army. Science and technology suffered as new inventions were stopped. Industry suffered because managers were unwilling to try anything new. Literature, art and music were all stifled. In art, Stalin only approved of socialist realism – painting that glorified the working people of the Soviet Union, showing them working harder and harder as in Source A on page 207. In music, Stalin liked loud brash pieces which portrayed events in Soviet history. By eliminating older figures, Stalin was able to promote younger men who owed their success to him. This made them completely loyal. Examples of these younger men include Lavrenti Beria, who became the head of the NKVD in 1938, and Georgi Malenkov, who was expected to be Stalin's successor.

The show trials

Stalin also used the purges as an opportunity to rid himself of the Old Bolsheviks who knew the truth about Lenin's political testament and Stalin's relationship with Lenin. In August 1936, Kamenev and Zinoviev were given show trials; these were repeated over the next two years to include all of Lenin's former colleagues. The pattern always remained the same. The defendants were accused of ridiculous crimes – arson, destruction of railways, poisoning of workers, conspiracy with the Whites during the Civil War from 1918 to 1920 – which they could not possibly have committed, and in each case they were linked with Trotsky.

The results of the show trials were always the same. The defendants confessed and were found guilty. They were often threatened that if they did not confess their families would also be arrested. Some had recordings of a woman weeping in the next room played to them and were told that it was their wife. The verdicts were broadcast to the world by Radio Moscow and the 'guilty' men were shot.

Not so public were the fates of millions of ordinary Soviet citizens, who were victims of the 'knock on the door', when the NKVD arrived in the small hours. In 1937–38 alone 681,692 people were shot by the secret police and many more found themselves in slave labour camps called **Gulags**. These camps were often in Siberia or in Northern Russia, where the weather during the winter was extremely cold. Here the victims worked with little food for ten years or more. Many died from exhaustion. Others were taken by rail to Vladivostok on the Pacific coast and then by ship to Kolyma in north-eastern Siberia. Here they were left to freeze to death. Their bodies have only recently been discovered.

The work of the NKVD was helped by thousands of accusations by neighbours who wanted their next-door flat, or by people who had been passed over for promotion or who just had a score to settle. As a result, millions of Soviet citizens disappeared without trace and without ever knowing why they had been arrested.

Questions

1 Explain the meaning of the following terms: purges, show trials, socialist realism, NKVD.

2 Why were so many of the delegates to the XVIIth Party Congress eliminated?

3 Why did Stalin purge the following groups of people: poets and musicians, the Red Army, scientists?

4 What effects did the purges have on the Soviet Union?

Chapter 10 *The rise and fall of the communist state. The Soviet Union: 1928–91*

211

The revision of history

To Stalin, simply removing his opponents was not enough; he wanted to obliterate them and any details of their lives and achievements in the triumph of communism in the Soviet Union. He had always wanted to rewrite the history of the Soviet Union since 1917, eliminating the part played by Trotsky and the other Old Bolsheviks and exaggerating his own contribution.

Stalin wanted to destroy the reputations of the other Bolshevik leaders. This could explain why he had put them on trial and had them executed. He picked on Trotsky in particular, because Lenin had chosen Trotsky as his successor. Stalin accused Trotsky of treason and said that he had done nothing to help the Soviet Union, claiming that he himself had been responsible for the successes in the Civil War from 1918 to 1920.

So in the 1930s Stalin began to rewrite the history of Russia and the Soviet Union in the twentieth century, making out that he was much more important than he really had been before he came to power. Existing textbooks and encyclopaedias were destroyed or altered. Children in school had to paste over pages in their books with the new versions of what had happened. References to the victims of the show trials were rewritten, and paintings and pictures were produced that showed Lenin and Stalin close together. Photographs were edited to remove the faces of people who had been purged. Drawings were produced showing the young Stalin in positions of importance and surrounded by his closest supporters from the 1930s.

At the same time Stalin began to refer to the Party as the Lenin–Stalin Party, rather than the Communist Party and introduced the term Leninism; he claimed that only he knew the real meaning of the word. He was also responsible for the building of Lenin's Mausoleum in Red Square in Moscow and the permanent display of Lenin's body. All of these actions were intended to create the impression that Joseph Stalin was the one and only true heir to Lenin.

The cult of personality

For Joseph Stalin, being obeyed was not enough; he expected love and worship, not just respect and obedience. Stalin made sure that everyone knew about his successes. Huge rallies were held in his honour. Many photographs were published showing him receiving gifts from children, or being applauded by workers or meeting ordinary people.

But such photographs were outnumbered many times by the paintings produced by Soviet artists showing Stalin meeting smiling people, opening factories and dams, and always looking rather taller and fitter than he actually was. In fact, Stalin hardly ever met ordinary Soviet citizens and rarely left the Kremlin. These paintings were part of his attempt to make people believe that he was a superman, a genius at everything. He was described as the 'wisest man of the twentieth century', the 'genius of the age'. The Soviet people were told that he was never wrong. This protected Stalin from any further challenges.

The high point of the cult of personality was after the Second World War, from 1945 to 1953, when Stalin began to plan further purges. He could then claim to have saved the Soviet Union from the attacks of Hitler and to be protecting it from the evils of the West.

Source D

Thank you Stalin. Thank you because I am joyful. Thank you because I am well. No matter how old I become, I shall never forget how we received Stalin two days ago. Centuries will pass, and the generations still to come will regard us as the happiest of mortals, as the most fortunate of men, because we lived in the century of centuries, because we were privileged to see Stalin our inspired leader.'

▲ **An extract from a speech made in Stalin's honour in 1936.**

▲ A photomontage of Stalin and the children of the Soviet Union.

In the midst of all the mayhem created by the purges, Stalin introduced a new constitution in 1936. He described it as the 'most democratic in the world' and at first sight it was. It guaranteed freedom of the press, freedom of speech, freedom of assembly and freedom of religious observance. It also made clear, however, that the needs of the Party came before everything else and that the NKVD was subject to the control of the Party. So the constitution did not amount to very much. It was merely another example of what Stalin wanted people to believe, rather than what actually happened.

Questions

1   What methods did Stalin use to create an image for himself in the Soviet Union? Use the sources and the text.

2   Choose one source from pages 209 to 213 and explain in detail how Stalin used it to deceive the Soviet people.

3   Why was Stalin able to rewrite history so successfully in the 1930s?

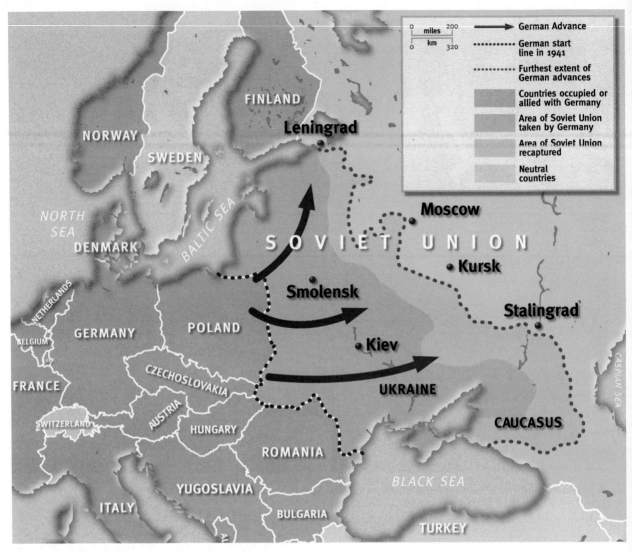

▲ Invasion of Soviet Union by Germany in 1941.

The impact of the Second World War on Soviet society

On 22 June 1941, Germany invaded the Soviet Union. The German generals were well aware of the numerical superiority of the Red Army and so Operation Barbarossa was an attempt to defeat it as quickly as possible. At first the successes of the German armed forces were spectacular. The Red Army was taken completely by surprise as Stalin had refused to believe a series of reports warning him of the German attack.

Consequently on 22 June a Soviet border unit was heard radioing to Moscow: 'We are being fired on. What shall we do?' The reply from Moscow was: 'You must be insane. And why is your signal not in code?'

For eight days after the invasion Stalin was in a state of shock. He did not return to public life until 3 July 1941 when he appealed to the peoples of the Soviet Union to defend their motherland. He did not mention communism or himself, and he referred to twelve different peoples of the Soviet Union specifically by name. Source B demonstrates the language he used.

He realised that he needed to call on the patriotism of the Russian people and their natural

▲ **A German soldier using a flame-thrower in an attack on a Soviet village.**

distrust of the West. At the anniversary parade of the Revolution in November 1941, Stalin reminded the peoples of the Soviet Union of the repeated invasions of Russia from the West throughout its history. The war itself became known as the Great Patriotic War – a name behind which all Russians and other peoples could unite.

Stalin's appeals might easily have failed. There were many peoples in the Soviet Union who had no love for Stalin or for Russia. In the Ukraine the Germans were greeted with gifts of bread and salt, which were signs of welcome. Many Ukrainians had been shipped off to Soviet labour camps in the past and they saw the Germans as liberators. Around 20,000

Source B

Comrades, citizens, brothers and sisters, men of our Army and Navy. It is to you I am speaking dear friends.

▲ **Stalin appealing to the people of the Soviet Union to defend their country.**

Source C

The Führer has decided to raze the city of Petersburg from the face of the earth. It is proposed to blockade the city and by means of artillery fire and ceaseless bombardment from the air to raze it to the ground. If this creates a situation in the city, which produces calls for surrender, they will be ignored.

▲ **An announcement made by the German forces besieging Leningrad in 1941.**

Tartars in the Crimea volunteered to join defence battalions and hunt for members of the Red Army.

Fortunately for Stalin, Hitler regarded Ukrainians, Tartars and others as *Untermenschen*, sub-humans. Many were killed and millions more were sent to labour camps in the West. Hitler made a similar mistake with Soviet prisoners of war. Of the 5,700,000 captured, 3,400,000 died in German hands. It soon became obvious that Hitler was a worse prospect even than Stalin.

As the Germans advanced in 1941, Stalin ordered a **scorched earth policy**. European Russia was devastated and as the Germans neared Moscow and Leningrad, people, livestock, equipment and even whole factories were moved to the East. By November 1941, 1,500 factories had been dismantled and moved, along with 10,000,000 people. The movement to the East and the conquests of the Germans cut industrial production by a third and agricultural production by two-thirds. As most horses had been sent to the army, workers – mostly women – had to plough the fields by hand. For four years all Soviet citizens went hungry.

Source D

One day an actor just fell dead on stage. We shuffled in front of him to hide him, and someone just pulled him into the wings. You had to keep on going.

▲ **A theatre producer describing the situation in Leningrad in 1941.**

Chapter 10 *The rise and fall of the communist state. The Soviet Union: 1928–91*

215

Leningrad: a case study

In September 1941 the German army reached Leningrad. Hitler regarded the city, which he referred to as St Petersburg, its old name, as the birthplace of communism and was determined to destroy it.

Leningrad was bombarded for nine hours a day for almost 900 days.

Leningrad suffered more than most places in the Soviet Union. By autumn 1941, all of the food had run out and cats and dogs were being hunted throughout the city. By January and February people were dying of starvation in the streets and the survivors were too weak to clear the dead bodies away. Sudden death became common.

A road was constructed across the frozen surface of Lake Ladoga, and some lorries managed to get through with food, but German aircraft attacked them constantly. For nearly 900 days the people of Leningrad were almost completely cut off from the outside world and 630,000 of them died, one-sixth of the population.

The writer of Source E, Tanya Savicheva, died in 1943 of dysentery. The disease was a result of her sufferings during the siege. She was the last survivor of her family.

How did the war affect the Soviet Union?

The overall impact of the four years of war is almost impossible to assess. In parts of European Russia one in four of the population was killed and tens of millions of people were made homeless. Some 1,710 towns and 70,000 villages were destroyed. The total cost in lives was about 28,000,000 people, or one-seventh of the pre-war population. Of these, 9,000,000 were soldiers and 19,000,000 were civilians.

The war also completed the work that Stalin had begun in the 1930s. Whole ethnic groups, which Stalin distrusted, were transported to Siberia – about 3,300,000 people in all. Membership of the Communist Party rose: 8,600,000 new members joined during the war,

Source E

Z – Zhenya died on 28 December 28, 12.30 in the morning, 1941.

B – Babushka died on 25 January 25, 3 o'clock, 1942.

L – Leka died on 17 March 17, 5 o'clock in the morning, 1942.

D – Dedya Vasya died on 13 April, 2 o'clock at night, 1942.

D – Dedya Lesha died on 10 May, 4 o'clock in the afternoon.

M – Mama died on 13 May, 7.30 am, 1942.

S – Savichevs died. All died. Only Tanya remains.

▲ Pages from a schoolgirl's notebook describe what happened to the Savicheva family.

most of them in the armed forces. As the tide turned in 1943, Stalin could claim to be the saviour of the Soviet Union and was able to demand even greater devotion and loyalty. He emerged from the war a far stronger figure than he had been before.

Stalin was also more convinced than ever of the need to be on guard against the nations of the West. His demands for a second front, which had begun as early as 1941, had only been heeded in the summer of 1944. He was confirmed in his belief, despite the enormous amounts of aid sent to him by Britain and the USA, that the West had wanted Nazism and Communism to destroy each other. So when he met the leaders of the other Allies at Tehran in 1943 and Yalta and Potsdam in 1945, he wanted to make sure that this could never happen again. He wanted a buffer zone between the Soviet Union and Germany. It was this that led to the creation of the Iron Curtain and the Cold War.

Stalin after the war

From 1945 to 1953 Stalin was at the peak of his power. Over and over again *Pravda* used the word 'Stalinist' to describe correct behaviour in the Soviet Union. **Dissent** and opposition were crushed more ruthlessly than ever before. The leading figure in these new purges was Andrei Zhdanov, who attacked artists, poets, musicians and scientists. He also began a systematic attack on Jews in the Soviet Union.

Rumours of further purges spread in the early 1950s. It appeared that nobody was safe, even Georgi Malenkov, who seemed to have been groomed to be Stalin's successor. In November 1952 the state press published details of the 'Doctors' Plot'. This was an entirely imaginary attempt by Jewish doctors to murder Stalin. It was yet another example of Stalin's distrust of almost everyone. Eventually, even Lavrenti Beria began to suspect that he was about to be purged.

Joseph Stalin suffered a brain haemorrhage on 2 March 1953. His personal doctor, Professor Vinogradov, was not on hand to treat him because he had been arrested the previous year for suggesting that Stalin should take things easy. Since then he had been subjected to repeated beatings on Stalin's orders. Lavrenti Beria, the head of the NKVD, and the only man who could call a doctor to Stalin, was sent for. He was found in a government villa with a woman and arrived at 3 a.m., plainly drunk.

Stalin died at 9.30 a.m. on 5 March 1953.

Source A

▲ Stalin lying in State in the hall of Trade Union House, Moscow.

Source B

A man goes to Stalin on his invitation as a friend. And when he sits with Stalin he does not know where he will be sent next, home or to jail.

▲ Nicolai Bulganin, the Soviet prime minister from 1955 to 1958 reportedly speaking to Nikita Khrushchev about Stalin.

Questions

Look back through this section for evidence of the following.

1 The effects of the war upon the Soviet Union and its peoples.

2 How the war strengthened Stalin's position in the Soviet Union.

3 Why the war changed Stalin's policy towards the West.

De-Stalinisation

What effects did Stalin's death have on the Soviet Union?

Stalin's successor was expected to be Georgi Malenkov; when Stalin died he became prime minister and Party secretary, but he was subsequently persuaded to give up one post and chose to be prime minister. The new Party secretary was Nikita Khrushchev. The most feared man in Russia was Lavrenti Beria. He was hated by all the other leaders, and was arrested and shot in December 1953. Copies of the *Great Soviet Encyclopaedia* were changed by having an entry on the Bering Sea substituted for the entry on Beria.

From 1953 the Soviet Union was governed by a committee, including Malenkov, Molotov, Khrushchev and Bulganin. By 1956 it was clear that Khrushchev was the man in power.

Why did Khrushchev emerge as the new leader?

The post of Party Secretary gave Khrushchev control of the Party machinery, which was essential. (Stalin had used exactly the same methods in the 1920s.) He was also able to isolate the other leaders by supporting one side and then the other, just as Stalin had. Khrushchev's part in the defence of Stalingrad during the war had won him the support of the army, especially Marshal Zhukov. He also promised reforms, especially improvements in the standard of living, and he appeared to offer something new as he was lively and outward-going. He was a completely different character to Stalin.

De-stalinisation

In February 1956, Khrushchev attacked Stalin in the Secret Speech, made at the Twentieth Part Congress and this denunciation was a key factor in his bid for power. His main criticisms were levelled at Stalin's Cult of Personality, which Khrushchev claimed had led him to abuse his power. He said that Stalin had been a dictator and an enemy of the people. The speech horrified the other leaders Malenkov, Molotov, Bulganin and Kaganovich, who had not been told of it in advance. It led to immediate attacks on Khrushchev in the Presidium, the Cabinet of the Soviet Union.

Why did Khrushchev make the Secret Speech?

The simple reason was that Khrushchev wanted to end the suspicion and fear that had marked Stalin's rule. He planned economic reforms, which would require initiative and imagination. These would not be possible under that shadow of Stalin.

The speech also gave him an advantage over his rivals in the Communist Party. If they continued to defend Stalin they would appear to be defending his methods. Additionally, it allowed Khrushchev to get himself off the hook. He had, after all, been a key figure in Stalin's regime and had carried out purges in the Ukraine. By spilling the beans on Stalin he made it appear that he had not been involved.

How did de-Stalinisation change the Soviet Union?

Stalin's reputation was affected immediately. In due course his body was removed from the Lenin Mausoleum in Red Square, where it had been placed after his death and Stalingrad was renamed Volgograd. Other places and streets were also renamed.

The size and power of the secret police were reduced, and the death penalty was abolished. Millions of political prisoners were released and

Source A

Stalin invented the idea of an 'enemy of the people'. He used this to carry out the most cruel actions against anybody who he suspected. The facts show that many abuses were carried out on Stalin's orders. He paid no attention to either the rules of the Communist Party or the laws of the Soviet Union. Stalin's behaviour not only affected life in the Soviet Union, but also our relations with foreign countries.

▲ **An excerpt from the Secret Speech.**

▲ **A scene from the film Dr Zhivago, adapted from Boris Pasternak's novel.**

the stories they told of the labour camps reinforced Khrushchev's statement. Many Communist Party members who had been expelled under Stalin were now reinstated and national minorities, who had been transported or condemned by Stalin, were allowed to return.

Controls on poets, writers, artists and musicians were lessened, but Khrushchev was only relaxing the system, he did not intend to change it. Freedom of expression was acceptable as long as the target was Stalin. Khrushchev did not approve of criticism of the Soviet system, or of himself. When Boris Pasternak's novel, Dr Zhivago, was awarded the Nobel prize for literature in 1958, he was attacked by the Soviet press. Pasternak was forced to refuse the prize and publicly apologised for his book.

Abroad, Khrushchev's actions were misunderstood. In Poland and Hungary there was unrest and Soviet forces were forced to intervene.

The outburst of criticism which destalinisation encouraged led to a clamp down in 1960 and 1961. The death penalty was reintroduced and 10,000 churches were closed down. Khrushchev had not realised that allowing partial freedom would only lead to demands for more.

In 1957 Malenkov, Molotov, Bulganin and Kaganovich had attempted to remove Khrushchev from power. They tried to force a vote in the Presidium, where they had a majority. Khrushchev, however, was able to refer the matter to the Central Committee of the Communist Party and won the day. All of his opponents were dismissed, except for Bulganin, who was prime minister.

Lazar Kaganovich telephoned Khrushchev with an appeal: 'Comrade Khrushchev, I have known you for many years. I beg you not to allow them to deal with me as they dealt with people under Stalin.'

Chapter 10 *The rise and fall of the communist state. The Soviet Union: 1928–91*

219

Khrushchev replied: 'You will be given a job. You will be able to work and live in peace if you work honestly like all Soviet people.'

Kaganovich became director of an industrial plant in the Urals. This, more than anything else, symbolised de-Stalinisation.

Khrushchev's attempts at modernisation

Why did Khrushchev want to change the Soviet Union?

In 1954, in a famous statement, Khrushchev asked the following question: 'What sort of communism is it that cannot produce sausage?' He realised that the Soviet Union had to produce more food and more consumer goods, so he set himself the task of modernising agriculture and industry in the Soviet Union. Khrushchev understood that the creation of Stalin's command economy had taken away local independence and initiative. He wanted to reduce central control and allow local leaders to decide agricultural and industrial policy. To allow this to happen he abolished all government ministries except those dealing with defence.

Agriculture

Khrushchev believed that he was an expert on agriculture and introduced three main policies to improve agriculture in the Soviet Union. The first policy was the Virgin Lands scheme, which involved ploughing up large areas of Kazakhstan, Western Siberia and the Urals. Around 13,000,000 hectares of land would be ploughed to produce 20,000,000 tonnes of grain. Hundreds of thousands of Komsomol members were summoned to Moscow and asked to volunteer to go to the new areas to begin the process of growing food on the steppes. Khrushchev claimed that the Virgin Lands scheme would solve the problem of food supply within two to three years.

A second policy was the amalgamation of collective farms. Between 1953 and 1958 the numbers fell from 90,000 to 70,000 and then fell even further. The debts of the collective farms were written off and the prices paid by the state were increased. The machine tractor stations were closed and their equipment was handed over to the collective farms. Khrushchev believed that this would make them more them independent and therefore more efficient. Finally, Khrushchev also personally backed the introduction of maize as animal fodder and persuaded many collective farms to grow it. He hoped that this would release grain for human consumption.

Industry

In industry Khrushchev followed a similar policy to agriculture. He set up more than 100 **sovnarkhozy**, or regional economic councils. These controlled areas of the country and were encouraged to be independent and take decisions – for example, they could decide what goods to produce. Many of the controls on workers were relaxed. A seven-hour working day was introduced and workers were allowed to change their jobs.

Year	Amount
1954	86 million tonnes
1955	104 million tonnes
1958	135 million tonnes
1961	133 million tonnes
1963	109 million tonnes

▲ **Grain harvests in the Soviet Union, 1954–63.**

Questions

1 Why did Khrushchev become the leader of the Soviet Union in the years after the death of Stalin?

2 Draw up two lists, one headed 'Stalin', one headed 'Khrushchev'. Write down the differences between the two leaders.

3 In what ways did de-stalinisation change the Soviet Union?

▲ **A map showing the location of Kazakhstan and the Virgin Lands.**

What went wrong with agriculture?

Although Khrushchev claimed that he was handing over decision-making to local people, in practice, because he believed that he was an expert, he rarely listened to advice. He continually interfered in decisions at all levels.

Too little research had gone into the Virgin Lands scheme. Not enough investment had been put into fertiliser. Maize was planted in areas of the Soviet Union where the climate was unsuitable. Much of the crop failed. By 1960 the Virgin Lands scheme had failed. In 1963 hurricanes lashed Kazakhstan and tore away the topsoil from the Virgin Lands. Some 6,000,000 hectares were destroyed forever. Not enough attention had been given to the problems of transporting crops. Kazakhstan was too remote and the railway network was inefficient. Even where there was a successful crop it often rotted by the roadside before it could reach the cities.

What went wrong with industry?

The sovnarkhozy did not work because managers did not believe that they had any real authority. Everyone was used to being told what to do, as they had been under Stalin. Khrushchev tried to group the councils into regions, but this made things even worse. The muddle just got bigger and bigger. Eventually, no one knew what they were supposed to do.

Why did Khrushchev's reforms fail?

At the heart of the matter was the fact that Khrushchev was caught between two stools. He realised that Stalin had stifled initiative and understood that greater incentives were needed to persuade workers to produce more, but he was not prepared to allow real independence from the control of the Communist Party. Most chairmen of collective farms were Communist Party officials, who knew little about agriculture. Regional Councils could decide what they were going to produce, but were not allowed to use the profit motive as an incentive to increase productivity.

From 1956 Khrushchev began to pour money into space research. This was part of his plan to compete with the USA. It was also an attempt to weaken the power of the military in the Soviet Union by replacing the manpower of the Red Army with missiles. Production of consumer goods suffered. Khrushchev's spending on foreign aid and sport also meant that there was less money available for consumer goods. By 1962, food prices were increased and Khrushchev found himself facing a crisis at home.

On 1 June 1962 there were strikes and demonstrations against increases in the price of meat in the city of Novacherkassk. One slogan carried by workers said: 'Turn Khrushchev into sausage meat.' The following day tanks and armed troops stopped a march heading for the local Party headquarters and shooting began. As a result, many people and children were killed.

The basic problem was that none of Khrushchev's promises were actually kept. There was some improvement in living standards, but there were still shortages of food and everything else.

Why was Khrushchev forced to resign in October 1964?

Almost all of Khrushchev's polices in the Soviet Union had failed. He had tried to make up for this by successes abroad, but this had not always happened. In particular, Cuba was seen as a failure. Khrushchev appeared to have given in to Kennedy when he agreed to remove the missiles from Cuba. The significance of Kennedy's agreement to leave Cuba alone was not appreciated. The removal of US missiles from Turkey and Italy was not made public at the time and only took place three months later so that Khrushchev was unable to claim the credit for that.

Other Party leaders were also embarrassed by his personal behaviour – for example, when he took off his shoe at the United Nations. He was often rude to other leaders and rarely listened to advice. Inside the Kremlin he could be very uncouth. Servants described how he would sweep food off his plate into his mouth with his hands.

Eventually all this failure became too much. In October 1964 he was sacked.

Khrushchev was not put on trial. Instead he was allowed to retire to the suburbs of Moscow and write his memoirs, which were published in the West. In his will he asked a sculptor, whose work he had ridiculed while he was in power, to design his monument. The sculptor agreed.

The decline and fall of the Communist state

What effects did Khrushchev's fall have on the Soviet Union?

The Communist Party leaders had been frightened by Khrushchev's attempts at reform. They believed that he had gone too far in criticising Stalin and in giving power to the regional councils. They saw the chaos and confusion that Khrushchev had created and decided not to take such risks ever again.

Khrushchev's successor, Leonid Brezhnev, began to reverse the process of reform that Khrushchev had started. He gave up any idea of change and for the next eighteen years until Brezhnev died (in 1982) the Soviet Union stagnated. One Soviet historian has stated that Brezhnev suffered a stroke in 1976, which left him clinically dead and an invalid for the next six years.

In 1965 Brezhnev ordered a crackdown on dissidents. Thousands of writers and other intellectuals were arrested and some were put on trial. When this failed, Brezhnev appointed Yuri Andropov as the new head of the KGB (Committee of State Security), which is the

Source A

Hare-brained scheming, hasty conclusions, rash decisions and actions based on wishful thinking, boasting and empty words, bureaucratism, the refusal to take into account the achievements of science and practical experience.

▲ **An extract from *Pravda* describing Khrushchev.**

Questions

1   What were the key features of Khrushchev's reforms in agriculture?

2   In what ways did Khrushchev try to change industry in the Soviet Union?

3   Why did Khrushchev's reforms fail?

4   *Pravda* described Khrushchev as 'hare-brained', 'hasty' and 'rash'. Was this a fair assessment of the policies that he tried to put into practice in the years from 1957 to 1964?

Source A

▲ Leonid Brezhnev.

Source B

Lack of skilled labour, alcoholism, absenteeism and lack of effort on the part of civil servants who manned the vast organisation which tried to plan the economy.

▲ Reasons for the failure of the tenth Five-Year plan.

By 1985, **Izvestia** believed that there was a black market in the Soviet Union worth 7,000,000,000 roubles. In fact, the real figure was probably much higher. The Soviet economy just could not produce what the citizens of the Soviet Union wanted. They had televisions, clothes, cheap flats, cheap public transport and other public services, but consumer goods and food were very scarce and queuing could take a whole day. A car cost the equivalent of seven years' wages, and even then repairs might be impossible. So the Soviet people turned to the black market.

Source C

▲ Yuri Andropov.

secret police force. He began to lock dissidents away in mental hospitals in an effort to break their spirit. Andropov began to attack corruption throughout the Soviet Union. Many Communist Party officials took bribes or acquired Party property. Andropov attempted to track down the guilty and put an end to their crimes.

The most significant problem that Andropov faced was that members of Brezhnev's own family were heavily involved. Brezhnev's daughter, her lover and his sons were all involved. Andropov was unable to do anything about them until Brezhnev died and Andropov himself took over. This meant that for eighteen years the Soviet Union drifted, increasingly out of control. At the Twenty-Sixth Party Congress in 1981, Brezhnev listed the reasons for the lack of success of the tenth Five-Year Plan. (See Source B.)

The basic problem was that the Soviet Union was a fourth-rate economy, trying to be a superpower. Since the 1950s, vast amounts of money had been spent trying to compete with the USA. The space race and nuclear arms had absorbed limitless amounts of cash. The countries of eastern Europe had been supported financially as had other communist regimes around the world, such as Cuba. Worst of all, the Soviet Union became involved in the Afghanistan War in 1979. The cost in terms of cash, equipment and lives was immense and turned many ordinary Soviet citizens against the government.

To pay for its foreign policy, the Soviet Union needed to make money abroad. Unfortunately, the Soviet Union had few saleable exports. Cars and other manufactured goods produced behind the Iron Curtain were regarded as a joke in the West. Only raw materials and grain could be sold as exports, but the Soviet Union did not have enough grain for its own consumption and it lacked the technology to exploit its vast reserves of raw materials.

Leonid Brezhnev made no attempt to change the Soviet Union. His successor, Yuri Andropov, wanted to crack down on corruption, but fell ill with kidney disease soon after taking over; he died in February 1984. His illness was hidden from the people of the Soviet Union for as long as possible. Andropov was succeeded by Konstantin Chernenko, a 72-year-old, who was already seriously ill and who died thirteen months later in March 1985. For nearly twenty years nothing of importance had happened inside the Soviet Union. The next leader was quite different.

Mikhail Gorbachev

All three previous leaders had grown up and began their careers under Stalin. Their immediate reaction to problems was to reinforce Party discipline. Gorbachev realised that these methods could no longer work. The question he had to face, however, was, was it too late?

What did Mikhail Gorbachev try to achieve?
Gorbachev came to power with two slogans 'Perestroika' and 'Glasnost'.

Perestroika referred to 'economic restructuring' in the Soviet Union. Gorbachev believed that the Soviet Union could only survive if the economy was rebuilt, doing away with the command economy that had existed since Stalin. However, he had no clear plan of what was needed and was not aware of the scale of the task that faced him. He soon found out, for example, that 24,000 of the 46,000 state enterprises were running at a loss, that the 'black' economy was probably 30 per cent of the total output of Soviet industry and that 10 per cent of workers regularly arrived for work drunk.

Glasnost referred to new sense of 'openness', both within the Soviet Union and also with the West.

Gorbachev realised that the Soviet Union's survival depended on the West. He needed investment and new technology, but most of all he needed arms agreements, which would allow him to reduce the Soviet Union's massive defence spending and balance the budget. In the 1980s,

Gorbachev's policies
Perestroika referred to 'economic restructuring' in the Soviet Union. Gorbachev wanted to break down the state monopolies, which controlled most industries, and introduce some forms of competition. He hoped that this would get the Soviet economy 'going again' and encourage enterprise. He realised that for too long industry had been stifled by control and direction from the centre. Prices would also no longer be subsidised by the state.

Glasnost led to censorship of the press being relaxed and western ideas and music began to flood into the Soviet union, including the first 'McDonalds' in Moscow. The Orthodox Church emerged from the restrictions imposed on it and real religious freedom was allowed for the first time for many years. The powers of the KGB were restricted and it was then abolished. Its records were made public. The Lubianka Prison was closed. Free elections were held in 1990. Gorbachev himself was often seen in the streets of Moscow meeting Soviet citizens and arguing about the changes.

the Soviet Union was running a 35,000,000,000 rouble annual budget deficit.

Although Gorbachev wanted to reform the existing system within the Soviet Union, he remained a communist and was committed to the preservation of the Soviet Union. He only banned the Communist Party after the hard-liners led a coup against him in August 1991.

Why did Gorbachev's attempts at reform fail?

It was too little too late. Gorbachev wanted to alter the system, not change it. By the late 1980s shortages were so severe that this would not work. The problems he faced had been building up since the death of Stalin. The only serious attempt to solve them by Khrushchev had failed. Gorbachev realised that action needed to be taken very quickly, so he tried to introduce reforms without allowing any time for changes to take place. The result was chaos.

Gorbachev banked on getting help from the West, especially financial support from the G7 countries, which included the USA, Britain, West Germany, Japan and France. He believed that if he made concessions on arms, they would provide cash. He was wrong. The West was not prepared to help Gorbachev out of a hole. It also wanted to take advantage of his difficulties and push him further. The West wanted to see an end to the threat from the Warsaw Pact in Europe.

As Gorbachev tried to maintain the power of the Communist Party in the Soviet Union, more and more people were tired of communism, of drab lives with little food. When the countries of eastern Europe threw off communism in 1989, because they wanted to run their own affairs for the first time in 40 years, Soviet citizens in the republics wanted to do the same. In 1989 Gorbachev was compelled to withdraw Soviet troops from the Baltic republics of Latvia, Lithuania and Estonia and allow them to become independent.

The policy of Glasnost backfired on Gorbachev. He believed that allowing greater freedom would encourage the Soviet people to accept communism and work together. Instead, just like Khrushchev, 30 years earlier, he discovered that allowing some freedom only encouraged people to ask for more. As he walked around the streets of Moscow, he did not find the friendly welcome he had expected. He got abuse, criticism and further demands. Russia and the Soviet Union had never known democracy. The people were not used to being involved in the process of government; they were accustomed to being told what to do. They could not get used to the ideas of responsible argument and criticism overnight.

Glasnost and Perestroika revealed one of the fundamental weaknesses of the Soviet Union; it was made up of many different peoples, cultures and nationalities. It was held together by the Red Army. Once the top was unscrewed, they all wanted to get out. In particular, they wanted to put an end to domination by Russians from Moscow, which had lasted since the October Revolution. Only strict discipline applied from Moscow had kept the Soviet Union together. When Gorbachev loosened it, the Soviet Union simply disappeared.

Source A

▲ Mikhail Gorbachev.

Questions

1 Explain the meaning of the following terms: Glasnost, Perestroika.

In August 1991 Gorbachev was arrested by Communist Party hardliners while he was in the Crimea. Tanks rolled onto the streets of Moscow and it seemed that all of the reforms were about to be swept away. For three days the world held its breath as the Cold War appeared to be returning.

Gorbachev was saved by the people of Moscow led by Boris Yeltsin, the Chairman of the Russian Federation. He appeared outside the White House, the home of the Russian Parliament, and dared the military to attack him. In fact, the will of the army was already being undermined by many ordinary Russians, who surrounded the tanks and urged the soldiers to go away. After three days they left, driving out of the city in long columns. There was no fighting and very little bloodshed.

It soon became clear that the real power in the Soviet Union now lay with Boris Yeltsin and not with Mikhail Gorbachev. When Gorbachev tried to make a speech after his rescue, he was interrupted by Yeltsin, who made it clear that he had brought about Gorbachev's release. It was the signal that Gorbachev had failed in his attempt to save the Soviet Union. The processes of Perestroika and Glasnost had only served to undermine the structure that Gorbachev had tried to protect. Criticism and restructuring had brought about the break-up of a state that was only held together by force.

Just as the countries of eastern Europe had broken away from the communist bloc, so the fourteen republics of the Soviet Union now began to assert their independence. By the Olympic games of 1992, the Soviet Union had ceased to exist and in its place was a team representing the Commonwealth of Independent States. The break-up of the Soviet Union was not achieved without bloodshed. Two republics, Armenia and Azerbaijan, fought over the disputed territory of Nagorno-Karabakh and civil war broke out in Georgia.

The process went even further. The Russian Confederation was made up of more than 50 autonomous regions and republics, and many of these took the opportunity to try to break away from the control of Moscow. From being one of the most controlled and disciplined of countries, the former Soviet Union became highly volatile and lawless. The collapse of the Soviet Union was complete.

Source B

▲ Yeltsin outside the Russian parliament during the attempt to overthrow Gorbachev in August 1991.

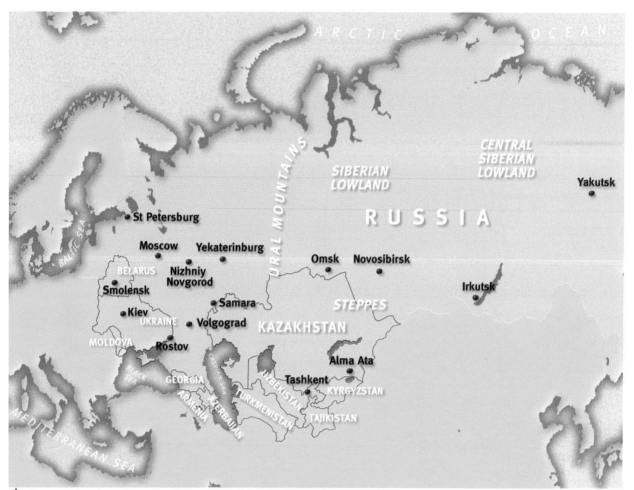

▲ A map showing the new Commonwealth of Independent States.

Source C

▲ Boris Yeltsin.

Questions

1 Why did Glasnost and Perestroika not have the results that Gorbachev expected?

2 Were the problems that developed under Brezhnev and Gorbachev the fault of the leaders themselves or the fault of the Soviet system? Draw up two lists for each of the leaders.

Overview

How far did the Soviet people benefit from communist rule in the period 1928~91?

Why did the communist state last for so long in the Soviet Union?

Chapter 10 *The rise and fall of the communist state. The Soviet Union: 1928~91*

227

CHAPTER 11

Superpower relations. 1945~90

Introduction

The dropping of the atomic bomb on Hiroshima on 6 August 1945 opened a new and potentially dreadful chapter in the history of the world. The lesson was not lost on Joseph Stalin, the Soviet dictator, who had long suspected that the West wanted to destroy the Soviet Union. He ordered the construction of the Iron Curtain and a barrier of buffer states to protect the Soviet Union from the West.

The breakdown of the wartime alliances led to a rivalry between the superpowers, in which each tried to outdo the other in military might and worldwide influence. This was the Cold War. The possible consequences of rivalry were brought home during the Cuban Missile Crisis in October 1962. Only at the last moment did the leaders of the superpowers pull back from the brink and turn to détente.

From 1963 the superpowers drew closer together, until Leonid Brezhnev ordered the Soviet army into Afghanistan on Christmas Day 1979. Suddenly the Cold War hotted up again. Looking back, however, it was no more than a final flourish. The Soviet Union was almost bankrupt and the West was able to extract arms reduction agreements from Mikhail Gorbachev after he became leader in 1985.

The Afghan War destroyed the morale of the Soviet army and with it the communist bloc and the Soviet Union. In 1989 the Cold War was over.

The origins of the Cold War and the partition of Germany

For four years, from 1941 to 1945, Britain, the USA and the Soviet Union worked together in the Grand Alliance. But within months of the end of the war, relations between the Allies had become so poor that they were almost unable to co-operate in any way. The Cold War, as it became known, began almost as soon as the Second World War ended.

What was the Cold War?
The Cold War was a war in which the two superpowers – the USA and the Soviet Union – never came to blows, at least directly. Both tried to impose their ideologies – capitalism and communism – on other nations and gain superiority by the use of propaganda, spying and the building up of vast stores of weapons.

The Cold War began in Europe, as the superpowers tried to sort out the devastation caused by the Nazis. But once the threat of Nazi domination was removed, the choice, or lack of it, between capitalism and communism became more and more important. From Europe, the Cold War spread worldwide, as more and more countries gained their independence from European empires in the 1950s and 1960s. Both superpowers attempted to draw newly independent countries into their own sphere of influence.

Since the break up of the Soviet Union and the collapse of the Soviet bloc in eastern Europe, it has become clear that the Cold War was partly caused by a joint misunderstanding of the aims and motives of East and West. Joseph Stalin and US President Harry Truman in particular made little effort to reach agreement.

Stalin still clung to his policy of 'Socialism in one country', his belief that the Soviet Union had to be as secure as possible. He believed that the West wanted to see the destruction of the Soviet Union. Truman believed that the West had been too soft with the Soviet Union at the end of the war and was determined to put that right. He was heavily influenced by the writings of George Kennan, who worked for George C. Marshall, Truman's Secretary of State. Kennan believed that the Soviet Union was determined to undermine the democracies of the Western world.

So what led the two sides to have such profound fears of each other? Why did the war-time alliance break down so quickly and so completely?

First of all, relations between the Soviet Union and the West had been bad since the Revolution in 1917 (Russia had not been allowed to join the

Source A

Superpowers

- 1945: US atomic bomb.

- 1949: Soviet atomic bomb.

- 1949: the USA began the development of the hydrogen bomb, or H-Bomb.

- 1952: US hydrogen bomb.

- 1953: Soviet H-bomb.

- Mid-1950s: nuclear weapons developed by the USA; began to be tested in the 1950s and became available in the early 1960s.

- 1957: the Soviet Union tested the first Intercontinental Ballistic Missile (ICBM). The USA responded by building its own ICBMs.

- Early 1960s: nuclear weapons available.

- 1966: Soviet Union developed Anti-Ballistic Missiles (ABMs); that could shoot down ICBMs. These were almost immediately followed by Multiple Independently-Targeted Re-entry Vehicles (MIRVs). These carried more than one warhead so they could hit more than one target and were, therefore, very difficult to shoot down.

- 1968: USA began to develop ABMs and MIRVs.

- 1982: USA deploys Cruise and Pershing missiles in Europe. Soviet Union deploys SS-20s.

- 1983: USA announces Star Wars.

▲ **The Arms Race from the 1940s to the 1980s.**

League of Nations in 1920) and had got worse in the 1930s. Some historians believe that the Cold War began before 1939 and that the Second World War was simply an interlude when Stalin had to work with the West. There was also no actual 'alliance' as such between the allies. Although they met on a number of occasions, the leaders of the Big Three never signed any formal treaty to fight the Axis.

▲ **The Big Three: Churchill of Britain, Roosevelt of the USA and Stalin of the Soviet Union at Yalta in 1945.**

What was the Soviet view?

In 1945, Stalin was determined to build a buffer zone against further German attacks. Germany had invaded Russia twice during the twentieth century, in 1914 and 1941. In the Second World War the Soviet people suffered terribly and 28,000,000 had died. Stalin was determined that this should never happen again.

Stalin did not trust the West. He remembered that the Western Allies had intervened in the Russian Civil War in 1918–19 and he suspected that they had encouraged Hitler in the 1930s. Britain and France had not taken up an offer of an alliance with the Soviet Union in 1938.

The Allies had ignored all of Stalin's appeals for a Second Front in 1942 and 1943, and had delayed invading France until 1944. This made Stalin very suspicious. He believed that they had wanted the Soviet Union to destroy itself fighting Germany on its own.

What was the Allies' view?

The Allies had spent nearly six years fighting against Hitler; they did not want to see another dictator take his place. Winston Churchill had urged Roosevelt to 'shake hands with the Russians as far east as possible'.

Churchill believed that the Allied armies should advance as far east in Europe as possible and liberate as many countries as they could from Nazi control. He was afraid that the Red Army would not leave the countries of eastern Europe that it liberated from the Nazis.

Churchill based his fears on the Soviet treatment of Poland. In 1944 the Red Army had not helped the Poles during the Warsaw uprising, and the Soviet Union seemed only too pleased to have a weakened Poland to deal with. When Poland was occupied, Stalin set up a pro-communist government – the Lublin Poles – and ignored the Polish government, which had fled to London at the outbreak of war. Churchill was also suspicious because Stalin had never declared war on Japan until the very last moment.

Source C

One hell of a people who to a remarkable degree look like Americans, dress like Americans and think like Americans.

▲ **A description of the Soviet people from the American magazine *Life* in 1943. By 1943 the Soviet Union and the USA were firm allies in the war. Previously many American people despised the Soviet Union because of its communist government.**

Why did rivalry develop between the superpowers after the Second World War?

The Yalta Conference

In February 1945 Roosevelt, Churchill and Stalin met at Yalta in the southern Soviet Union to plan the end of the Second World War. In the West, Allied forces were about to cross the Rhine and invade Germany, in the East the Red Army was poised to invade eastern Germany and Hungary; it was obvious that the German armed forces would not be able to hold much longer. The Allies needed to decide how the final onslaught on Germany was to be organised and what needed to be done with Germany after the final surrender.

The Allies were determined to avoid a repetition of the situation that had occurred after the First World War, when the Nazi Party had been allowed to develop and build up resentment of the Treaty of Versailles. This time, they wanted to occupy Germany and keep the country under firm control. The question was: how was Germany to be divided? Eventually the Allies decided that each would take responsibility for the areas in which their armed forces were fighting when the German armed forces finally surrendered.

This decision created one problem. Berlin, the capital of Germany, would be in the Soviet zone. Stalin agreed that Berlin would be occupied jointly by all four Allies.

- They agreed to divide Germany into four zones; each one would be occupied by one of the four Allies.

- Stalin agreed to accept France as one of the powers and the USA agreed to give France part of its zone.

- Berlin would also be divided into four sectors.

- The boundaries of Poland would be altered. Poland would be given land in the West, which would be taken from Germany, and would lose land to the Soviet Union.

Source A

We really believed in our hearts that this was the dawn of a new day. We were absolutely certain that we had won the first great victory of the peace. The Russians had proved that they could be reasonable and there wasn't any doubt in the minds of the President or any of us that we could live with them peacefully.

▲ Harry Hopkins, Roosevelt's closest adviser, describing US feelings in early 1945.

- The Soviet Union would declare war on Japan three months after the end of the war with Germany.

- Stalin promised to allow free elections in the countries of eastern Europe that had been occupied by the Soviet army.

The actual details of the agreements made at Yalta were left to be decided later. This meant that a second conference had to be held to work out the areas to be occupied by each of the four Allies.

The Allies met for a second time in Potsdam, outside Berlin, in July 1945. By then relations between East and West had already begun to worsen. It was becoming clear that Stalin was going back on his promises to allow free elections in eastern Europe.

Another reason was the change of leadership. President Roosevelt had always been inclined to trust Stalin and Roosevelt had believed that Stalin would keep his promises. He also believed that the Soviet army would be needed in the final attack on Japan, so he was prepared to leave the Soviet Union in control of eastern Europe. Churchill did not think that this was a good idea. By the time of the Potsdam conference in July, it was clear that Churchill had been right.

The new president, Harry Truman, who took over when Roosevelt died on 12 April, took a much tougher line with Stalin. He announced that he was going to 'get tough with the Russians'.

When Truman met Molotov, the Soviet Foreign Secretary, in April 1945, he immediately told him off for failing to keep the agreements made at Yalta. Molotov is reported to have said: 'I have never been talked to like that in my life.' And this was a Soviet politician who had survived all of Stalin's purges.

Finally, at Potsdam, Harry Truman knew that he no longer needed the Red Army for an invasion of Japan. He could afford to be much 'tougher'.

What happened at Potsdam?

The Potsdam conference was the last of the conferences between the leaders of the Allies during the Second World War.

These are some of the agreements that were reached at Potsdam.

- Germany was divided into four zones and Berlin was divided into four sectors.

- Each zone would be occupied by one of the four Allies, Britain, France, USA and the USSR.

- Decisions on the government of Germany would be taken jointly and at some time in the future the country would be reunited.

- The Nazi Party would be dissolved and war criminals tried and punished.

- There would be free elections in Germany, freedom of speech and a free press.

- Germany would pay reparations for the damage caused by the war. Most of this would go to the Soviet Union.

- The Soviet Union agreed to hand back to the West food to the value of 25 per cent of the reparations.

- All three Allies agreed to take part in the United Nations.

Source B

▲ Clement Attlee (British prime minister from July 1945), Harry Truman and Joseph Stalin together at the Potsdam conference in 1945.

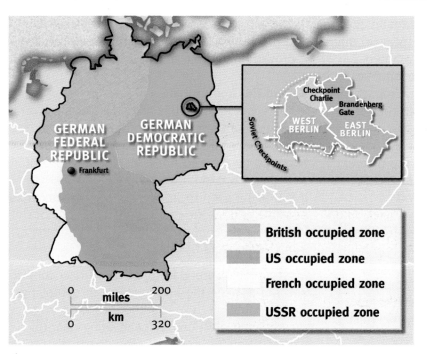

▲ **The eventual division of Germany and Berlin.**

Poland has borders with the
Soviet Union, but does not
have any with Great Britain
and the USA. I do not know
whether a democratic
government has been
established in Greece, or
whether the Belgian
government is genuinely
democratic. The Soviet Union
was not consulted when
those governments were
being formed. We did not
claim the right to interfere in
those matters, because we
realise how important
Belgium and Greece are to
the security of Great Britain.

▲ **An extract from a letter from
Stalin to Truman and
Churchill, 24 April 1945.**

But there were also disagreements at Potsdam. The new US
president, Harry Truman, tried to force the USSR to allow free
elections in the countries of eastern Europe that had been
occupied after the end of the war. He said that he wanted to 'get
tough with Russia'. But when Britain and the USA referred to
Poland, Stalin simply referred to Greece. Here Britain was
supporting the Greek government against communist influence. This
led to a civil war, which dragged on for several years. Eventually
the British government was forced to withdraw support when it ran
out of money in February 1947. This proved to be a turning point
in East–West relations and led directly to the Truman Doctrine.

Stalin was angry that Truman had not told him about the
development of the atomic bomb until the very last minute and
did not consult him about using it against Japan. Truman also
refused to share atomic secrets with the Soviet Union. This created
a belief in the Soviet Union that the bombs had been dropped as
a warning. In fact, Stalin knew all about the bomb; his spies had
passed on the information, but he distrusted Truman's secrecy.

It was now clear that there were very serious differences between
the two sides.

What were the differences between East and West?
Clearly, Stalin believed that Europe had been divided into two
spheres of influence at Yalta and Potsdam. Britain and the USA
could do as they liked in the West, but at the same time, the
Soviet Union could do as it liked in the East.

Questions

1 What were the causes
of the breakdown of
trust between the
wartime Allies?

2 How far does Source A
on page 229 help
explain the causes of
the Cold War?

3 What were the aims of
Stalin and the West in
1945? Draw up two lists
of their aims for Europe.
In what ways did their
aims differ?

A major difference occurred over Germany. Stalin wanted Germany to be kept weak, to avoid any possibility of a third war. The West wanted Germany to be allowed to recover economically. Britain and the USA remembered the impact that the Treaty of Versailles had had in the 1920s and 30s, and did not want that to happen again. This meant that the zones of Germany and the sectors of Berlin received very different treatment from the occupying forces. The Soviet sector was stripped of machinery and equipment, which was taken to the Soviet Union to help rebuild the country after the appalling damage inflicted by the war. The Western Allies wanted to rebuild their sectors and quickly began to reorganise industry and trades unions. To the West, Stalin appeared to be little more than a merciless predator; to Stalin, the West appeared to be laying the foundations for a strong Germany – something he feared more than anything else.

In December 1946, Britain and the USA agreed to unite their zones in Germany for economic purposes. In January 1947, **Bizonia** was created. This was the first step on the road to the recovery of Germany. But in the Soviet Union it was greeted with fury. Not only were the Western Allies acting without the agreement of the Soviet Union, but also they appeared to be planning to rebuild Germany, when Stalin wanted to keep it as weak as possible.

What impact did the differences between East and West have?

To protect eastern Europe from Western influence, in 1946 Stalin built the Iron Curtain, a 1,600-kilometre fence cutting off the communist countries of eastern Europe from the non-communist West. At some points, the 'curtain' became a series of fences protected by razor wire, dog runs, photo-electric beams, remote-controlled weapons and guard towers. The most famous example of the Iron Curtain was the Berlin Wall. However, this was not built until 1961.

The Iron Curtain became the most important symbol of the Cold War. Between 1945 and 1948 all the countries behind the Iron Curtain, which had been occupied by the Red Army at the end of the war, were brought under Soviet control and pro-communist governments were installed. It proved impossible for the West to intervene.

Behind the Iron Curtain

In the years immediately after the Second World War, most of the countries of eastern Europe fell under Soviet influence, because they had been liberated by the Red Army. Making Soviet control permanent was not so easy. Stalin wanted to avoid being seen to interfere directly as much as possible and so the methods used by the Soviet Union to gain control of countries behind the Iron Curtain were usually peaceful.

Most nations were glad to be rid of Nazi control and did not see the Red Army as an occupying force. At first the Soviet authorities tried to gain majorities at elections by persuading political parties to amalgamate with the communists. They also tried to infiltrate the civil service, the police and trades unions. Only when this failed to work did they resort to stronger measures.

Source D

"IF WE DON'T LET HIM WORK, WHO'S GOING TO KEEP HIM?"

▲ **A British cartoon of 1946 showing the Allies discussing the future of Germany.**

The first countries to fall under Soviet control were Romania and Bulgaria, which had both been allies of Germany during the war. Pro-communist governments were set up in Romania in March 1945 and in Bulgaria in November 1945. In November 1945, Enver Hoxha came to power in Albania and set up the People's Republic of Albania in the following year.

In Czechoslovakia, the communists were unable to win a majority in the Assembly and so carried out a coup in February 1948. The foreign minister, Jan Masaryk, died mysteriously in a fall from a window in March and the president, Eduard Benes, resigned in June. This handed control to the communists.

In Hungary, the communists did not take real control until May 1949, after a general election gave complete victory to the communist-controlled National Independence Front. But Stalin also had a significant failure. President Tito of Yugoslavia refused to co-operate with the Soviet Union, despite having set up a communist government and signing a series of agreements with the communist bloc. In June 1948, Yugoslavia was expelled from COMINFORM, the Communist Information Bureau (see page 236).

The Truman Doctrine, Marshall Plan and the Soviet response

In February 1947, the British government told the US government that it could no longer afford to support the Greek government in its civil war against communists. President Truman agreed to take over the responsibility and provided

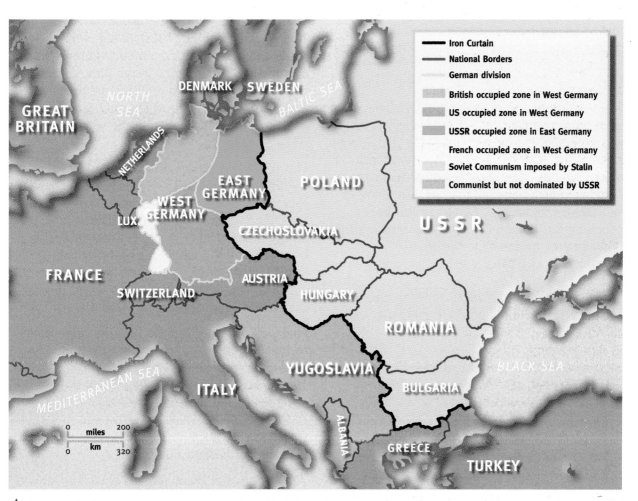

▲ Europe during 1945–48, showing the Iron Curtain and the countries under Soviet control.

US$400 million of aid. In March 1947, Truman published the Truman Doctrine. He offered to help any government that was being threatened either from within or from without its own borders.

Truman was careful not to mention the Soviet Union and did not specify what form aid might take, but his meaning was obvious. He was not going to allow the Soviet Union to take over any more countries in Europe.

Why was the Truman Doctrine published?

Truman wanted to help the countries of Europe recover from the effects of the Second World War. He had seen the devastation, and he wanted the USA to play a part in recovery. Marshall Aid was annonced the following month.

Truman was also trying to stop any other countries in Europe becoming communist. Already the Iron Curtain had cut Europe in two; he did not want that to go any further. Truman hoped that he might be able to persuade some of the countries of eastern Europe to break away from communism. Marshall Aid was also intended to help here.

While the Truman Doctrine did not actually mention the Soviet Union, it was obvious that it was intended as a warning to Stalin that Truman was not going to let him get away with any more attempts to increase Soviet influence in Europe. Truman had said that he was going to 'get tough with Russia'. Stalin reacted by criticising the Truman Doctrine and accusing the USA of trying to dominate the world.

In 1947 Stalin set up COMINFORM, which co-ordinated the activities of communist parties throughout Europe in an effort to counteract Truman.

Source A

I believe that it must be the policy of the United States to support free peoples who are resisting attempted subjugation by armed minorities or by outside pressures.

▲ An extract from the Truman Doctrine.

Source B

The Truman Doctrine meant in reality the rearmament of Greece and Turkey, and building bases in these countries for American strategic bombers. These actions were justified by outspoken statements about defending democracy and peace.

▲ From a history book published in the Soviet Union, outlining the Soviet view of the Truman Doctrine.

How did Marshall Aid work?

Marshall Aid was an attempt to rebuild Europe after the Second World War, named after the US Secretary of State George C. Marshall. It put the ideas of the Truman Doctrine into effect. In June 1947, President Harry Truman offered grants of American money to all European countries. Truman intended that Marshall Aid would be made available to all countries in Europe but eventually only countries in the West accepted it. For example, Italy, one of the members of the Axis, received US$601 million, and Spain, which had remained neutral during the war, received US$62.5 million.

The USSR and other eastern countries attended the first meetings in 1947, but withdrew when they discovered that they would have to join the Organisation for European Economic Co-operation (OEEC). The OEEC would decide how Marshall Aid would be spent, not the individual countries. The most important point was that Marshall Aid had to be spent in ways that would help develop capitalism.

This would have given the USA the opportunity to influence the countries of the East and undermine communism, which was exactly what Truman had hoped would happen. In the end, seventeen countries received a total of US$13.75 billion, which allowed them to recover from the war much more quickly than the countries of Eastern Europe.

When the Soviet Union realised what Truman was up to, the Soviet government forced other eastern bloc countries – Czechoslovakia in particular – to withdraw applications for Marshall Aid. Stalin set up a Soviet version of Marshall Aid, called COMECON (Council for Mutual Economic Assistance). However, the Soviet Union had far fewer resources to offer the countries of eastern Europe. In the long run COMECON became a drain on the Soviet Union's resources and helped to bring about its bankruptcy in the 1980s.

The Berlin blockade

The Iron Curtain meant that Marshall Aid had little impact on eastern Europe, except in the three Western sectors of Berlin. From 1945 to 1948 travel between the four sectors in Berlin was easy. People could live in one sector and work in another, so East Berliners were soon

Our policy is not directed against any country or doctrine, but against hunger, poverty, desperation and chaos. Any government that is willing to assist in the task of recovery will find full co-operation on the part of the United States government.

▲ **From a speech in which George C. Marshall, US Secretary of State, explains Marshall Aid.**

able to see the improvements that Marshall Aid had on life in the West. Stalin, however, saw West Berlin as capitalist island behind the Iron Curtain. In 1948 he decided to try to get rid of it.

In June 1948, to put pressure on the West and try to force the Allies to remove their forces, Joseph Stalin ordered that all traffic between West Germany and West Berlin should be stopped. He was able to close the road, canal and rail routes, but was not able to prevent Great Britain, France and the USA from bringing supplies into West Berlin by air.

The main reason for the blockade was that Great Britain and the USA made it clear that they intended to rebuild the economy in their zones of Germany. In 1947 the British and US zones were joined together in Bizonia; the French zone was added in 1948. Stalin believed that Germany should be kept weak to prevent any risk of further trouble. He also wanted to get reparations from Germany to help rebuild the Soviet Union. So he opposed these changes.

A more immediate reason for the blockade was that in 1948 the Western Allies announced that they were going to introduce a new currency in the West, the Deutschmark, to kick-start the economy again. This would mean that East and West would be separate

Source C

▲ **A Soviet poster attacking the Marshall Plan.**

economically, and broke the agreements made at Yalta and Potsdam that decisions over Germany would be taken by the Allies, jointly. The Allies' reason for the introduction of the new currency was that they wanted to get Germany going again. They were tired of Stalin's attitude, which they saw as unco-operative and had decided to act without him.

How did the Allies react to the blockade of Berlin?

The most important reaction was that they were determined that Stalin should not succeed. The Allies believed that if they gave in, Stalin would behave as Hitler had done in the 1930s, and more and more countries would be taken over. General Lucius Clay, the US Commander in Berlin, said: 'If West Berlin falls, West Germany will be next.' Clay actually offered to try to fight his way out of West Berlin – an offer that Truman turned down very quickly. Instead, the Allies began to bring supplies into West Berlin by air.

From June 1948 to May 1949, everything that West Berlin needed was brought in by air. Allied planes flew round the clock, one landing every 90 seconds. Soviet fighter aircraft did all they could to prevent the airlift and 79 pilots lost their lives in accidents. But Stalin did not dare to start shooting. Eventually the Allies were bringing in 8,000 tonnes of provisions every day, twice the amount that was needed. Even coal was brought in by plane. A total of 277,264 flights were completed before the airlift finally ended in September 1949.

In May 1949 Stalin gave up. It was obvious that the West was not going to give in, so he ended the blockade. Some Russian historians now claim that the blockade was really an attempt to take Allied attention away from the communist revolution in China, which took place in 1948–49.

The Berlin blockade marked the complete breakdown of all the agreements made by the Allies at the end of the Second World War. It convinced the West that there was no point in hoping that Stalin would co-operate and keep the promises made at Yalta and Potsdam. The Cold War had really begun.

Source E

THE BIRD WATCHER

▲ A British cartoon from 1948. It shows Stalin watching the Allied 'storks' flying supplies to Berlin.

NATO, the Warsaw Pact and the Arms Race

NATO

The Berlin blockade convinced the West of the need for greater security. In April 1949, twelve countries signed the North Atlantic Treaty Organisation (NATO), including Britain, the USA and France. NATO, which came into being in September 1949, was a military alliance, which committed each member to the defence of all of the others. It established the principle that if one member was attacked, the others all had to declare war on the aggressor without question. Since 1949 this has never happened. The creation of NATO also led to US military forces being stationed in western Europe. From 1949 bombers arrived in Britain and other European countries.

Questions

1 What is the meaning of the following: Truman Doctrine, Marshall Aid, the Marshall Plan, COMECON?

2 Why did the Soviet Union distrust the Truman Doctrine?

3 Why did Stalin refuse to allow the countries of eastern Europe to accept Marshall Aid?

4 Why did Stalin begin the blockade of Berlin in June 1948?

5 What point do you think the cartoonist was trying to make in the source opposite?

However, the clearest signal that co-operation between East and West was at an end, was the creation of the Federal Republic of Germany (West Germany) in May 1949. Although the Western Allies continued to occupy their three zones, a parliament was elected and Konrad Adenauer became the first chancellor of post-war Germany. To help recovery, Germany was made a full member of the Marshall Plan. The Soviet reply to these developments was to establish the German Democratic Republic (East Germany) in October 1949. There were now two separate German states. This meant that the agreements made at Yalta and Potsdam were no longer of any importance.

The need for a military alliance was reinforced when, in July 1949, the Soviet Union exploded its first atomic bomb. The two superpowers were now equal. The USA could no longer assume that it could out-gun the Soviet Union, and so it began to try to develop new weapons, which were more powerful than those of the Soviet Union. This was the beginning of the Arms Race. From 1949 until the 1980s the two superpowers poured vast sums of money into the development of new weapons of mass destruction.

How did the death of Joseph Stalin change relations between the superpowers?

Joseph Stalin died in 1953. At first his death seemed to make very little difference to the relations between the superpowers. In 1955, the Warsaw Pact was signed by the countries of eastern Europe. This was the first time that a military alliance had been set up by the Soviet Union; it was the communist equivalent of NATO. The Pact was set up as a direct result of West Germany becoming a member of NATO on 9 May 1955. The USSR was very concerned at this, because, as Stalin had pointed out in 1945, Germany had invaded Russia twice in the twentieth century. The Warsaw Pact was an attempt to protect the USSR by drawing the countries of eastern Europe even closer together.

The members of the Pact were the Soviet Union, Poland, Hungary, Czechoslovakia, Romania, Bulgaria, Albania and East Germany. The full title was the 'Pact of Mutual Assistance and Unified Command'. It had two important effects.

1 It created a joint command of the armed forces of the alliance.

2 It set up a Political Committee to co-ordinate the foreign policies of the members.

The Pact increased the influence of the Soviet Union in eastern Europe and led to more Soviet troops being stationed there. This made the crushing of the anti-Soviet Hungarian Rising of 1956 all the easier.

But despite the creation of the Warsaw Pact, relations between the superpowers began to change.

Co-existence

The new Soviet leader, Nikita Khrushchev, believed in co-existence. He believed that the Soviet Union should accept that the West had a right to exist and that, rather than trying to destroy the West, the Soviet Union should try to compete with it and prove that its way of life was better than the Western way of life. This marked a complete break with the policy adopted by Stalin since the 1920s.

Stalin had maintained his policy of 'Socialism in one country' until the end of his life. It was his belief that it was essential to build up and protect the Soviet Union from all forms of Western influence. He had constructed barriers across Europe to keep out Western ideas and to keep in the Soviet people. This had resulted in permanent confrontation between the superpowers. Khrushchev wanted to replace confrontation with co-existence. His break with Stalin's policy was announced in his 'Secret Speech' at the Twentieth Party Congress in 1956.

Unfortunately, Khrushchev's actions were misunderstood, both abroad and inside the Soviet Union. While he believed in co-existence, he was not prepared to sacrifice the security of the Soviet Union. He had also to retain the support of the Soviet military leaders. This meant he had to maintain spending on arms and match any improvements made by the USA. Consequently, while Khrushchev was in power, there was increased spending on the arms race.

The Arms Race

The bomb that was dropped on Hiroshima in Japan on 6 August 1945 exploded with the force of 20,000 tonnes of high explosive. It was 2,000 times more powerful than any other bomb dropped during the Second World War. Once the Soviet Union had developed atomic weapons in 1949, the USA began the development of the hydrogen bomb, or H-bomb. This was perfected in November 1952. But the Soviet Union exploded its first H-bomb only nine months later. This led to the development of nuclear weapons by the USA; these began to be tested in the 1950s and became available in the early 1960s.

In 1957 the Soviet Union tested the first Intercontinental Ballistic Missile (ICBM). This missile was capable of carrying a warhead from one continent to another, or from the Soviet Union to the USA. Until then the only way of

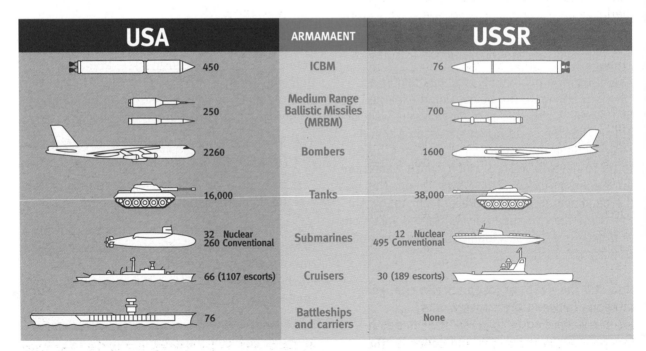

USA	ARMAMAENT	USSR
450	ICBM	76
250	Medium Range Ballistic Missiles (MRBM)	700
2260	Bombers	1600
16,000	Tanks	38,000
32 Nuclear 260 Conventional	Submarines	12 Nuclear 495 Conventional
66 (1107 escorts)	Cruisers	30 (189 escorts)
76	Battleships and carriers	None

▲ The Arms Race between the USA and the Soviet Union showing the armaments each superpower had.

dropping an atomic bomb was by plane. Now there was a new threat. The USA responded by building its own ICBMs.

The next step came in the 1960s. Both sides developed Anti-Ballistic Missiles (ABMs). These were missiles that could shoot down ICBMs. But these were almost immediately followed by Multiple Independently Targeted Re-entry Vehicles (MIRVs). These carried more than one warhead so they could hit more than one target and were, therefore, very difficult to shoot down.

Khrushchev and competition with the West

From 1957, Khrushchev began to travel the world, meeting foreign leaders in a series of summits. On his travels he deliberately tried to attract newspaper coverage by using unexpected behaviour. On a trip to Britain he walked off the red carpet on a visit to a factory and went over to talk to the workers. In the USA, during a visit to an exhibition, he got involved in a debate about kitchens with Vice-President Richard Nixon.

Khrushchev began to compete with the USA throughout the world. From the 1956 Olympic Games in Melbourne, Soviet sportsmen and women challenged the US domination of the medal table. At Rome in 1960, the Soviet Union won more medals than any other country. This pattern continued until the 1980s. Soviet athletes were supported by the state so that they could concentrate on training.

Khrushchev was also determined that the Soviet Union should win the Space Race. In 1957 the first satellite, called Sputnik, was launched. In the same year the first animal, a dog called Laika, was sent into space, and in 1961 the first astronaut, Yuri Gagarin, followed. Khrushchev's success was achieved by vast expense on the space programme. This expenditure eventually proved to be ruinous and was one of the main reasons for the bankruptcy of the Soviet Union in the 1980s.

Khrushchev also began to offer Soviet aid to the large number of countries that became independent in the 1950s and 1960s as the European empires were broken up. Soviet technicians, equipment and loans were made freely available to African and Asian nations. This led to increased support for the Soviet Union at the United Nations. This support was a severe drain on the Soviet economy and was yet another reason for its collapse in the 1980s and 1990s.

In the short term, however, Soviet successes had two main effects.

1 They hit the headlines, just as Khrushchev had wanted them to; all over the world public opinion was focused on the Soviet Union and on Khrushchev in person.

2 They proved that Soviet technology was superior to Western technology.

Source C on page 242 outlines what Khrushchev himself thought of this Soviet success.

The US reaction was one of great alarm, as Source D on page 242 shows.

In the USA, Soviet successes in space led President John F. Kennedy to order US scientists to get a man on the moon by the end of the 1960s.

Source A

▲ **Successful Soviet athletes, during the 1960 Rome Olympic Games.**

Why did relations between the USA and the Soviet Union change after Khrushchev came to power in the USSR?

The US government found Khrushchev hard to handle. His lively personality, popular style and unpredictability gave him an automatic advantage over Dwight Eisenhower, the US president from 1953 to 1961. Eisenhower – or 'Ike' as he was always known – seemed uninspiring and dull by comparison. This was one reason why the US people voted for the much younger and much more charismatic Kennedy in 1960.

Khrushchev's policies were difficult to understand. Co-existence seemed to suggest that relations with the West were going to improve but, at the same time, the increased competition that Khrushchev brought about seemed to create a new type of threat. At least with Stalin the West had known exactly where it was, but Khrushchev appeared to be trying to beat the West at its own game. There were also signs in the late 1950s that the Cold War in Europe was beginning to hot up.

▲ Sputnik, the first satellite launched into space by the Soviet Union in its bid to win the Space Race.

Source C

The Sputniks prove that socialism has won the competition between the socialist and capitalist countries. The economy, science, culture and the creative genius of people in all spheres of life develop better and faster under socialism.

▲ Khrushchev, speaking about the success of the Soviet Union.

Source D

Americans were extremely disturbed. Strategic Air Force units were dispersed and put on alert, short-range rockets were installed in Turkey and Italy. Money was poured into missile and bomber programmes.

▲ The views of one American historian.

Questions

1 Explain the meaning of the following: NATO, the Arms Race, the Warsaw Pact, co-existence.

2 Draw up two lists, one headed Stalin and the other headed Khrushchev. Write down examples of relations between the superpowers under the two leaders. Explain the ways in which these relations were different.

3 Explain why relations between the superpowers changed after the death of Stalin.

The nature of the Cold War: Poland, Hungary, Berlin, Cuba; the differences between communist and non-communist societies

In February 1956 Khrushchev criticised Stalin in the Secret Speech at the Twentieth Party Congress. In Poland and Hungary this was taken as a sign that he was going to allow ties between members of the Warsaw Pact to be relaxed. First in Poland and then in Hungary, opposition to Soviet domination developed. But Khrushchev did not intend to weaken the ties between the Soviet Union and other countries of eastern Europe, and he had no intention of allowing a more lenient attitude towards West Germany.

Poland

Rioting, which led to more than 100 deaths, broke out in Poland in June 1956, but the real trouble began in October when the rioters were put on trial. On 21 October, Wladislaw Gomulka became the new leader of the Polish Communist Party. Khrushchev had to decide between allowing Gomulka to remain in power or using force, as the Polish Defence Minister demanded. He decided to back Gomulka and removed some unpopular Stalinists from the government.

However, Gomulka had to promise that Poland would remain a loyal member of the Warsaw Pact, and the Communist Party remained firmly in control. The Defence Minister, Marshal Rokossvky, was summoned to Moscow and accused of taking part in a conspiracy to overthrow Gomulka.

Hungary

Serious unrest developed in October 1956, almost simultaneously with that in Poland. On 24 October, Imre Nagy became prime minister of Hungary. He had already been prime minister from 1953 to 1955 and was known to be a liberal. This led to fighting in Budapest between Hungarians and Soviet troops.

Khrushchev tried to deal with the situation by withdrawing the Soviet troops from Hungary and allowing Imre Nagy to become the leader of the Hungarian government. Nagy set up a new government, which included non-communists. Then on 30 October he announced free elections, and on 2 November, Hungary's withdrawal from the Warsaw Pact.

Rumours spread that US forces were about to come to the aid of the new government. This encouraged resistance. In fact, there was never any intention, by the West, of interference.

Khrushchev could not accept this, and on 4 November, ordered the Soviet army to invade Hungary and crush the uprising. There was bitter street fighting; 7,000 Soviet troops and 30,000 Hungarians were killed. Nagy was arrested and later shot. The West protested, but did nothing because it was afraid that military action would lead to war. This caused a deep sense of betrayal felt by many Hungarians.

Source A

▲ **Soviet tanks on the streets of Budapest in November 1956 as they attempted to crush the Hungarian uprising.**

Berlin

The problems in Poland and Hungary were of Khrushchev's own making. He had not appreciated the effects that the Secret Speech would have in eastern Europe. But Berlin was a problem that he had inherited.

The end of the Berlin blockade in May 1949 had convinced many East Berliners and East Germans that life was better on the other side. Since May 1949 hundreds of thousands of people had escaped from the East to the West. On average the number ranged between 20,000 to 25,000 each month.

Why did so many people defect to the West?

Many defectors were well educated professionals – for example, engineers, teachers, doctors, lecturers. They were just the sort of people that the communist bloc could not afford to lose as it tried to modernise its industry and agriculture. So what attracted these people to the West?

In the East, life was dominated by the Communist Party, which became more important than the elected government. No other political parties were permitted and elections involved a selection from a list of candidates supplied by the communists.

The media were also controlled by the Communist Party. There were no legal means of finding out what was happening in the world on the other side of the Iron Curtain. Newspapers and the radio and television could only report the official version of the news.

People were subject to the secret police – in the Soviet Union, the KGB. These organisations operated outside the law and there was little that an ordinary citizen could do about their actions. Freedom of expression was restricted, and although Khrushchev relaxed some of the controls that Stalin had put into place and reduced the powers of the secret police, he did not allow complete freedom. Criticism of the Communist Party and the Soviet way of life was not allowed. **Consumer goods** were limited and often of poor quality. Sales of foreign goods were restricted. Foreign travel was difficult and currency sales were strictly controlled in an effort to obtain foreign exchange.

On the other hand, there were some benefits in the East. All citizens of the countries of eastern Europe had a job. In the USSR, according to the government, the last unemployed person found a job in 1932. Prices were controlled and held at low levels. Rent, electricity, gas and telephone charges were minimal by Western standards. Public transport was very cheap and very reliable. But these advantages were outweighed by the possibility of greater freedom, much higher earnings and a much higher standard of living in the West.

How did Khrushchev try to deal with Berlin?

Khrushchev wanted to plug this hole in the Iron Curtain and end the stream of defectors. In November 1958 he demanded that the three Western powers should leave West Berlin. The West refused and called for talks on the reunification of East and West Germany (in fact, at the Rome Olympics in 1960 there was a united German team, but nothing more). Khrushchev refused to discuss unification and in April 1960 threatened another blockade. In September 1960, East Germany forced West Berliners who wanted to travel to East Berlin to obtain a police pass. This was the first time that any restriction had been placed on travel between the four sectors in Berlin.

Finally, on 13 August 1961, the East German government closed the border between East and West Berlin and on 15 August began to build the Berlin Wall. East and West Berlin became completely cut off from each other and remained so until November 1989.

Why did Khrushchev decide to build the Berlin Wall?

The building of the Berlin Wall was not an isolated event. It took place in August 1961 and followed a series of incidents, which appeared to show that Khrushchev held the upper hand in East–West relations.

In 1959, Fidel Castro had overthrown the pro-US government in Cuba. At first Castro appealed to the USA for financial aid, but when this was refused, he turned to the Soviet Union.

▲ **The Berlin Wall, dividing East and West Berlin.**

In May 1960, the Soviet Union shot down a U2, a US spy plane, and put the pilot Gary Powers on trial. Only a few days later Khrushchev met the US President, Eisenhower, at a summit meeting in Paris. When Eisenhower refused to apologise for the U2 incident, Khrushchev gleefully stormed out of the meeting and returned to Moscow. The exit from the building was caught on film by the world's press and he made the most of the opportunity. A visit by Eisenhower to Moscow was immediately cancelled.

In April 1961, an attempt to overthrow the Cuban leader Fidel Castro with US support ended disastrously at the Bay of Pigs on the south coast of Cuba. In June 1961, Khrushchev and Kennedy met for a summit in Vienna. Khrushchev apparently decided that he could take advantage of his young and inexperienced opposite number. And so he took the opportunity to build the wall.

Kennedy returned from Vienna in June 1961 convinced that he had to show Khrushchev that he meant business. In the next two years he ordered three increases in the US defence budget, and an increase in the number of spying missions by U2s.

Questions

1 Draw up two lists of events from 1956 to 1961. One should be events that would have worried the USA; the other should be events that would have worried the Soviet Union.

2 Which is the longer list? Can you explain why one list is longer than the other?

Source C

CHERRY PICKER

LAUNCH PAD WITH ERECTOR

LAUNCH PAD WITH ERECTOR

MISSILE READY BLDGS.

OXIDIZER VEHICLES

FUELING VEHICLES

▲ **A photograph of missile sites in Cuba with labels added by the American government.**

Events in Cuba

The overthrow of Fulgencio Batista by Fidel Castro in January 1959 was a serious blow to the USA. Cuba had been dominated by the USA since 1898, when it had been liberated from Spain. A great deal of US money had been invested in Cuba and much of the industry was US owned. The island was also only 90 miles from the nearest US soil.

In 1959 and 1960, Castro attempted to get US aid for the development of Cuba, but was turned down by President Eisenhower. Instead, Eisenhower reduced the amount of Cuban sugar bought by the USA by 95 per cent. This meant ruin for Cuba. Only then did Castro turn to the Soviet Union in 1960. The Soviet Union agreed to buy 1 million tonnes of Cuban sugar every year. This tied the two countries closely together. In the following months, Castro nationalised US businesses and property in Cuba.

US fears of Castro led to a series of unlikely attempts to get rid of him. The CIA (the Central Intelligence Agency) tried to smuggle poison into Cuba and to kill him with an exploding cigar; in

April 1961 at the Bay of Pigs, 1,400 exiled Cubans tried to overthrow Castro's government with CIA support. Castro's agents had infiltrated the scheme and it was a disaster. The Cubans were all either killed or captured. President Kennedy, who had known about the invasion, but had not been involved in its planning, was made to look foolish.

In December 1961, Castro announced that he was setting up a communist government in Cuba. This was a very serious blow to the USA. Communism was now established for the first time in the Western hemisphere and right on the USA's doorstep. This presented a real challenge to Kennedy. His response was to increase US military spending.

For Khrushchev, however, Castro's decision showed how successful his policies of co-existence and competition had been. It was a clear sign, at least in his mind, that the Soviet Union held the upper hand and he was determined to take full advantage.

The Missile Crisis

On 14 October 1962 a U2 on a flight over Cuba took photographs which showed that the Soviet Union was building missile bases in Cuba. This confirmed reports that the CIA had been receiving for a month. The following day the CIA reported that there were at least sixteen Soviet missiles in Cuba already. On the same day twenty Soviet ships were spotted in the Atlantic, apparently bound for Cuba, carrying what appeared to be missiles.

Kennedy realised that he must act. He summoned the National Security Council (NSC) and began a series of meetings, which lasted from 16 to 22 October. The majority of the members of the Security Council advised military action against Cuba, but the president, supported by his brother, Robert Kennedy, decided to blockade Cuba.

On 22 October, President Kennedy went on national television to explain his policy to the US people. He hoped that his message would also be heard in the Soviet Union:

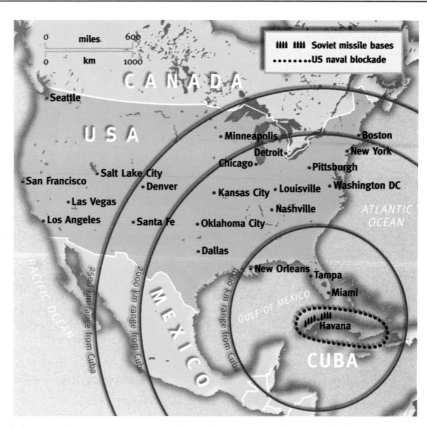

▲ American cities that could be reached by missiles fired from Cuba.

The transformation of Cuba into an important strategic base is an explicit threat to the peace and security of the Americas. This action contradicts the repeated assurances of Soviet spokesmen that the arms build-up in Cuba would be defensive.

Our objective must be to prevent the use of these missiles against this or any other country, and to secure their withdrawal from the Western hemisphere.

All ships bound for Cuba will, if found to contain cargoes of offensive weapons, be turned back. Any nuclear missile launched from Cuba will be regarded as an attack by the Soviet Union on the United States.

I call upon Chairman Khrushchev to halt this reckless and provocative threat to world peace.

On 23 October, Khrushchev replied with a statement at the UN accusing the USA of interfering in Cuba's internal affairs:

Cuba belongs to the Cuban people. The Soviet government warns the government of the United States that it is playing with fire and the fate of the world.

The blockade came into effect on 24 October: 180 ships were used, including a fleet of Polaris submarines, 156 ICBMs were put on combat readiness, troops were moved into the south eastern states of the USA and the Strategic Air Force was put on full alert.

But almost immediately some Soviet ships turned back. On 24 October the remaining Soviet ships slowed down and then stopped.

Khrushchev now sent two more letters to Kennedy. The first contained the following offer:

Source D

▲ A cartoon published in 1962 during the Cuban Missile Crisis.

This is my proposal. No more weapons to Cuba and those in Cuba withdrawn or destroyed. You reply by ending your blockade and also agreeing not to invade Cuba.

The second was much more menacing:

You want to rid your country of danger. But Cuba also wants the same thing. You have surrounded the Soviet Union with missiles, your rockets are aimed against us. Do you believe that you have the right to demand security for your own country while not recognising it for us?

While Kennedy was deciding how to respond to the two messages, news arrived that a U2 had been shot down over Cuba, killing the pilot. In an effort to avoid further complications Kennedy apologised:

I regret this incident and will see to it that every precaution is taken to prevent recurrence.

The US government then accepted the offer made by Khrushchev in the first letter. Kennedy wrote on 27 October:

Your proposals, which seem acceptable, are as follows.

1 *You would agree to remove these weapons systems from Cuba.*

2 *We would agree*
   a to remove the measures now in effect, and

   b to give assurances against an invasion of Cuba.

In other words, the missiles would be withdrawn in exchange for a US promise to leave Cuba alone. Khrushchev summed up the agreement in one final letter on 28 October:

I regard with trust the statement you made that there would be no attack, no invasion of Cuba. It is for this reason that we have instructed our officers to stop building missile facilities, to dismantle them and to return them to the Soviet Union.

Not only did this letter bring the whole crisis to a peaceful conclusion, but it also sounded a real note of hope for the future.

One further meeting took place late on 27 October. Robert Kennedy met the Soviet Ambassador and agreed informally that US missiles would be removed in time from Turkey and Italy. However, since the missiles were part of a NATO force, this could not be announced immediately. This helped to give the impression that Khrushchev had given in. The missiles were removed three months later, almost unnoticed.

Why did the Cuban Missile Crisis end like this?

Much of the credit must go to the good sense of the two leaders. Most members of the US NSC advised military action; Kennedy refused to be pushed into war even though he realised that he had to make a stand. In Source E he describes his situation. For his part, Khrushchev realised that he had gone too far. He was simply not prepared to go to war for Cuba or probably for anything else. This was another sign of a new understanding between the superpowers. Both leaders realised the need to allow the other to save face. So Kennedy publicly agreed that the USA would leave Cuba alone and privately agreed to remove missiles from Turkey and Italy. Khrushchev publicly agreed to remove the missiles from Cuba and also accepted Kennedy's invitation to begin discussions about *détente*.

Source E

It isn't the first step that concerns me, but both sides escalating to the fourth or fifth steps, and we don't want to go to the sixth step.

▲ **The thoughts of President Kennedy regarding resolution of the Cuban Missile Crisis.**

Source F

John F. Kennedy had won. The Soviet government was backing down. The Russians did dismantle the bases. They took everything away. It should be noted that three months after the crisis, the United States removed all its missiles from Turkey and Italy.

▲ **Written in 1980 by an American historian.**

After the crisis was over, both the people involved and others gave their views about the reasons why nuclear war was avoided. Source F outlines what an American historian wrote in 1980. On the other hand, Source G outlines what Nikita Khrushchev wrote in his memoirs, *Khrushchev Remembers*.

Source G

We sent the Americans a note saying that we agreed to remove our missiles and bombers on condition that the President gave us his assurance that there would be no invasion of Cuba by the forces of the United States. Finally, Kennedy gave in. It was a great victory for us, a spectacular success without having to fire a shot.

▲ **From the memoirs of Nikita Khrushchev.**

Questions

1 Draw up a timeline from 16 October to 28 October. On it list all the events of the Cuban Missile Crisis, as well as all of the statements and letters from the two leaders.

2 Outline any differences between the public statements of the leaders and their private letters. Give explanations for these differences.

3 Explain how the crisis was settled peacefully.

4 Both Kennedy and Khrushchev claimed to have won. Explain why they were both able to claim victory.

Détente: Cuba to Afghanistan and the roles of Reagan and Gorbachev

How did the Cuban Missile Crisis change relations between the superpowers?

During the Cuban Missile Crisis, Dean Rusk, the US Secretary of State, commented: 'We're eyeball to eyeball and I think the other fellow just blinked.' This famous comment summed up the nature of the crisis exactly. For two weeks in October 1962 the two superpowers squared up to each other, but then backed down. In one of his letters to Khrushchev, Kennedy used the word *'détente'*. He meant a lessening of tension, a drawing together of the two superpowers. Khrushchev responded to Kennedy's invitation and the process of *détente* began in 1963.

The first real sign of *détente* was the Hot-Line, which was set up. This was a direct tele-printer between the Kremlin and the White House. It enabled the two leaders to communicate almost immediately in the event of a crisis, like Cuba. In fact it was hardly ever used, except during the Afghanistan War from 1979 onwards, but it symbolised the attempts that the two sides were making attempts to get on with each other.

In 1963 the Test Ban Treaty was signed. This stopped nuclear tests above ground. As far as the superpowers were concerned, this was a relatively unimportant restriction as most tests were carried out underground. But once again it symbolised a new degree of co-operation.

Brezhnev, Vietnam and Czechoslovakia

However, from 1965 relations between the superpowers took a turn for the worse. In October 1964, Nikita Khrushchev was dismissed and replaced by Leonid Brezhnev. He appeared to be less interested in *détente* and more interested in maintaining the military power of the Soviet Union. He began to increase spending on the arms race.

Relations between the superpowers were also affected by two crises. In 1965, President Johnson authorised the deployment of US troops in Vietnam for the first time. Until then the USA had only sent military advisers. Now they took part in the fighting. US involvement grew until 1969, when the newly elected President Nixon decided to withdraw US forces. The last US combat troops left Vietnam in 1973.

Brezhnev sent Warsaw Pact forces into

Source A

▲ A British cartoon showing how the Cuban Missile Crisis was seen by many as a trial of strength.

Source B

	1964	1974
USA		
ICBMs	834	1054
SLBMs	416	656
Soviet Union		
ICBMs	200	1575
SLBMs	120	720

SLBMs were Submarine-launched Ballistic Missiles

▲ The Arms Race 1964-74.

◄ South Vietnamese civilians scrambling on to a US helicopter to leave South Vietnam in 1975.

Czechoslovakia in August 1968. Since January 1968, the Czech government had shown increasing independence from the Soviet Union. In April a programme was announced allowing freedom of speech, the press, assembly and religion. By July the situation was so serious that the Czech prime minister, Alexander Dubcek, was summoned to Moscow, and when he refused to go, the entire Soviet Politburo visited Prague.

Presidents Tito of Yugoslavia and Ceausescu of Romania both visited Prague to offer support to the Czech government, but this did not prevent an invasion by 200,000 troops on 20 August 1968. Dubcek was dismissed and became Czech Ambassador to Turkey.

Despite the invasion of Czechoslovakia, the Nuclear Non-Proliferation Treaty was signed in 1968. The superpowers guaranteed not to supply nuclear technology to other countries. Once again this was symbolic rather than significant. Neither the Soviet Union nor the USA wanted to give control of nuclear weapons to foreign countries. It was just too risky. The real breakthroughs came in 1969 after the election of Richard Nixon as US president in 1968.

Nixon and the SALT talks

Nixon was determined to improve relations between the East and West. He was committed to withdrawing US troops from Vietnam and also made real efforts to improve relations with communist China. He was helped in his attempts to improve relations with the Soviet Union by Leonid Brezhnev, the Soviet president. When Brezhnev had succeeded Khrushchev in 1964 he had tried to develop Soviet industry, but failed. He soon gave up any further attempts, but realised that somehow or other he had to reduce the enormous budget deficit of the Soviet Union.

Brezhnev now wanted to reduce Soviet military spending so that he could sort out the problems facing the Soviet economy. The most obvious way was by cutting expenditure on arms. So in 1970 Brezhnev agreed to begin Strategic Arms Limitation Talks. They soon became known as SALT and, later, SALT I.

The SALT talks led to the signing of the SALT I treaty in 1972. This limited the increase in numbers of nuclear missiles. There would be a five-year delay on the building of more missiles. At the end of the five-year period a further agreement would be necessary. A separate treaty restricted the number of ABMs (Anti-Ballistic Missiles).

At the same time the two sides agreed to begin Mutual and Balanced Force Reduction Talks (MBFR). These continued until the 1980s, when there had been more than 300 meetings with almost no agreements. Both sides also agreed to allow each other to use spy satellites to make sure that the numbers were being kept to. Additionally, the USA signed a trade deal to export wheat to the Soviet Union, and both sides agreed to develop artistic and sporting links. In 1975 Soviet and US astronauts linked up in space for the first time.

SALT I was the first time that the superpowers had reached an agreement on arms limitation, but the talks only dealt with strategic weapons, long-range nuclear weapons. They did not cover multiple warhead missiles or battlefield weapons (tactical nuclear weapons). In fact, the USA continued to produce multiple warheads, at the rate of three a day, throughout the 1970s. The Soviet government announced: 'SALT talks show that despite differences an improvement in relations between the Soviet Union and the USA is quite possible.'

Source C

▲ Protests against the siting of American Cruise missiles at Greenham Common, Britain.

Arms reduction and human rights

Détente soon covered other areas, however, when in 1975 the USA and the Soviet Union, along with 33 other countries, signed the Helsinki Agreement on Human Rights. This guaranteed that they would respect human rights and fundamental freedoms, including the freedom of thought, conscience, religion or belief for all without distinction of race, sex, language or religion. SALT II began in 1974 and continued until 1979. Agreement was reached on further reductions in strategic weapons, which were to last until 1985.

But even before agreement was reached on SALT II, relations between the superpowers began to break down. In 1977 President Carter of the USA criticised the Soviet Union's human rights' record at the Belgrade conference. He wanted to link the issue of human rights to arms reduction. The Soviet Union was not prepared to do this. The real crisis in superpower relations, however, came in 1979.

The year 1979 was one of turmoil around the world. In Iran the Shah, who was pro-Western, was overthrown and an Islamic

	USA	Soviet Union
ICBMs	1,000	1,600
SLBMs	650	700

▲ The numbers of missiles agreed at SALT I.

Weapons Allowed	USA	Soviet Union
ICBMs	1,054	1,398
SLBMs	656	950

▲ The numbers of missiles agreed at SALT II.

republic was set up. The US embassy in the capital, Tehran, was attacked and hostages seized. The USA suspected that the new Iranian government would be pro-Soviet. In Nicaragua, guerrillas seized power, with communist support. Cuba sent armed forces to Africa to help rebels in Angola.

In Europe, new Soviet SS-20 missiles were deployed in the eastern bloc, and there was a build up of conventional forces in the Warsaw Pact. In December, NATO replied by announcing that Cruise and Pershing missiles would be deployed in Europe.

Afghanistan

Then, on Christmas day the Soviet Army invaded Afghanistan. The President, Hafizullah Amin, was arrested and executed, and a pro-communist government was set up. President Brezhnev announced that the Soviet Union 'had responded to an urgent request from the Kabul government for help'.

Almost immediately the good relations between the USA and the Soviet Union broke down. Exports of US grain to the Soviet Union were stopped. The USA refused to ratify SALT II and the USA boycotted the 1980 Olympic Games, which were held in Moscow.

Questions

1 Explain the following terms: *détente*, ICBM, SALT.

2 Draw up a timeline of the sequence of events in *détente* from 1963 to 1979.

3 Explain the forms that *détente* took in the 1960s and 1970s.

4 Explain why relations broke down between East and West in 1979.

Source D

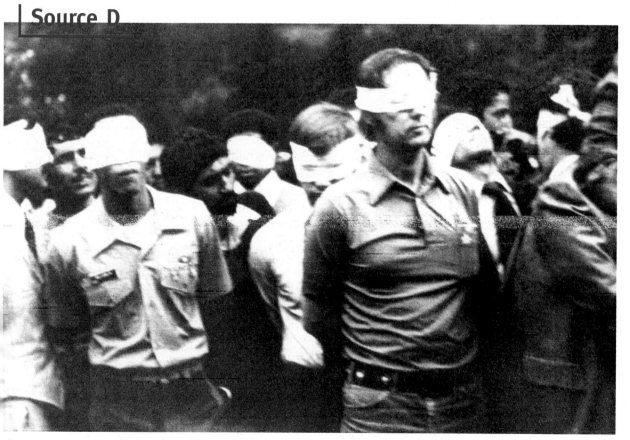

▲ **US citizens who were taken hostage at the US Embassy in Iran in 1979.**

Reagan's presidency

For the next five years there was almost no progress towards *détente*. In 1981, Ronald Reagan became US president. He made no secret of his hatred for the Soviet Union. He called it 'The Evil Empire'. But Reagan had become president after being Governor of California, where he had made his name by reducing taxation. He knew that one way of reducing taxes was cutting expenditure, and defence was an obvious target. He made it clear that he was prepared to discuss arms limitation, but was only prepared to negotiate from strength. If things did not work out, he was not prepared to compromise.

In 1981, talks on Intermediate Range Missiles (SS-20s and Cruise) began. Reagan offered the **'Zero Option'**; both sides would dismantle and remove all their weapons from Europe. Brezhnev refused.

In December 1981, martial law was imposed in Poland to stop the activities of the trade union Solidarity, led by Lech Walesa, who was arrested at the same time. Solidarity had been set up the previous year in the Gdansk shipyards, after several years of protests against rising food prices. President Reagan reacted by stopping high technology exports to the Soviet Union. This was a serious blow as the Soviet Union was depending on imports of technology to develop its industry.

Walesa was released from prison in October 1982, but at the same time a new trade union law was passed, which meant that Solidarity was banned. For the next seven years Solidarity campaigned against the communist government.

In 1982 Strategic Arms Reduction Talks (START) began. But all talks soon became deadlocked. Reagan then announced plans for the Strategic Defence Initiative (SDI) – Star Wars as it became known – a plan to use lasers to destroy missiles from space. The Soviet Union immediately condemned Reagan's actions, but the leadership was beginning to realise that it was in a no-win situation. Whether Reagan was serious or not, the Soviet Union had neither the finance nor the technology to build an equivalent to SDI.

Superpower squabbles

The next few years were marked by a series of petty incidents. In 1983, the Soviet Union condemned the US invasion of Grenada to crush a communist take-over, and in 1984, along with the other communist countries, it boycotted the Los Angeles Olympics.

The situation was made even more difficult by the prolonged illness of Leonid Brezhnev. This prevented any decisive action being taken. When Brezhnev died in 1982, he was succeeded by Yuri Andropov. But Andropov was taken seriously ill almost immediately in 1983, with kidney disease. He was last seen in public in August 1983 and died in 1984. Andropov, in turn, was replaced by Konstantin Chernenko, who was already in his 70s. He was himself already seriously ill and died thirteen months later in March 1985.

The changes in leadership and the ill-health of successive leaders had profound effects on the Soviet Union. Decisive action to change policies was impossible and the Soviet economy was allowed to drift still further. The corruption, which had developed under Brezhnev, continued and this meant that swift and decisive action was essential if the Soviet Union was to be saved from economic ruin.

How did the appointment of Mikhail Gorbachev change relations between the superpowers?

Gorbachev was the first leader of the Soviet Union who had grown up in the post-Stalin period. He came to power with two policies, Perestroika and Glasnost.

Perestroika referred to 'economic restructuring' in the Soviet Union. Gorbachev believed that the Soviet Union could only survive if the economy was completely rebuilt, doing away with the command economy which had existed since Stalin.

Glasnost referred to a new sense of 'openness', both within the Soviet Union and also with the West. The powers of the KGB were restricted and criticism of the government was allowed. Free elections were held in 1990.

Gorbachev knew that the Soviet Union was

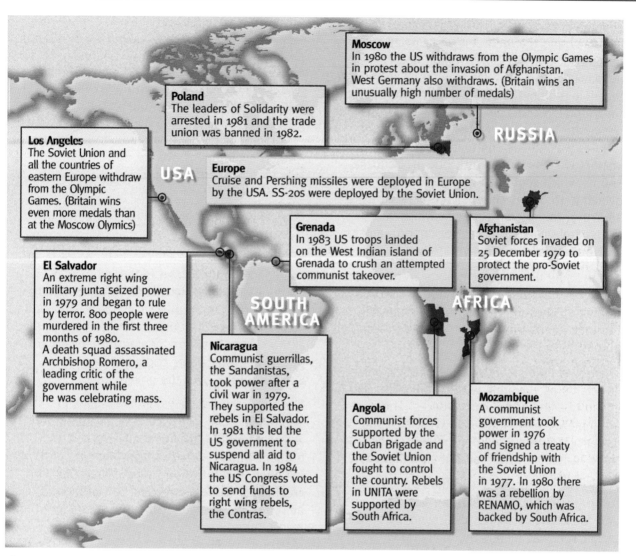

Moscow
In 1980 the US withdraws from the Olympic Games in protest about the invasion of Afghanistan. West Germany also withdraws. (Britain wins an unusually high number of medals)

Poland
The leaders of Solidarity were arrested in 1981 and the trade union was banned in 1982.

Los Angeles
The Soviet Union and all the countries of eastern Europe withdraw from the Olympic Games. (Britain wins even more medals than at the Moscow Olymics)

Europe
Cruise and Pershing missiles were deployed in Europe by the USA. SS-20s were deployed by the Soviet Union.

Grenada
In 1983 US troops landed on the West Indian island of Grenada to crush an attempted communist takeover.

Afghanistan
Soviet forces invaded on 25 December 1979 to protect the pro-Soviet government.

El Salvador
An extreme right wing military junta seized power in 1979 and began to rule by terror. 800 people were murdered in the first three months of 1980.
A death squad assassinated Archbishop Romero, a leading critic of the government while he was celebrating mass.

Nicaragua
Communist guerrillas, the Sandanistas, took power after a civil war in 1979. They supported the rebels in El Salvador. In 1981 this led the US government to suspend all aid to Nicaragua. In 1984 the US Congress voted to send funds to right wing rebels, the Contras.

Angola
Communist forces supported by the Cuban Brigade and the Soviet Union fought to control the country. Rebels in UNITA were supported by South Africa.

Mozambique
A communist government took power in 1976 and signed a treaty of friendship with the Soviet Union in 1977. In 1980 there was a rebellion by RENAMO, which was backed by South Africa.

▲ The collapse of détente, 1976–84.

bankrupt and that its survival depended on the West. He needed investment, new technology and most of all arms agreements, which would allow him to reduce the Soviet Union's massive defence spending.

Why was the Soviet Union bankrupt?

For 40 years the Soviet Union had supported communist regimes around the world through COMECON. In 1977 Cuba had joined. Cuba depended almost totally on the Soviet Union for aid. Military expenditure had continued to rise,

despite Brezhnev's attempts at arms limitation. No leader dared offend the military in case he was overthrown by a coup. Military expenditure prevented increased spending on consumer goods.

The space programme had been very ambitious and very expensive. In 1975 Soviet and US astronauts had met in space, but that would be almost the last symbol of genuine superpower status for the Soviet Union.

Inside the Soviet Union, prices were controlled and subsidised. This was a heavy drain on the government's budget. The weakness of the economy and the inefficiency of Soviet industry had meant that the Soviet Union had increasingly come to rely on imports of food and technology from the West. This had to be paid for in foreign currency. The Soviet Union became desperate for foreign exchange. The sale of roubles was strictly controlled and foreign visitors were encouraged to buy in 'Beriozka' shops, which contained goods that were not available to Soviet citizens. This was an extra source of the foreign currency, which was desperately needed to pay for imports and to revive the Soviet economy.

At the same time, Soviet exports were almost always of poor quality – the notorious Lada car or cheap Qualiton records, for example. Virtually the only goods that the Soviet Union could sell abroad were raw materials.

There was little incentive to workers to raise standards as everyone was guaranteed a job, cheap housing and public services. There was an immense black market in Western goods and currency. Tourists would be offered roubles at three to five times the official exchange rate.

Even Brezhnev had realised that something had to be done about spending on arms, but in the end the Afghanistan war destroyed all of his plans. This was merely the final straw.

The roles of Reagan and Gorbachev
Just like Mikhail Gorbachev, Ronald Reagan also wanted to cut military expenditure. In 1983, the USA spent US$300,000,000,000 on defence – almost as much as the entire British budget. In 1986, almost as soon as Gorbachev became leader the two presidents met and agreed to remove Intermediate Range Missiles (SS-20s and Cruise) from Europe. The Intermediate Nuclear Forces (INF) Treaty, as it was called, was signed in 1987.

Further talks were held to discuss the reductions in conventional forces. But before these reached any conclusions the eastern bloc disintegrated and the Soviet Union did nothing to stop it.

Source E

We are now catching up with the United States in some of the old traditional industries, which are no longer as important as they used to be. In newer fields, for example computers and industrial research and development, we are not only lagging behind, but are also growing more slowly.

▲ A description of Soviet industry.

The spark was provided in Poland, where the trade union Solidarity had been campaigning since 1980. In 1989 price rises led to strikes and mass protests. The Communist Party gave in and allowed free elections, hoping to hang on to power. The plan went badly wrong and Solidarity took over the government.

The same thing happened in Hungary. In September 1989, Hungary opened its borders with Austria and East Germany opened its borders with Austria. Massive numbers of refugees began to flood west. When the communist leaders appealed to Gorbachev for help, he told them that they must sort out their own futures.

The collapse of the communist bloc
Suddenly the peoples of eastern Europe realised that they no longer had to fear that the Red Army would crush opposition as it had done in Hungary in 1956. In November 1989 the communist governments of East Germany, Czechoslovakia and Bulgaria all resigned and the Berlin Wall was torn down. In Romania in December, Nicolai Ceausescu , the Stalinist dictator, was murdered.

In December Gorbachev met George Bush, the new US President, and they declared that the Cold War was over.

▲ Gorbachev and Reagan meeting in Geneva in November 1985.
A sign of improved relations between the two superpowers.

Questions

1 Explain the following terms:
START, Glasnost.

2 Draw a timeline of events from 1979 to
1984, showing the breakdown in relations
between the Superpowers. Explain which
events angered the USA and which events
angered the Soviet Union.

3 Explain the aims of Mikhail Gorbachev
and Ronald Reagan. Why were two such
different people able to get on so well?

4 Explain why Mikhail Gorbachev was
determined to get agreement on arms
reductions with the USA.

Overview

5 Do you agree that the breakdown
of the wartime alliance created a feeling
of mistrust which lasted from 1945
right through to the end of the Cold
War in 1990?

The collapse of the Warsaw Pact and the Soviet Union. The dates show the year which each country became independent.

Why did the Cold War end so suddenly?

One reason for the sudden end to the Cold War was that the Soviet Union had been bankrupt for years and in the end just ran out of cash. There was no incentive in the state-run industries to improve productivity and the Soviet government was unable to pay for the imports, which it needed to revitalise its economy. The cost of supporting communist regimes and revolutions around the world, and subsidising the standard of living of the Soviet people, was simply too much for a fourth rate economy.

The Afghan War was the final straw. For ten years from 1979 to 1989 the Red Army struggled to defeat Muslim guerrillas. The cost in lives, equipment and money was immense. But even more significant was the loss of faith in the Soviet leaders as more and more families lost sons in the mountains of Afghanistan. Gorbachev finally ordered the withdrawal of Soviet troops in 1989, but only after ten years of fighting.

Most importantly, the government was unable to pay the wages of the Red Army. In fact, by the late 1980s, it could not afford an army at all. When the Red Army units in East Germany were almost destitute, the West German government offered to pay the expenses for their removal and the cost of their rehousing in the Soviet Union. The bill came to £30,000,000,000.

Mikhail Gorbachev refused to consider using force to keep control of eastern Europe as his predecessors had. To him the prospect of bloodshed was unacceptable, and so he was not prepared to order the Red Army into Poland, Hungary or Czechoslovakia. Since the states of eastern Europe had only been kept in the communist bloc by the threat of retribution from the Red Army, Gorbachev's withdrawal of that threat meant the collapse of Warsaw Pact, the destruction of the Iron Curtain and the end of the Cold War.

Appeasement — The policy followed by Britain in the 1930s to try to avoid war with Nazi Germany.

Apartheid — The system of separating Whites, Blacks and Coloureds practised in South Africa after 1948.

Anti-Semitic — Being hostile or prejudiced against Jews.

Armistice — When opposing sides agree to stop fighting; a truce.

Aryans — A white person of non-Jewish decent.

Autobahns — German motorways.

Autocratic — The behaviour of somebody who is an absolute ruler, or a dictator.

Bizonia — The uniting of the British and American zones of West Berlin in 1947.

Blacklisted — To be placed on a 'list' of wrongdoers, e.g. supposed communist sympathisers in the USA in the 1950s.

Black market — An illegal system for selling shortage goods at higher prices.

Blackout — A system of removing all traces of light to make it harder for enemy bombers to hit their targets.

Black Power — The movement towards Black separatism in the USA during the 1960s.

Blitzkrieg — A form of warfare involving rapid movement. Used by the Nazis in the Second World War.

The Blitz — The Nazi bombing attack on British cities in 1940–1.

Bonds — Certificates sold to civilians to help the government raise money – often during war.

Booby traps — A hidden explosive device intended to kill or injure anyone who touches it.

Boycott — Refusal to trade, deal or buy goods from someone, a country or group.

Censure — Criticism.

Civil rights — The rights of the individual in society e.g. voting, education.

Collaborate — To work with. In the war citizens who worked with occupying Nazi forces were called collaborators.

Coloureds — People of mixed race in South Africa.

Congress — The American parliament.

Conscientious objector — Someone whose principles prevent him or her from fighting in a war.

Conscription — Compulsory military service.

Constitution — A set of rules by which a country is governed.

Consumer goods — Products made for use in the home e.g. radios, washing machines.

Defect — A Cold War term for someone switching from East to West (or vice-versa).

Deferred — Men in key industries in the Second World War were able to put off or prevent their call-up to fight. These men had 'deferred' their call-up.

Dekulakisation — Ridding the Soviet Union of the richer peasants (Kulaks).

Desegregation — End the practice of Blacks and Whites having separate facilities.

Détente — The improvement in relations between East and West in the Cold War.

Dictator — A ruler with complete power who disregards the law.

Dirty tricks — Unfair or illegal practices to discredit an opponent.

Dissent — Disagreeing with the government – especially in the Soviet Union.

Dogfights — Fights between aircraft in war.

Doodle bugs — Another name for the German V1 bombs used during the Second World War.

Duma — The Russian parliament.

Easterners — People who supported the idea of attacking Germany from the east in the First World War.

Economic sanctions — Measures taken to limit trade with a country.

Executive privilege — Special treatment for the President.

Expletive deleted — A swear word has been removed.

Führer — Leader. Name adopted by Hitler in Germany.

Ghetto — A part of a city where minority groups live. The Jews in Nazi Germany lived in ghettos.

GIs — American servicemen.

Glasnost — Meaning 'openness'. The policy, especially in the Soviet Union since 1985, of the government or press being more open and sharing information.

Gosplan — The organisation responsible for setting targets in the Stalinist Soviet Union. The State Planning Commission.

Great Society — The name given to Lyndon Johnson's policies on equal opportunities, voting rights, education and poverty, etc. He wanted America to be a 'Great Society' free from such problems.

Guerrilla — A type of warfare using ambushes and sabotage rather than open battle.

Gulags — Forced (slave) labour camps in the Soviet Union, particularly during the Stalin era

Herrenvolk — Master race. The Nazis believed in Germany's superiority as a race and nation.

Honeymoon period — A period at the beginning of a government's life when it has extra support from the people.

Hoovervilles — Makeshift towns for poor Americans following the Crash.

Hyperinflation — A period of rapid price increases – especially in Germany in 1923/4.

Immigrants — People coming from abroad to live in a country.

Impeach — Put on trial – especially the US president.

Impregnable — Not able to be defeated.

Inaugural — First. The inaugural speech is made by the US president at the start of his term in office.

Incendiaries — Bombs designed to cause fires.

Incriminating — Something that will get you into trouble.

Integration — People of different colours having the same rights and facilities.

Issei — Japanese immigrants living in the USA.

Izvestia — A Russian newspaper. Until 1991 it was the official national publication of the Soviet government.

Kristallnacht — Literally, the Night of Broken Glass. The name refers to the broken glass of shop windows etc, smashed on the night of 9th November 1938 when Nazis throughout Germany and Austria attacked Jews and their property.

Laissez-faire — The policy of non-interference. The government makes as few rules for industry and society as possible.

Legislation — Laws.

Luftwaffe — The German airforce.

Migrants — People who move from one part of the country to another (usually looking for work).

Milestone — A particularly important moment.

Militant — Especially active or forceful.

Monopoly — Being the only one allowed to do something, e.g. make radio broadcasts.

Munitions — Weapons. Munitions factories made war goods.

Nisei — Children of Issei, i.e. whose parents are Japanese immigrants, but who are themselves born in the USA.

Non-aggression — Peace. Agreement not to make war.

Pass Laws — Laws restricting the movements of Blacks in South Africa.

Panzer divisions — German tank division.

Perestroika — The policy of restructuring or reforming, especially the economic and political system in the Soviet Union since 1985.

Phoney war — The period in 1939–40 when there was little fighting.

Prohibition — The banning on the making and selling of alcohol.

Propaganda — Information altered or presented in such a way as to make a special impression.

Puppet government — A government set up by another power, e.g. the Vichy government set up by the Nazis in Second World War France.

Purges — Removing opponents – especially in the Stalinist Soviet Union.

Rationing — Restricting food supplies in the war.

Red Scare — A period of anti-communist hysteria in the USA in the 1950s.

Reparations — Payments made by Germany as compensation for damage caused in the First World War.

Reichstag — The German parliament.

Rugged individualism — The policy of 'standing on your own two feet', not relying on government help.

Scorched earth policy — The policy of destroying everything of use to the enemy as an army retreats.

Show trials — Special public trials where the results were fixed beforehand.

Socialism — Political/economic theory which states that the people should own and control the means of production, i.e. factories, etc.

Social welfare — President Kennedy's policy of reducing poverty and improving education and housing in rural and urban America.

Soviet — A Russian word meaning 'council', originally set up in the 1905 Revolution.

Sovnarkhozy — Regional economic councils set up by Khrushchev in the Soviet Union.

Stakhonovites — The name given to workers in the Soviet Union who were offered incentives to increase production.

Stalemate — A situation where neither side can win.

Stockbroker — Someone who buys and sells shares for a client.

Strategic hamlets — Villages set up by the Americans in Vietnam to separate local peasants from the Vietcong.

Swastika — The Nazi emblem.

Tariff — A tax or duty placed on goods (usually being imported into a country).

Trekking — During the Blitz people avoided air raids by leaving the towns and cities in the afternoon and moving to the countryside. They would return the next morning after the air raid.

Untermenschen — Derogatory German name for Slavs and Russians.

Vietcong — Communist guerrillas in South Vietnam.

Zero option — During the period of détente and arms reduction, President Reagan offered the 'Zero Option', whereby both the Americans and the Russians would dismantle all their nuclear weapons.

INDEX